WEST ACADEMIC PUBLISHING'S LAW SCHOOL ADVISORY BOARD

FAMILY LAW SIMULATIONS

Second Edition

Jessica Dixon Weaver
SMU Dedman School of Law

Jamie R. Abrams
American University Washington College of Law

Keeshea Turner Roberts
Widener University Delaware Law School

BRIDGE TO PRACTICE SERIES®

WEST ACADEMIC

860 Blue Gentian Road, Suite 350
Eagan, MN 55121
1-877-888-1330

Published in the United States of America

ISBN: 979-8-89209-775-8

This book is dedicated to my late father, Ernest L. Dixon.
I am blessed to have had such tremendous love and support from him throughout my life. Dad, I still hear your words of encouragement!

Jessica Dixon Weaver

To my beloved grandparents, Patsy J. Pullen and Joseph Pullen, Jr.—
I am forever grateful for the love, strength, and guidance you poured into me.
You never stopped believing that I could do all things through Christ who strengthens me.

Always and forever—love you both.

Keeshea Turner Roberts

ACKNOWLEDGMENTS

My sincere appreciation goes to Ellen Pryor, my former SMU colleague, for introducing me to Louis Higgins and supporting my desire to become a book author. Thank you to Louis, Staci Herr, Sarah Bowser Agan, and Megan Hoffman for their support and patience throughout the writing process. I would also like to thank my former Dean, Jennifer Collins, for her support of my one-year sabbatical and scholarship goals over the time period that it took to complete the first edition of this work. This book would not have been possible without a generous grant from the George Ellis Endowed Faculty Research Fund. Thank you to the funder for enabling me to bring my vision to life for future family law lawyers.

An incredibly big thanks is due to Professor Jamie Abrams, who courageously and enthusiastically joined this book as a co-author of the first edition in the latter stages of its development. There are not enough words to express my gratitude for Professor Abrams' generous and kind spirit, her sharp and precise writing, and the wonderful ideas, suggestions and additions she brought to the book. This book would not have come to fruition during the year of a global pandemic without her. I am immensely grateful for the spark she provided to finish the first edition of the book, and the chapters she wrote, co-wrote and edited. Her research assistants, Neha Khan and Victoria Skinner, also provided valuable support in the editing process.

Professor Keeshea Turner Roberts, who joined the second edition as a co-author, brought a wealth of expertise, passion, and fresh perspective to the second edition. A seasoned family law scholar and educator, Professor Turner Roberts drew on her extensive background in both public interest practice and clinical legal education to enrich the text with real-world context, critical insights, and a commitment to inclusive, accessible teaching. She provided novel pedagogical approaches that will deepen students' understanding of doctrine and prepare them to think critically about the structural inequalities that shape family law and its impact on marginalized communities.

A special thanks goes to Donna Wolff, my library research assistant for the diligent research assistance she provided and her interest in my work. She completed projects big and small and was always prompt and thorough. She was an absolute pleasure to work with, and she also made life easier for my student research assistants. I thank the following former law students who served as excellent research assistants of the first edition: Regan Donnenfield, Caitlin Conner, Keisha Crane, Caroline Near, and Diana Dimon. I also would like to thank student research assistant Brianna Ballester for her assistance in updating the second edition of this book.

I would like to also thank Professors Cynthia Godsoe, Peggy Davis Cooper, and the 2019 Family Law Scholars and Teachers Workshop, as well as Professors Sasha Coupet, Taja-Nia Henderson, and the 2019 Lutie A. Lytle Black Women Law Professor Workshop and Writing Retreat for helping me improve my writing and editing of several chapters in the first edition of this book. Thank you to Naomi Cahn and the AALS Section on Family and Juvenile Law for partnering with me to present portions of the book at the 2020 AALS Annual Meeting.

Finally, I want to thank my wonderful husband, Charles Wesley Weaver for his dedication to the care and support of our daughter and me. I am appreciative that he picked up where my Dad left off and is my biggest cheerleader in life.

PROFESSOR JESSICA DIXON WEAVER

I would like to thank my loving husband, Franklin M. Roberts, for his unwavering love and patience throughout this journey. Your steady presence has been a source of strength and peace. To my son, Joseph Layne—you inspire me every single day. Your curiosity, determination, and joy remind me why I keep striving. Thank you for teaching me to work hard and never give up. To my family—thank you for your continued love, support, and encouragement as I continue this path. I carry each of you with me in all that I do. I also extend my deepest appreciation to my research assistants, Hannah Penrose and Jon Spain for going above and beyond on this project. Your interest in family law, enthusiasm for the work, and meticulous attention to detail have been invaluable. I am truly grateful for your contributions to this research.

PROFESSOR KEESHEA TURNER ROBERTS

COPYRIGHT ACKNOWLEDGMENTS

INTRODUCTION

I. The Vision and Framing of This Book

I began my legal career as a practitioner, and my first job as a lawyer was as a litigator. When students contemplate the practice of family law after taking a general bar course, it is often because of the range of extremely interesting issues that arise among families over time. Everyone comes from some type of family, so it is easy to relate to the emotional and legal complexities of parent-child relationships, marriage, divorce, child custody, and unfortunately, family violence. While a general family law course is a great introduction to the wide range of matters covered by lawyers, it does not prepare you for the actual practice of law.

The Family Law Education Reform Project ("FLER") highlighted this dissonance between what is taught in law schools about family law and what is necessary for law students to become proficient as family law practitioners.[1] The FLER final report outlines the areas that should be part of a family law curriculum if the goal is to prepare you for the practice of family law. It presents the "Four C's" of family law education: Content, Context, Conduct, and Competence.[2] The content of most general family law courses is largely appellate case law. FLER suggested a reordering of traditional family law case books to cover the ebb and flow of a variety of family law fact patterns that change over time.

Consistent with FLER's recommendations, the Family Law Simulations book uses several family law fact scenarios and builds upon them throughout subsequent chapters. This approach highlights the interplay of legal and social issues and considers both their short-term and long-term effects. This book also compels you to consider other vital aspects of the law necessary to be a competent family lawyer, such as the rules of professional conduct, civil procedure, and evidence.

FLER also advised that it is important to place family law in a larger context. The classifications of necessary context include "1) court and family dispute resolution processes; 2) issues of class, race, gender, age, and power; 3) financial issues; and 4) issues of policy and law reform."[3] Accordingly, the Family Law Simulations book includes fact patterns and simulations that challenge you to address each of these issues. Your professor will likely allow time for you to write and collectively comment on your simulated experiences so that there is room for self-reflection and self-evaluation as you form your professional identity as a family law lawyer.

The professional identity of attorneys includes a strong command of ethical duties, civility, cultural competency, and other inter-personal skills. Opportunities to develop these skills are often missing in traditional family law courses and are incorporated throughout these simulations. The Family Law Simulations book also incorporates the practice of collaborative problem-solving, which often takes place with not only other attorneys, but also with different professionals such as parent educators, custody evaluators, forensic accountants, mental health professionals, social workers, and mediators. Inclusion of other professionals within the drafting exercises and simulations demonstrates the value of cross-disciplinary learning and cooperation.

To develop competency as a future lawyer, you also need to hone your skills as a communicator, counselor, manager, and educator. One significant skill for an effective family law lawyer is active listening. Learning this skill involves repetitive role-playing that entails hearing the facts of the

---

[1] Mary E. O'Connell and J. Herbie DiFonzo, *The Family Law Education Reform Project Final Report*, 44 FAM. CT. REV. 524, 524 (2006).

[2] *Id.* at 529.

[3] *Id.* at 531.

client's case, acknowledging the emotions associated with the facts, and determining the client's short term and long term objectives. Being a good counselor and educator also involves building upon strong communication skills to guide clients through the process of a family law case. Learning good management skills includes managing the case from a technical and logistical perspective. These types of skills are not typically discussed in law school classes (with the exception of clinics), and they include boundary setting, self-management, and time-management.

I consider myself fortunate to have experience as both a practitioner and a legal clinician. Real live clients and cases taught me how to use all of the vital aforementioned skills on behalf of my diverse clients and their range of needs. I developed a keen sense of judgment and expertise over a period of time. I certainly made errors along the way. It is important for you to know that you can (and will) make mistakes, learn from them, and grow into excellent lawyers.

These experiences informed my vision for this book. It is designed to provide guidance and lawyering opportunities to prepare students for the actual practice of family law. In determining the topics to cover, I researched family law books, articles, and media coverage of family law issues, as well as consulted with family law attorneys and other family law professors. The family law scenarios chosen for the book are among the most commonly encountered problems of family law practitioners. The simulations involve drafting routine family law pleadings, often referred to as 'bread and butter' documents for family law lawyers. The simulations also include preparing for standard hearings and role-playing negotiation proceedings that are common for litigators.

As a dynamic field, family law grows and changes each year. What remains the same are the basic tools family law lawyers need to effectively advocate for their clients. This book offers you a bridge to the practice of family law.

The old adage that law school teaches you how to think like a lawyer is true; however, law schools are being challenged to do more to prepare you to be practice-ready. Two years after graduating from law school, a wise lawyer mentor shared this with me: "what they don't tell you in law school is that you ARE the job. As a lawyer with a state bar license, computer, paper, pen and phone, you can represent people as an advocate. That is all you need to earn a living as a lawyer." It is within this spirit that I write this book for future family law practitioners.

—Professor Jessica Dixon Weaver

II. Coverage

This book presents a robust compilation of case files that collectively cover core family law subject matters and skill sets. In total, there are twenty-five simulation assignments involving realistic family law case scenarios that introduce a diverse range of clients across various geographies. These chapters include "Research the Law" questions and "Ethical Considerations" to hone the skill of exploring key issues presented in family law. These prompts will develop your fluency in working with ethical standards and research sources when new issues arise in your practice. While this book is centered on the family law field, it focuses on developing transferrable skills that you can apply to any practice scenario that may emerge in your career.

These simulations are located in six different states: California, Florida, Massachusetts, Ohio, New York, and Texas. The Uniform Law Commission promulgates laws for adoption by states to achieve more uniformity from state to state. States can adopt provisions of these uniform laws, such as the Uniform Interstate Family Support Act (1996), the Uniform Premarital Agreement Act, and the Uniform Child Custody Jurisdiction and Enforcement Act (UCCJEA) (1997). Thus, while a simulation might be based in Florida, by applying the UCCJEA, for example, the content has sweeping relevance to many more states that likewise follow the UCCJEA. Your professor will help spotlight, as appropriate, how your home state law compares to the geographies selected for each simulation. Your professor may use the "Bring it Home" features of the chapters to empower you to research how your home state handles a particular legal issue, if your course emphasis is more localized. The "Research the Law" exercises further reinforce how you would always review your home state law, in its current and updated form, to use sources that are correct and credible.

This book uses simulation exercises as the springboard to practice lawyering across various subject matters within the family law field. In so doing, it builds a well-rounded and versatile skill set. While you might only negotiate a parenting plan in Chapter Nine, the skill of negotiation transfers across every subject matter. This book accordingly adopts a Skills Matrix illustrating how it holistically develops over a dozen lawyering skills. The Skills Matrix contains an "X" next to the type of experiential learning that is refined and applied in each chapter. This Skills Matrix demonstrates how the chapters of this book teach substance and skills in dynamic and intertwined ways. Use this matrix to capture your professional identity formation and to envision what other courses in your legal education might support your ongoing development.

The specific goals of this book depend on whether you are taking the course as a stand-alone experiential learning course or if the book is being used as a supplement to a survey family law course. If you are using this book comprehensively, you will be able to perform the following lawyering tasks:

1) Draft family law pleadings;
2) Reflect on your cultural competencies to work successfully with diverse clients and stakeholders;
3) Observe the many essential intersections between other disciplines and family law;
4) Develop and collect facts in a family law case through both client intakes and discovery;
5) Research the law to extract rules and apply them to different family law scenarios;
6) Consider common ethical issues facing family law lawyers;
7) Counsel clients in their legal options, rights, and obligations;
8) Prepare for family law proceedings, such as negotiation, a mediation, and hearing by developing arguments and narratives.

If you use portions of the book, the Skills Matrix and the individual chapter learning outcomes will establish more particularized learning objectives.

Finally, self-reflection about the practice of law is important for any lawyer. It is rare that practicing lawyers have the time and space to consider the implications of a case and how it impacts them personally and professionally. Throughout the book, your professor may ask you to journal about your reflections, feelings, or reactions during a drafting or simulation assignment. Take the time to learn more about yourself as a student and future lawyer. Self-reflection can help you in several ways. It primarily helps you determine if family law would be a rewarding career for you. It can also help you determine your strengths and weaknesses before you hit the ground running. Finally, it will help you to appreciate the journey and growth of becoming a lawyer as your career unfolds.

III. Some Administrative Details

For purposes of keeping the timeline of case scenarios current, a system of using YR-00, YR-01, YR-02, etc. is used throughout the book. YR-00 is the year in which you are using the book, and YR-01 is last year, or this current year minus one. YR-02 is two years ago, and so on. YR+01 indicates a future year, i.e., the present year plus one. This may result in a day falling on a weekend day, rather than a weekday. This should not distract you from achieving the identified learning outcomes for each chapter. If the date calculation falls on a weekend, use the next business day for fact scenario and the simulation exercise.

It should also be noted that some of the state family law statutes do not appear in their entirety. There is a set of three asterisks (* * *) when there is a missing statute or a set of missing statute sections. For teaching purposes, only the most relevant statute sections are included in the chapter. Your professor may supplement the state law when necessary to achieve the learning objectives.

Family law can and often does change every couple of years because of state legislative amendments to the family code, a related legal code, or a Supreme Court ruling. If a change should occur prior to a supplement or a new edition of this book, abide by the current rule in your state or in the country. Your professor will guide you through any state or federal reforms and can adjust the research questions or facts accordingly.

Be creative and open to ad libbing in the simulations to make them unique to your class or group. Ask the "what if" questions and explore how the law or an argument for a client might be improved. Allow this book to help you imagine what your family law practice will look like once you graduate!

TABLE OF CONTENTS

FAMILY LAW SKILLS MATRIX

	Ch. 1, Practicing Family Law	Ch. 2, Family Dissolution	Ch. 3, Prenups & Cohabitation Agreements	Ch. 4, Intimate Partner Violence	Ch. 5, Parentage	Ch. 6, Child Custody and Access	Ch. 7, Child Support	Ch. 8, Property Distribution and Alimony	Ch. 9, Negotiation	Ch. 10, Mediation	Ch. 11, Final Orders
Interview clients, witnesses, and other stakeholders	X	X						X			
Communicate effectively with individuals and entities of all backgrounds, cultures, communities, perspectives	X	X	X	X	X	X	X	X	X	X	
Analyze and advise clients re: options to achieve their objectives, including strengths and weaknesses of case	X	X	X	X	X	X	X	X	X	X	
Refer clients and third-parties to services and support as appropriate (e.g., counseling, bankruptcy, public benefits)		X		X	X	X				X	
Communicate with client in writing and orally		X		X		X	X	X	X	X	
Follow ethical rules of profession and manage malpractice risks	X	X	X	X	X	X	X	X	X	X	X
Interpret family law statutes accurately and thoroughly	X	X	X	X	X	X	X	X	X	X	X
Find family law primary sources that are binding and persuasive						X	X	X	X	X	
Use family law secondary sources and practice guidance to strengthen practice and economize work	X	X	X	X	X	X	X	X	X	X	X

	Ch. 1, Practicing Family Law	Ch. 2, Family Dissolu-tion	Ch. 3, Prenups & Cohabita-tion Agree-ments	Ch. 4, Intimate Partner Violence	Ch. 5, Parentage	Ch. 6, Child Custody and Access	Ch. 7, Child Support	Ch. 8, Property Distribu-tion and Alimony	Ch. 9, Negotiation	Ch. 10, Mediation	Ch. 11, Final Orders
Engage in or review discovery (e.g., preparing for discovery, cost-effective strategizing, discovery requests, discovery responses)						X	X	X		X	
Identify, analyze, adapt, and prepare court forms	X			X	X		X	X		X	X
Advocate for client in written and oral context		X	X	X	X	X	X	X	X	X	X
Apply relevant court procedures and practices		X		X	X	X	X	X		X	X
Negotiate and mediate claims using alternative dispute techniques to promote collaboration and settlement			X						X	X	
Draft and review contracts to meet client's objectives		X	X	X	X				X	X	X

Compiled using sources from:
https://www.afccnet.org/Portals/0/Committees/TheFamilyLawEducationReformProjectFinalReportWeb.pdf
https://www.leocussen.edu.au/wp-content/uploads/2016/11/Competency_Standards_for_Entry_Level_Lawyers-1.pdf

FAMILY LAW SIMULATIONS

Second Edition

CHAPTER ONE

PRACTICING FAMILY LAW

I. INTRODUCTION

Welcome to the practice of family law! There is never a dull moment in a family law practice. You are tasked with obtaining a legal result in a case that is usually one of the most difficult and emotional situations your client has experienced. The case may center around a couple divorcing, a father seeking to establish paternity, or a parent fighting to obtain custody of her children. Sometimes there are situations involving family violence that can be fraught with anxiety and concern for your client's well-being. At its core, family law is about providing legal services to help people resolve and manage the most important relationships in their lives. Being a family law lawyer means that you must care about people and their hardships. You must be able to handle the technical aspects of lawyering while encouraging clients to rise above challenging circumstances and difficult times with people they love (or used to love) dearly.

Learning Outcomes:

(1) Explore family law career options and professional identity as a family law lawyer.

(2) Observe the basic ways a court operates to serve parties in family court matters.

(3) Identify the basic requirements for drafting pleadings and how to use forms within a family law practice.

(4) Connect the family law field to other subject matters that are relevant in a family law practice, including cultural competence.

(5) Examine common ethical concerns faced within family law practice, specifically the common conflicts of interests that arise.

II. OVERVIEW OF FAMILY LAW PRACTICE

A. SATISFYING AND SUSTAINABLE CAREERS IN FAMILY LAW

Family law requires you to be willing to learn many things that you might not typically think would be part of a divorce and child custody case. If you have already taken a basic family law course, you know that the actual practice of family law encompasses many different practice areas, including civil, juvenile, probate, criminal, bankruptcy, tax, business, employment, immigration, intellectual property, and real property law. Family law lawyers help their clients by shepherding them through the legal system, assisting them with various social services, and managing the different emotions evoked by their circumstances.

Perhaps the most enjoyable part of being a family lawyer is the fact that no two cases are alike. Meeting a new client is like opening a window into a person's life, and the opportunity to get to know a wide variety of people is enriching. Most family law lawyers are sociable and able to find common ground with a host of different people. Because family law lawyers must learn some of the most intimate details about their clients' lives, good communication and honesty with clients are critical components of being an effective advocate. Clients are often motivated more by emotional feelings about a situation involving a family member than a desire for money or tangible outcomes. Developing a client-centered approach means that in addition to determining the legal services a client needs, a family law lawyer must also have the emotional intelligence to discern a client's deeper objectives. This knowledge will aid in reaching an optimal solution earlier in a case, and it often will save the client money in the long run. The ability to offer solutions and connect people with useful resources is also a satisfying and essential part of being a family law lawyer.

The terms 'attorney and counselor' on business cards often indicate more than just your role as legal counsel! Because of the prevalence of family violence and other health issues like substance abuse and mental or physical disabilities, the practice of family law also involves becoming knowledgeable about a host of other disciplines like social science, psychology, medicine, psychiatry, and special education. Family law lawyers wear many hats. It is important that you determine whether you would like to be a general practitioner or someone who concentrates on a certain area of family law. For example, if you have an undergraduate degree with a mathematical background, you might thrive practicing family law coupled with bankruptcy, probate, or tax law. Others with a social science or humanities degree might excel pairing family law and juvenile or criminal law together.

One way to start thinking about the many choices you have as a practitioner is to figure out who you are as a person, and what you enjoy doing. Are you the type of person that has a short attention span or likes working on something over a long period of time? You might have some cases that take six months to one year, or some that go on for two to three years. Are you a person that likes variety at work or someone who likes to do repetitive tasks? Family law is anything but boring! It is exciting, dynamic, sometimes sad, and often fast-paced. You will always have different facts with each case, but some cases are more prone to being similar (and therefore repetitive) than others. Are you an emotionally sensitive person or do you have a tough resilience to hardship? Some lawyers are unable to take on domestic violence or child abuse cases because it is too much trauma for them to handle. Knowing your personality traits, talents, strengths, and vulnerabilities is important as you consider the plethora of legal areas you have to choose from after you obtain your law degree.

Family law lawyers must also consider how they want to live their lives. Being a lawyer is often stressful. You often take home the problems and dilemmas your clients face in their family lives. Often your clients need to meet after the workday or on weekends. Sometimes you might have less than 24 hours to file an emergency temporary restraining order so that you can protect your client from an abusive partner or spouse. You may need to spend an entire afternoon meeting with family members on a case to determine what kind of witnesses they will make in court at a contested custody hearing. If you yearn for strict, dependable working hours, family law may not be the practice area for you. If you can be flexible and set work-life boundaries for yourself, it can be a great way to make a living as a lawyer.

Because of these demands, when selecting your family law path, you and your family should also consider your lifestyle choices. If you have a significant other, spouse, children, or elderly parent (or can anticipate having any of these), preparing them for your work life is also critical to the health and happiness of your whole family. Being a litigator can be hectic and unpredictable. Given the cyclical nature of attorney workloads, it is key for you also to figure out the best way to manage your time. Building a professional identity involves assessing your values in balancing work, family, and wellness to find a career that is successful, satisfying, and sustainable. Thinking critically about your professional goals and values will pay big dividends as you grow in this profession. Learning good time management will take you a long way as a family lawyer, as well as in your personal life.

There are, of course, various jobs within family law that you can obtain with varying professional demands. Family law lawyers can work as solo practitioners or at small, mid-size, and large firms representing a wide variety of clients. Government attorneys practice family law as district attorneys or prosecutors in child welfare or child support cases. These attorneys represent the state in cases against parents who are accused of child abuse and neglect, or in cases to establish paternity and obtain child support. Public defenders represent parents and children in child welfare cases, and city or county attorneys can also represent victims of domestic violence in family and criminal court. Family law lawyers can also work for non-profits that provide specific legal services at the intersections of family law and immigration law, disability law, and education law. There are also niche areas of family law such as private adoption and assisted reproduction technology (ART) law that are highly specialized.[1] These practice areas are often more transactional in nature and may require knowledge of international laws.

Professional Identity Formation: If you have worked in a family law firm, with a family court judge, or in a government or non-profit office with a focus on family law, discuss your experiences and impressions with the class. Did the work motivate you or discourage you from working in certain positions within the family law field?

B. THE FAMILY COURT SYSTEM

According to the Court Statistics Project of the National Center for States Courts, an overview of 2023 state court caseloads shows that family court cases are 6% of the total docket for the U.S. legal system.[2] Where courts use one general jurisdiction, domestic relations cases comprise 24.8% of the total docket.[3] Based on statistics from thirty-three states, 26.4% of domestic relations cases involve divorce or marriage dissolution and 22% involve civil protection orders, with child support cases following closely behind at 18.4%.[4] Custody and paternity cases make up 4.5% and 7.4%, respectively, with a remaining 4.7% categorized as "other," and 2% of cases involving adoption.[5]

---

[1] While the term "specialized" is used here, it is not meant to indicate that attorneys can be board certified for adoption law or ART law. State certifications that allow attorneys to advertise a specialization in an area of family law are available in family law (generally), child welfare, juvenile, and elder law.

[2] S. Gibson, N. Waters, M. Hamilton, E. Stephens, M. Moffett, H. Caspers, E. Taylor, eds., 2024 Court Statistics Project (CSP) STAT, *Trial Court Caseload Overview*, National Center for State Courts, (https://www.ncsctableauserver.org/t/Research/views/TrialDashboards/Overview?%3Aembed=y&%3AisGuestRedirectFromVizportal=y), last updated October 2024.

[3] *Id.*

[4] *Id.*

[5] *Id.*

In most large cities around the U.S., the family court system is set apart from other civil courts with its own set of judges and associate judges. A unified family court system is a set of fully integrated courts that handle all legal cases involving families and children. Once a family matter is assigned to a specific family court, that same court (and ideally the same judge) will hear all present and future family law matters brought forward in that jurisdiction. The idea behind this type of system is that families are better served by continuity in the judicial fact finder and administrative staff. The same judge will have both knowledge and familiarity with the factual backgrounds and the types of legal and social issues faced by families in his or her court. It prevents family members from forum shopping for judges who might be more favorable to an argument and ideally fosters better decisions that serve the best interests of children. It also allows judges to become extremely knowledgeable in the area of family law and related disciplines, which has a positive impact on decision-making and court resolutions in difficult cases. Most states have either a statewide unified family court system or a family court division in selected areas of the state.[6]

If you practice in a small or rural town, there will likely be just a few civil court judges who preside over a variety of legal matters. These judges do not have the benefit of listening to family law issues all day, every day, so lawyers may have the additional task of educating the judge on certain issues. It may also be more difficult to have complete impartiality in smaller geographies where stakeholders often know each other outside of the proceeding. One of the benefits of practicing in a smaller jurisdiction is that judges may have more time to work with lawyers and families to reach a mutually beneficial outcome. It is wise to speak to lawyers who have practiced before specific judges to learn what the judges expect, how they run their courtroom, and how best to navigate issues. This is more important in a town where there are only two judges, as opposed to a city where there may be as many as six to twelve family law judges and associate judges.

In all geographies, it is useful to develop strong working relationships with the court coordinators and clerks because they will be key allies when you are trying to set hearings, resolve problems with pleadings and court filings, and obtain guidance in dealing with specific judges. Your rapport with judges and court personnel is crucial to attaining your client's objective in family law cases. Building relationships is part of being a good lawyer in any field. Start with just being civil and polite—there should be no expectation that court personnel work for you. Be assured that any negative interaction with you will likely be relayed to the judge who will be deciding your client's case. Be mindful to adhere to the rules of professional conduct in your locality. Work daily to cultivate and retain a reputation as a respectful professional in all interactions with all personnel.

Often, in larger towns and cities, the family court also offers family court services to all families to assist parents with litigation and mediation. These services may provide tools and guidance for co-parenting after a case is resolved and offer neutral psychological assessments and resources for counseling. Parents who are representing themselves *pro se* often take advantage of family court services, but they are also helpful for parents who are represented by legal counsel. Some judges may require use of family court services to reduce the issues that arise with children during divorce or family separation.

The best way to experience what the family court system is like is to clerk in a family law practice, government attorney's office, or with a family court judge. It is invaluable to observe or work on family law cases as they are being prepared for court proceedings; witness the interactions between lawyers, clients, and the judge; and then watch the hearings or trial before a judge or jury. You can learn useful lessons about a host of different skills necessary to become a successful

---

[6] Barbara A. Babb, *Reevaluating Where We Stand: A Comprehensive Survey of America's Family Justice Systems*, 46 FAM. CT. REV. 230, 232 (2008); *see also*, State Family Courts, FindLaw.com, last reviewed on July 18, 2023, *available at* https://www.findlaw.com/family/family-legal-help/state-family-courts.html.

litigator. It will also shed light on how fulfilling you would find a family law career to be. You might be dissuaded or energized by all the activity found in a family court room!

C. USING FORMS AND DRAFTING PLEADINGS

The modern practice of law is more accessible because of technology and standard forms. Developing a successful family law practice includes honing and developing the art of drafting a simple motion or pleading. Pleadings generally require a plain and concise statement that sets forth a cause of action or defense in consecutively numbered paragraphs. Information is set forth in discreet sections so that the responding party can address each allegation individually. A pleading is designed to give fair notice of the claim to the person from whom the petitioner is seeking relief.

Each state family law code sets forth the grounds for claims and the general requirements to petition the court. As with all lawsuits, jurisdiction and venue must be established. In family law cases, residency is an additional qualifying factor to determine if a court may rule upon a matter. Lawyers collect a substantial amount of information from clients at the very beginning of a case to determine the type and number of claims to set forth in a pleading.

The goal of a pleading is to ask the court for something on your client's behalf. It is the cornerstone of your case, framing the issues before the court. To draft a simple pleading, identify the parties clearly and unmistakably. Who is bringing the case and from whom do they seek relief? The next task is to identify the nature of the "ask" that brings you to the court. Are you petitioning for dissolution of a marriage and custody of children or a modification of an existing order? Put the other party on notice of the basic facts that support your request. Discovery will follow so the pleading need not contain all of the factual details, but you should have sufficient information to satisfy the ethical requirement for meritorious pleadings. The relief sought must be stated, and if this relief is monetary, a general range of amounts must be set forth based on a state's rules of civil procedure. If the petitioner demands a judgment and alternative relief, this also must be clearly stated in the pleading. In the digital world, most pleadings are filed electronically.

Given the professional demands on lawyers discussed in Section II, it is tempting to download a form and change the necessary words and numbers in lieu of drafting. While most professionals benefit from not having to 'recreate the wheel,' it is important for all practitioners to know what is required in various pleadings. Practitioners need to anticipate that forms are not always available, and you may need to draft filings outside of your office.

Every state is different. You must be knowledgeable about the state rules of civil procedure, rules of evidence, and any local rules of a particular county and/or court. For example, some judges require a Certificate of Conference for certain motions. This certificate verifies the date and means by which you communicated to opposing counsel or the respondent regarding the matter that you are presenting to the court. It indicates to the court whether the respondent agrees with or opposes your motion. If you fail to include this certificate on pleadings that require it, your motion could be rejected or denied by the judge. Knowing the appropriate rules not only helps to achieve your client's objectives, but it also saves you and your client time and money.

Once you know the basics about drafting motions, as well as the state and local rules, using forms can be a cost-saver for your clients. Often firms establish their own signature style for pleadings and orders. It will not take you nearly as long to draft pleadings and discovery on a case once you have developed your own standard forms. One good way to customize your forms is to inquire with the judges' staff or judges themselves about their preferences. Another method may be to purchase the family law manual produced by your state bar, which includes both the forms and the relevant state statutes necessary to file family law pleadings. This manual is usually several volumes and is a comprehensive collection of pleadings and motions. There are typically updates based on changes in the law, but you will need to be familiar with the local rules in the county or counties in which you practice so that you can ensure that your pleadings contain everything needed to make a proper filing. You may also have a well-established mentor or partner that gives you a copy of their forms as a template.

Most family law lawyers use forms promulgated by well-respected legal companies, the state bar, or the family law section of a local or state bar. There are many corporations, including Legal Zoom, Nolo.com, Rocket Lawyer, and Legal Solutions that also provide simple and complex legal forms for divorce, child custody, pre-marital agreements, discovery requests, etc. Some of these websites are designed for laypersons who are representing themselves *pro se* and want do-it-yourself paperwork. Others are for attorneys seeking to simplify their practice. If you use forms, they should be used as a starting point only.

There is no substitute for preparation. This is true when you are a brand-new attorney and when you are seasoned in your practice area. Forms can be out of date, rules can change, and human error is common when you attempt to use a cut and paste method of preparing pleadings and orders. Being a competent lawyer requires that you pay attention to detail. Do not allow forms to undermine your professional standards or your client's objectives.

Work to develop a strong sense of empowerment in drafting pleadings. In time, drafting pleadings will become part of your 'bread and butter' law practice. You will draft pleadings, for example, to secure a legal separation, to dissolve a marriage, to request a legal annulment, to establish paternity, to secure parenting rights and visitation, to enforce existing orders, and more. You will also respond to pleadings. These documents reply to initiated actions, refine the issues, and put the recipient on notice of what your client seeks from the court. Eventually you will assemble your own set of model pleadings for your practice area. The pleadings included in this book will help you build concise writing skills necessary for efficient and effective legal representation of clients.

D. KNOWLEDGE OF RELATED DISCIPLINES AND AREAS OF LAW

Knowledge of state family law statutes is just the foundation of what is required of competent family law lawyers. Family law is heavily interdisciplinary. It intersects with other fields such as social science, psychology, medicine and health. It also intersects with other areas of law such as criminal law, property law, tax law, and employment law. For example, it often overlaps with criminal law in domestic violence and child abuse cases. These types of cases involve review and analysis of psychological evaluations and medical records. Family law intersects with bankruptcy and probate courts when the family business dissolves with a marriage or when someone dies without having established parentage for a child. The variety of expert witnesses family law lawyers must be familiar with is robust because of the wide scope of professionals involved with families.

It is important to develop competency in these other disciplines in order to best serve your clients. Understanding and interpreting social studies, psychological evaluations, property valuations, division of a retirement or pension plan, and medical records takes time and improves with experience. Continuing Legal Education (CLE) is the best way to spend devoted time learning from the experts what you need to know to get the best outcome for your client.

E. *PRO SE* LITIGANTS

One unique aspect of family law is that parties more often than not represent themselves in court without hiring attorneys. Nationally, *pro se* litigants comprise 70% of the parties in family court. You will therefore be communicating with a non-lawyer for a good portion of your cases. Understanding how to communicate with unrepresented parties and learning what you can and cannot say will require familiarity with the ethical rules for professional conduct in your home state.

Model Rule 4.3 of the ABA Model Rules of Professional Conduct governs a lawyer communicating with a *pro se* party. It states:

> In dealing on behalf of a client with a person who is not represented by counsel, a lawyer shall not state or imply that the lawyer is disinterested. When the lawyer knows or reasonably should know that the unrepresented person misunderstands the lawyer's role in the matter, the lawyer shall make reasonable efforts to correct the misunderstanding. The lawyer shall not give legal advice to an unrepresented person, other than the advice to secure counsel, if the lawyer knows or reasonably should know that the interests of such a person are or have a reasonable possibility of being in conflict with the interests of the client.

Comment 2 of this rule states that a lawyer is not prohibited from negotiating the terms of a transaction or settling a dispute with an unrepresented person. As "long as the lawyer has explained that the lawyer represents an adverse party and is not representing the person, the lawyer may inform the person of the terms on which the lawyer's client will enter into an agreement or settle a matter, prepare documents that require the person's signature and explain the lawyer's own view of the meaning of the document or the lawyer's view of the underlying legal obligations."[7] Often *pro se* litigants seek help in understanding family law, the rules of civil procedure, or evidentiary rules. You must be careful not to explain legal concepts to an unrepresented person such that they rely on the information you give them.

While communicating with another attorney is usually easier than communicating with a *pro se* party, it is possible to amicably deal with an opposing party in a family law case. It does take more patience. You will often have to repeat your advice that they retain counsel.

In states that allow for limited representation, this may be a viable alternative to paying costly attorney's fees for some *pro se* litigants. Limited representation allows for review or drafting of certain documents and explanations of the court process. It sometimes allows for attorneys to assist *pro se* litigants with the final steps of a divorce or child custody matter. For a list of state resources that allow for limited representation or the "unbundling" of legal services, see this source: https://www.americanbar.org/groups/delivery_legal_services/resources/pro_se_unbundling_resource_center/pro_se_resources_by_state/.

Another issue that may arise with regard to *pro se* litigants is how judges interact with them in court. Many states have court-approved forms for *pro se* parties to support their access to courts.[8] These forms come with some explanation of the court process; however, it is still difficult for a lay person to have a complete understanding of how family law cases should proceed.[9] Since the number of *pro se* parties is so high, it will be important for you to understand how local judges deal with them. The Model Code of Judicial Conduct provides guidelines for judges to follow when handling matters that involve *pro se* litigants.

Ethical Considerations: What specific rules within the Model Code of Judicial Conduct govern judicial treatment of *pro se* litigants? If a judge does not abide by these rules, either by treating a *pro se* litigant unfairly or by giving a *pro se* litigant assistance prohibited by the rules, what is your recourse as a lawyer?

---

[7] MODEL RULES OF PRO. CONDUCT. r. 4.3 cmt. 2 (AM. BAR ASS'N 2020).

[8] Jessica Dixon Weaver, *Overstepping Ethical Boundaries? Limitations on State Efforts to Provide Access to Justice in Family Courts,* 82 FORDHAM L. REV. 2705 (2014).

[9] Tianna Gibbs, *Paper Courts and Parental Rights: Balancing Access, Agency, and Due Process,* 54 HARVARD CIVIL RIGHTS-CIVIL LIBERTIES L. REV. 549 (2019).

F. UNDERSTANDING CULTURAL DIFFERENCES

The practice of family law has evolved along with rules that have expanded the Constitution and the Bill of Rights to various groups of people who were formerly excluded from the American concept of freedom. Legislation and Supreme Court rulings have broken down significant barriers on the basis of race, national origin, gender, religion, disability, and sexual orientation. Courtrooms have witnessed transformations in the parties appearing inside the courthouse because of the integration of various cultures and groups of people within our society.

From 2010 to 2022, the nation's foreign-born population increased by 15.6%. According to a report released by the U.S. Census Bureau, the foreign-born population was 46.2 million (13.9% of the total population) in 2022 compared to 40.0 million (12.9% of the total population) in 2010.[10] Another significant change that accompanies the increase in foreign-born people living in the U.S. is the number of different languages spoken within families. For example, in 1980, 23.1 million people spoke a language other than English at home, a number that grew to 67.8 million people in 2019.[11] The increase in people who spoke a language other than English at home outpaced the increase in the total U.S. population. The overall population grew by approximately one-half (47 percent) between 1980 and 2019, while the population who spoke a language other than English at home grew threefold (194 percent) over the same period.[12] Many individuals come to family courts as *pro se* litigants, without a general sense of how the court system operates. We also are a nation comprised of many different races and ethnicities whose families do not necessarily reflect one type of normative family. Immigrants made up over one-fifth of the population in four states: California (26.5%), New Jersey (23.2%), New York (22.6%) and Florida (21.1%).[13] Because we live in a global world where there are more interracial marriages and more children who descend from various races and cultures, it is important to reflect on how different people live and operate as families, and how different ethnic or religious laws and social mores impact family law.

The term "cultural competence" for legal professionals means the ability to communicate, interact, negotiate, and intervene on behalf of clients from diverse backgrounds. It also requires you to adapt, work, and navigate successfully in new and unfamiliar cultural settings. Some law schools have a class dedicated to developing cultural competency for law students. Others will incorporate this skill into offerings such as clinics, professional responsibility, externships, and experiential learning courses.

Many corporations and universities are taking proactive steps to develop 'cultural intelligence' among their employees, students, and faculty. Cultural intelligence is similar to cultural competence. It is defined as a person's ability to gain, understand, apply, and adjust his or her cultural knowledge in order to relate and work effectively with people from different cultural backgrounds. It involves studying the culture of other races, ethnicities, nations, and religions. Cultural intelligence ultimately enhances communication skills to increase your ability to function and manage effectively in culturally complex contexts without fear or misunderstandings, as well as use your cultural knowledge to create innovative solutions.

---

[10] Shabnam Shenasi Azari, Virginia Jenkins, Joyce Hahn, and Lauren Medina, *The Foreign-Born Population in the United States: 2022*, U.S. Census Bureau, Report No. ACSBR-019, April 9, 2024, *available at* https://www.census.gov/newsroom/press-releases/2024/foreign-born-population.html.

[11] Sandy Dietrich and Erik Hernandez, *Language Use in the United States: 2019*, American Community Survey Reports, U.S. Census Bureau, August 2022, *available at* https://www.census.gov/content/dam/Census/library/publications/2022/acs/acs-50.pdf.

[12] *Id.* In 2019, seven of these languages had more than 1 million speakers. Spanish was the most spoken non-English language by far with 42 million speakers. As of 2019, Chinese (including Mandarin and Cantonese) was the only other detailed language with at least 3 million speakers. The other languages with over 1 million speakers were Arabic, French, Korean, Tagalog, and Vietnamese.

[13] Azari, et al., *The Foreign-Born Population in the United States: 2022*, *supra* note 10.

If you are unfamiliar with these terms, here are some suggested background readings to prepare you for practicing in a diverse community. You will use the last two sources in the simulation that follows.

Simulation reading:

a) Serena Patel, *Cultural Competency Training: Preparing Law Students for Practice in Our Multicultural World*, 62 UCLA L. REV. DISC. 140 (2014), *available at*: https://www.uclalawreview.org/cultural-competency-training-preparing-law-students-for-practice-in-our-multicultural-world-2/.

b) Cultural Intelligence Center, https://culturalq.com/about-cultural-intelligence/.

c) Susan Bryant, *The Five Habits: Building Cross-Cultural Competence in Lawyers*, 8 CLINICAL REV. 33 (2001), *available at*: http://academicworks.cuny.edu/cl_pubs/258/.

d) Susan Bryant and Jean Koh Peters, *Reflecting on the Habits: Teaching about Identity, Culture, Language, and Difference in* TRANSFORMING THE EDUCATION OF LAWYERS: THE THEORY AND PRACTICE OF CLINICAL PEDAGOGY (Susan Bryant, Elliott S. Milstein & Ann C. Shalleck, eds., 2014), *available at*: https://www.law.georgetown.edu/wp-content/uploads/2017/10/chapter15-methodological-doubt-belief-excerpt.pdf.

III. CASE FILE—HECTOR GONZÁLEZ

A. SIMULATION ROADMAP

You have had an initial consultation with Hector González, a potential client. After meeting with him, your paralegal prepared the following memorandum. Your law practice has historically involved representing middle to upper class women in divorce and custody proceedings. You have recently begun offering free family law clinics monthly at a local church primarily serving the immigrant community. You first met Hector at this clinic. Spanish is Hector's first language. He has acquired proficient English skills over the years, but he is stronger in his spoken English skills than his written English. Hector first came to the U.S. with his mother and father when he was twelve from Honduras. His parents worked hard to provide for their three children. They hold strong, traditional, Catholic values. His parents fervently believe that children should be raised in a marital family.

Recognizing that you are unfamiliar with Hector's culture, you will create a Venn diagram to visualize how you and your potential client may align and may differ in your thinking. Your goal is to prepare to represent him with a strong degree of cultural competence. To complete this assignment, you can use your own identity and cultural background for the Venn diagram situated within the law practice scenario described in the preceding paragraph.

The second part of the simulation is a family law court room observation. If time and space permit, you and/or your class will attend a morning or afternoon docket for a family court in your local county. This assignment will provide you with a realistic snapshot of how family law operates in practice, highlighting courtroom dynamics, the roles of various participants, and the emotional complexity of family law matters. You will write a 2-page reflection paper that addresses the family matters you observed.

B. INITIAL CLIENT CONSULTATION MEMORANDUM

TO:	Attorney
FROM:	Paralegal
RE:	Initial Consultation with Hector González

Legal services sought by prospective client:

Hector González lives in Dallas, Texas, and is the father of a three-year-old son, Hector González, Jr. He recently found out that there is a chance that his son may not be his. He is distraught at the thought of his namesake being the son of another man. He wants to establish paternity for his son.

Background facts:

He was twenty years old when he found out that his girlfriend, Samantha Fuentes, was pregnant. She was nineteen at the time. For both of them, this was their first child. They had only been dating for ten months before Samantha learned that she was pregnant. Hector definitely wanted to be a father to his child. He wanted his son to have his surname. He believed at the time Hector Jr. was born that he was the father, but he acknowledges that some of his friends have gotten burned paying child support for a kid they later found out was not their biological child.

After the birth of his son:

At the hospital, a "nice lady" named Ms. Jenkins approached Hector and Samantha the day after the birth to discuss the birth certificate. She first asked if he and Samantha were married. Samantha said "no." Ms. Jenkins told Hector that in order for his son to have the last name "González," he needed to sign a document called an Acknowledgement of Paternity. She asked whether he understood written English, but he did not want to admit that he did not read in English as well as he speaks English. He nodded "yes." Ms. Jenkins gave him a form with English on one side of the page and Spanish on the other side. He read the Spanish version of the document as Ms. Jenkins read the document out loud in English. The first thing she said was, "this is a legal document." Ms. Jenkins mentioned that Hector should talk with an attorney if he had any questions about his paternity or signing "El Reconcimiento De Paternidad (AOP)."

Ms. Jenkins then read from the document about the benefits, rights, and responsibilities of paternity. She said that signing the acknowledgment would allow the child to inherit from Hector and assist the child in receiving military and/or social security benefits from him as the father. Ms. Jenkins stated that the document would give Hector standing in court regarding custody and visitation issues. He recalls hearing the words "child support" multiple times. He got the sense that this document was connected to his payment of child support in the future. He interrupted her to ask, "Do you know what happens if I lose my job and am unable to make child support payments?" She advised him that she believed there were penalties that he would face, but that this was a legal question that he would need to ask an attorney. Ms. Jenkins mentioned that he and Samantha could get DNA testing done first to find out if he was the biological father, but Samantha immediately told her that this would not be necessary because Hector was the father of their child. Hector nodded in agreement, sure that he was the only person that Samantha had been intimate with because he believed her to be a virgin when they first met.

After reading over the filing instructions for the AOP, Ms. Jenkins left the two of them to discuss the form. Samantha took the form, signed it, and handed it to Hector to sign. Even though Hector wanted to ask about the cost of DNA testing and whether it was offered at the hospital, he did not want to upset Samantha by asking too many questions. It had been just eight hours since she gave birth, and she had a long labor with complications.

While Hector was pretty sure that he was the father of the baby, he wanted to wait on signing this AOP form. He thought about how angry Samantha might be if told her he wanted to wait. He thought about how upset she would be if he asked for DNA testing. He wanted his name to be on the birth certificate, so he signed the form. He called Ms. Jenkins back into the room. She took the AOP, stating that she was going to fax it to the State Bureau of Vital Statistics. She left the room for about twenty minutes. She returned with the birth certificate form in her hand. The couple left the hospital all smiles, with their son, Hector González, Jr., together as a family. Hector moved into Samantha's apartment. Everybody in Hector's family treats Samantha and Hector Jr. like his wife and son, even though he and Samantha never got married.

Recent facts that caused him to question son's paternity:

Hector and Samantha broke up one year later, and he moved out. He began paying Samantha $200 per month informally along with purchasing clothes and toys for his son over the next two years. Samantha allowed Hector to visit their son every other weekend and at least one evening each week. The arrangement they had was going smoothly until Samantha's ex-boyfriend, Carlos Garcia, showed up, claiming to be the father of his child. Hector confronted Samantha about Carlos' claim of being Hector's father. He challenged how Carlos could even think that he was the father. Samantha admitted that she had previously lost her virginity to Carlos and not to him. Hector angrily stormed out of her apartment and has not spoken to Samantha in over a week.

Hector is confused about the AOP and does not know whether he is really the legal father of Hector Jr. or if Carlos can now become the legal father. Hector is presently working as a dock loader at a package delivery company. He does not have much money to retain a lawyer, but his parents will help him out if it means preserving his right to be a father. He wants to know his options. He brought his copy of the signed AOP to the consultation. It is attached. It does not have a file stamp from the Texas Bureau of Vital Statistics.

Parentage statutory provisions:

You also asked me to send you the most updated versions of the key parentage statutory provisions. I have attached those excerpts to this memorandum for your reference. I left a complete copy of the parentage statute on your desk.

ATTACHMENT 1 of 2

STATE OF TEXAS
ACKNOWLEDGEMENT OF PATERNITY

<u>This is a legal document</u>. Type or Print in black ink. Parents are to be given a copy of both sides of this completed document.

We declare under penalty of perjury that

Hector	George	González
Biological Father's first	middle	last name

is the biological father of

Hector	George	González, Jr.
Child's first	middle	last name

born on

08	23	YR-03	in	Dallas	Dallas	Texas
m m	d d	y y y y		city	county	state

to

Samantha	Ana	Fuentes	n/a
Mother's first	middle	last name	maiden name if different

May 4, YR-23	123-45-6789	17 Dahlia Lane	Dallas	TX	75235
Father's date of birth	social security number	address	city	state	zip code

January 15, YR-22	987-65-4321	840 Western Lane, Apt. 19A	Dallas	TX	75233
Mother's date of birth	social security number	address	city	state	zip code

We further declare on penalty of perjury that:

- We have been given written and oral notice of the benefits of having paternity established; the availability of paternity establishment and child support services; and the legal consequences of, the rights and responsibilities of, and the alternative to signing this Acknowledgment. **Written notice is on the back of this legal document.**
- No other man is acknowledged as the biological father of this child.
- There is no court order naming another man as the biological father of this child.
- A genetic test has not determined that another man is the biological father of this child.
- We understand that the effect of this Acknowledgment of Paternity is a legal finding of paternity that may be challenged only under limited circumstances. Challenge is barred after 4 years.

Mark only the one correct statement from each of the following:

☑ There **has not** been genetic testing of the man listed above to determine if he is the biological father of this child.	**Or**	☐ Genetic testing **has** determined that the man listed above is the biological father of this child.
☑ The mother **was not** married to someone other than than the biological father at the time of the child's birth or within 300 days prior to the child's date of birth.	**Or**	☐ The mother **was** married at the time of the child's birth or during the 300 days before the child's birth; and that man has completed the Denial of Paternity below or has a Denial of Paternity filed with the Bureau of Vital Statistics.

Full Signature of Biological Father   date 08/23/YR-00   Full Signature of Mother

Denial of Paternity

We declare under penalty of perjury that ______________________________

Presumed Father's first   middle   last name

the presumed father of the child, is not the biological father. We understand that filing of this denial with an acknowledgment removes the presumed father's legal duty to support the child and terminates his right of custody or visitation with the child.

Full Signature of Presumed Father   date   Full Signature of Mother   date

ATTACHMENT 2 of 2

THIS IS WHAT YOU'LL SEE ON THE BACK OF THE AOP

This is a legal document. If you are not sure that the man named in this Acknowledgment is the biological father of the child, you should **NOT** sign this document. You may want to get a genetic test. **The biological father who signs this Acknowledgment becomes the legal father of the child when this document is filed with the Department of State Health Services, Texas Vital Statistics.**

Signing this legal document gives you certain rights and responsibilities. Signing this document is voluntary. You should consult an attorney if you have any concerns about signing this document. This document requires an Entity Code completed in the lower right corner by an individual certified by the Office of Attorney General to administer Acknowledgments of Paternity.

Benefits, Rights and Responsibilities of Paternity

Establishing parentage makes it easier for a child to receive benefits such as social security, military and veteran's benefits, health care coverage and life insurance, as well as inheritance.

This Acknowledgment has the same effect as a court order establishing paternity. Both parents have parental rights and duties as provided by state law. Either parent has the right to seek primary custody of the child. A parent not living with the child may have the right to visit and maintain a relationship with the child, either as both parents agree or as ordered by the court. By signing this Acknowledgment, you may be ordered to pay child support and medical support.

This document may be completed before the birth of the child, at the time of birth, or at any time after the birth of the child prior to any court hearing in a proceeding involving the child. If this document is signed before the birth of the child, it is binding for any child born no later than 300 days after the signature date on this document. When this Acknowledgment is properly filed with Texas Vital Statistics, it creates a parent-child relationship between the man and the child. Establishment of paternity is required for a father's name to be entered on a birth certificate.

Child Support services can be obtained through the Office of the Attorney General, Child Support Division or by hiring an attorney.

Denial of Paternity

If a child's mother is married to a man other than the biological father at the time of birth or within 300 days of the ending of a marriage (by a finalized divorce), the (ex) husband is presumed to be the legal father. To complete this document for a child that has a presumed father, the presumed father must deny paternity by completing the Denial of Paternity section. The mother must agree that the presumed father is not the biological father by also signing the denial section. The acknowledgment section must also be completed by the biological father and mother, or the denial will not be accepted. Upon the filing of this document, the presumed father is legally determined not to be the father of the child. His legal duty to support the child is removed. Likewise, his legal right to custody or visitation with the child is terminated.

Change of Mind

If any party to this document changes his/her mind about acknowledgment or denying paternity, he/she may file a Rescission of Acknowledgment of Paternity (VS-158) to rescind this document. The Rescission of Acknowledgment of Paternity must be filed within sixty (60) days after this legal document is filed with Texas Vital Statistics or before the date a proceeding related to the child is initiated, whichever occurs first. After sixty (60) days, or the date a proceeding for the child was initiated, a lawsuit is required to challenge this document. Fraud, duress, or material mistake of fact in signing this form must be proven during the lawsuit.

<u>If a Party is a Minor</u>

Minors are authorized to complete the Acknowledgment of Paternity without parental consent. Minors are allowed to rescind or challenge this document in the same procedures as persons eighteen (18) or older.

All parties must receive oral notice of the above information before completing this Acknowledgment. You can receive oral notice of the information by calling 1-866-255-2006 and select option 1, "Notice of Rights and Responsibilities of a Parent."

If you have questions, you may call the Paternity Opportunity Program at 1-866-255-2006.

September 2011

C. RELEVANT STATUTORY LAWS

Texas Family Code

Title 5. The Parent-Child Relationship and the Suit Affecting the Parent-Child Relationship

Subchapter D. Voluntary Acknowledgment of Paternity

§ 160.305. Effect of Acknowledgment or Denial of Paternity

(a) Except as provided by Sections 160.307 and 160.308, a valid acknowledgment of paternity filed with the vital statistics unit is the equivalent of an adjudication of the paternity of a child and confers on the acknowledged father all rights and duties of a parent.

(b) Except as provided by Sections 160.307 and 160.308, a valid denial of paternity filed with the vital statistics unit in conjunction with a valid acknowledgment of paternity is the equivalent of an adjudication of the nonpaternity of the presumed father and discharges the presumed father from all rights and duties of a parent.

* * *

§ 160.307. Procedures for Rescission

(a) A signatory may rescind an acknowledgment of paternity or denial of paternity as provided by this section before the earlier of:

(1) the 60th day after the effective date of the acknowledgment or denial, as provided by Section 160.304; or

(2) the date a proceeding to which the signatory is a party is initiated before a court to adjudicate an issue relating to the child, including a proceeding that establishes child support.

(b) A signatory seeking to rescind an acknowledgment of paternity or denial of paternity must file with the vital statistics unit a completed rescission, on the form prescribed under Section 160.312, in which the signatory declares under penalty of perjury that:

(1) as of the date the rescission is filed, a proceeding has not been held affecting the child identified in the acknowledgment of paternity or denial of paternity, including a proceeding to establish child support;

(2) a copy of the completed rescission was sent by certified or registered mail, return receipt requested, to:

(A) if the rescission is of an acknowledgment of paternity, the other signatory of the acknowledgment of paternity and the signatory of any related denial of paternity; or

(B) if the rescission is of a denial of paternity, the signatories of the related acknowledgment of paternity; and

(3) if a signatory to the acknowledgment of paternity or denial of paternity is receiving services from the Title IV-D agency, a copy of the completed rescission was sent by certified or registered mail to the Title IV-D agency.

(c) On receipt of a completed rescission, the vital statistics unit shall void the acknowledgment of paternity or denial of paternity affected by the rescission and amend the birth record of the child, if appropriate.

(d) Any party affected by the rescission, including the Title IV-D agency, may contest the rescission by bringing a proceeding under Subchapter G 1 to adjudicate the parentage of the child.

§ 160.308. Challenge After Expiration of Period for Rescission

(a) After the period for rescission under Section 160.307 has expired, a signatory of an acknowledgment of paternity or denial of paternity may commence a proceeding to challenge the acknowledgment or denial only on the basis of fraud, duress, or material mistake of fact. The proceeding may be commenced at any time before the issuance of an order affecting the child identified in the acknowledgment or denial, including an order relating to support of the child.

(b) A party challenging an acknowledgment of paternity or denial of paternity has the burden of proof.

(c) Notwithstanding any other provision of this chapter, a collateral attack on an acknowledgment of paternity signed under this chapter may not be maintained after the issuance of an order affecting the child identified in the acknowledgment, including an order relating to support of the child.

(d) For purposes of Subsection (a), evidence that, based on genetic testing, the man who is the signatory of an acknowledgement of paternity is not rebuttably identified as the father of a child in accordance with Section 160.505 constitutes a material mistake of fact.

* * *

§ 160.609. Time Limitation: Child Having Acknowledged or Adjudicated Father

(a) If a child has an acknowledged father, a signatory to the acknowledgment or denial of paternity may commence a proceeding under this chapter to challenge the paternity of the child only within the time allowed under Section 160.308.

(b) If a child has an acknowledged father or an adjudicated father, an individual, other than the child, who is not a signatory to the acknowledgment or a party to the adjudication and who seeks an adjudication of paternity of the child must commence a proceeding not later than the fourth anniversary of the effective date of the acknowledgment or adjudication.

D. THE SIMULATION—CULTURAL COMPETENCIES IN CLIENT COUNSELING

To be a culturally competent lawyer, you recognize the need for reflection on how you see your client and his legal problems. After considering the Texas Family Code excerpts, you also realize that you need to obtain additional information from Hector to determine if he needs legal representation at all.

1. Create a Venn Diagram, as suggested in the law review article by Serena Patel (on page 9), to map the similarities and differences between you and your client, Hector González. After you finish the Venn Diagram, review the concept of cultural intelligence using the Cultural Intelligence Center link in Section F. of this chapter. There are a series of quizzes to test your personal cultural intelligence using this link: https://www.quiz-maker.com/cp-np-discover-your-cultural-i. Take the first two quizzes, which should take you approximately 15 minutes total (you do not need to take all seven quizzes). Be prepared to discuss your scores. After completing these two quizzes, review your Venn Diagram and determine whether there are background questions you should ask Hector about his culture that would aid you in representing him.

2. **Experiential Learning and Self Reflection:** Observe a docket in a family court or civil court that presides over family law matters for a minimum of two hours. Draft a two-page written reflection of your observations documenting the types of cases heard, the motions, evidence, witnesses presented by the litigants, and the court's rulings. You may reflect on any relevant issues presented by the cases you observe, including but not limited to access to justice, the impact of socioeconomic status on case outcomes, and/or how litigants and attorneys navigate procedural challenges. Before and during your court observation, consider the reflection questions below.

   Court Observation Reflection Questions:

   - How do the roles and/or actions of the judge, attorneys, and parties contribute to the tone of the proceeding?

- Are there any power dynamics that exist between the parties and their attorneys in the courtroom? Does the judge allow the parties to speak before the court during the proceeding?
- Does the judge appear impartial and attentive, or are there any moments that suggest bias or favoritism?
- Do all parties seem to have equal access to representation and the opportunity to present their case?
- Does language, culture, or other barriers affect any party's ability to fully participate in the proceeding?
- How do your own experiences or biases shape the way you perceive the proceedings?
- Was there anything about the process that surprised you? If so, does it challenge your previous understanding of family law?

3. Review the Hector González AOP. Is there anything vital that is missing? What information do you need to confirm about the client's situation before you can analyze the case and the legal services he needs?
4. Optional Statutory Spotlight.

Bring it home! Statutory spotlight.

Your family law course may study law using general rules and trends or it may use your home state statutes and rules to more specifically prepare you for local practice. Compare and contrast your home state statutes with the paternity laws in this chapter. Your professor may provide a state statutory supplement to replace the statute provided here or you may research your home state rules independently.

CHAPTER TWO

FAMILY DISSOLUTION

I. INTRODUCTION

This chapter explores the main focus of family courts today—the dissolution of families. Both marriage and divorce rates have declined over the last seventy-five years. In the 1949s, 78% of all households were comprised of married couples, and now approximately 47% of the American households were headed by married couples.[1] For over a decade, "less than half of American households have included a married couple."[2] Even with the expansion of the institution of marriage to same-sex couples, many individuals have opted to create families outside of the 'keystone' of society.

Marriage is both a contract and a status. Traditionally, it was defined by the roles that men and women held within the status as husband and wife.[3] Husbands worked in the public market space as the 'breadwinner,' and wives stayed in the private space of the home to raise children, as the 'homemaker.' The roles of men and women have changed over time with the availability of birth control, equal opportunities for women in higher education, and a greater number of career options for women who work outside of the home. The rite of passage to adulthood changed from getting

---

1 USA Facts Team, How has marriage in the U.S. changed over time, USA FACTS (Feb. 11, 2025), https://usafacts.org/articles/state-relationships-marriages-and-living-alone-us/.

2 *Id.*

3 Legal marriage was not available to all people in the U.S. *See infra* pp. 84–86. The traditional role of husband and wife has also not been the same within different racial groups and for same sex couples. *See generally* Teresa Amott and Julie A. Mattaei, RACE, GENDER, AND WORK: A MULTICULTURAL ECONOMIC HISTORY OF WOMEN IN THE UNITED STATES (1996) and Amanda M. Pollitt, et. al., *Gender Conformity, Perceptions of Shared Power, and Marital Quality in Same- and Different-Sex Marriages*, 32 GENDER & SOCIETY 109 (2018).

married and having children to establishing a personal identity and career. These changes, as well as changes in the U.S. economy that have affected the availability of living-wage jobs, are a few of the reasons cited for the marriage decline by some family law scholars.[4] There are many other reasons for the decline in marriage rates that are covered in more detail during a basic family law course.

Marriage has increasingly become a union focused on love and companionship rather than a framework for having children and securing financial stability. Among those who do marry, 39% can expect their marriage to end in divorce.[5] The reasons for divorce vary depending on the survey, but some of the most common are incompatibility, infidelity, constant conflict, and financial problems.[6] While divorce previously held a negative stigma, it is far more accepted today when married couples decide to part ways. Remarriage is commonplace and blended families comprise 40% of married couples.[7] Blended families often share childcare responsibilities with new partners. This can add to the complexity of shared parenting and child support between ex-spouses. While most marriages end within the first eight years, there has been growth in the prevalence of couples divorcing after being married for thirty or forty years.[8] Since people are living longer due to better health and medical technology, couples are less willing to 'settle' and stay in a bad marriage.

Divorce can be accomplished amicably outside of court or through contentious litigation. More than 95% of divorce cases settle through mediation.[9] Collaborative law is a more recent model of alternative dispute resolution where lawyers negotiate the family dissolution before going to court. It is increasingly used among couples to divide property and determine child custody; however, if the settlement negotiations break down, each spouse must hire a new attorney to proceed with litigation. Well-versed family law lawyers are trained to represent clients in a variety of ways, utilizing litigation, collaboration, negotiation, and contract law.

This chapter focuses on separation and divorce. These matters are driven by the statutory provisions that establish both the grounds and procedure for divorce. Collecting information from your client and applying the law to those facts are critical skills for all lawyers. In this chapter, you will meet clients, ascertain their objectives, and draft documents applying the law to your client's facts.

Learning Outcomes:

(1) Collect information from a diverse spectrum of clients seeking to dissolve their marriages.

(2) Issue-spot relevant legal matters necessary for a dissolution of marriage proceeding.

(3) Identify the various grounds and requirements for obtaining a divorce.

(4) Examine the waiting periods and separation requirements among the states.

(5) Draft a separation agreement and a *Petition for Dissolution of Marriage.*

---

4 *See* JUNE CARBONE AND NAOMI CAHN, MARRIAGE MARKETS: HOW INEQUALITY IS REMAKING THE AMERICAN FAMILY (2014).

5 Belinda Luscombe, *The Divorce Rate Is Dropping. That May Not Actually Be Good News,* TIME (Nov. 26, 2018), https://time.com/5434949/divorce-rate-children-marriage-benefits/.

6 Ann Gold Buscho, *Why Do People Divorce?,* PSYCHOLOGY TODAY (Feb. 22, 2020), https://www.psychologytoday.com/us/blog/better-divorce/202002/why-do-people-divorce.

7 A.W. Geiger and Gretchen Livingston, *8 facts about love and marriage in America*, THE PEW RESEARCH CENTER, Feb.13, 2019, https://www.pewresearch.org/fact-tank/2019/02/13/8-facts-about-love-and-marriage/.

8 Rose M. Kreider and Renee Ellis, *Number, Timing, and Duration of Marriages and Divorces: 2009*, Current Population Reports, U.S. Census Bureau 70–125 (May 2011); Naomi Cahn and June Carbone, *Who is at Risk for a Gray Divorce? It Depends*, Institute for Family Studies (May 1, 2017), https://ifstudies.org/blog/who-is-at-risk-for-a-gray-divorce-it-depends.

9 Jeff Landers, *Divorcing Women: Is It Best To Settle Or Litigate?,* FORBES (May 22, 2014), https://www.forbes.com/sites/jefflanders/2014/05/22/divorcing-women-is-it-best-to-litigate-or-settle/?sh=2777ae714618.

II. OVERVIEW OF THE LAW

Every state has family law statutes that govern marriage, divorce, property distribution, alimony, child support and custody. These statutes vary, but most of them are grounded in public policy that supports the institution of marriage and the well-being of children. The sources of these statutes include the Uniform Marriage and Divorce Act, the American Law Institute's Principles of the Law of Family Dissolution, and common law.

Dissolution of Marriage

A dissolution of marriage terminates the contract and status rights of a marital couple. Often referred to as a divorce, it is effectuated by a decree or order that ends the marital relationship. In the past, there were two types of divorce—an absolute divorce and a limited divorce. An absolute divorce is a dissolution of a marriage ordered as a result of marital misconduct or other statutory cause arising after the marriage ceremony. A limited divorce, also referred to as a 'divorce from bed and board,' is a legal separation whereby the marital parties' status changes because they are precluded from cohabitation but technically still married. Today most couples seek an absolute divorce based on one or several grounds, the most common of which is irreconcilable differences or irretrievable breakdown. This type of divorce is known as a 'no-fault' divorce because it does not attribute blame to any one party. Fault-based grounds for divorce can include adultery, cruelty, abandonment, voluntary separation, felony criminal conviction, habitual drunkenness or drug addiction, and confinement to a mental hospital.

Counseling a client about which ground(s) to plead is important because this choice affects the amount of evidence necessary to prove that the marriage should be dissolved. The burden of proof in a divorce action lies with the petitioner. The legal standard varies depending on the ground. For a no-fault divorce, a court may dissolve a marriage if one party can show by a preponderance of the evidence that there has been an irretrievable marital breakdown, and there is no reasonable prospect of reconciliation. No specific cause or blame is assigned to either party. A fault-based divorce may take longer because fault-based grounds typically require corroborating evidence. The legal standard ranges from preponderance of the evidence to clear and convincing. Discovery costs make fault-based divorces more expensive. The pace of the court docket can also delay a final ruling. Fault-based divorce also leads couples down a path of 'airing their dirty laundry' publicly, which can be damaging to the family unit if there are shared children to co-parent long after the divorce is final. Marital fault can also have steep financial implications in states that consider fault when dividing property and deciding alimony awards.

If a couple has no children and has been married less than five years, there may be very little shared property to divide. Often this type of divorce is known as a simple divorce. It may be an agreed separation that requires less paperwork and can be accomplished in a shorter amount of time.

Marriage dissolutions that involve children and lengthier partnerships can be more complex. This type of divorce will include property division, child custody and visitation, and child support. In some instances, a dissolution addresses spousal support or alimony, usually when one spouse ceased working to care for the home and raise the couple's children for many years. Ultimately, the divorce allows a couple to disentangle themselves such that they can continue their lives independently.

Waiting Periods

States impose statutory waiting periods to allow couples time for reconsideration and 'cooling off' before divorce. Waiting periods can govern the amount of time that must pass before a divorce can be filed or before it can be finalized. Statutory waiting periods can vary between sixty days to two years. For example, California provides that no judgment of marriage dissolution is final until six months have expired from the date of service of the petition or the date the respondent makes an appearance (whichever occurs first). A few states also have waiting periods after a divorce is finalized before a person can remarry. This period ranges from thirty days to six months. Twenty-nine states, however, do not have any statutory waiting period.[10] Because of the variety among states, choice of law can make a big difference in how quickly a couple can divorce, as well as how quickly they can remarry.

Choice of Law

If you have taken a basic course in family law, you are familiar with the jurisdictional issues that can arise when a couple or individual shops around for forums that allow for quick divorces. While complete coverage of jurisdictional family law matters is beyond the scope of this book, it is important to know what the domicile and venue requirements are in the state and county in which you practice. Forum choices can affect the length of time a couple must be separated before filing for divorce, whether a couple can file for divorce using fault-based grounds, and how long an individual must reside in a state or county before being able to access the family court system. State law also governs the terms upon which spouses can divide property, seek alimony, and obtain child custody or visitation. Child support awards are very similar across the states, but there may be differences in enforcement and modifications. Chapters Five, Six, and Seven introduce these substantive topics.

Research the Law: Compare and contrast the rules governing venue and domicile for dissolution of marriage between your home state and one neighboring state. Consider how the procedural rules of jurisdiction might alter the substantive outcomes. Be prepared to discuss with the class one example of a procedural difference and why it would matter. What happens if both spouses file for divorce in two different jurisdictions?

Legal Separation

Some states require the spouses to separate before divorce. Legal separation is defined as either a trial or permanent time period when a couple remains married but formally lives separate and apart from one another. Often a court order provides for temporary maintenance, child custody, access, and child support during the legal separation. Legal separation is not allowed in Delaware, Florida, Georgia, Idaho, Mississippi, Pennsylvania, and Texas.

The basic difference between a legal separation and a divorce is that a court order or judgment of legal separation governs the rules for couples living apart from one another while a divorce decree is the actual termination of the marriage. In some cases, a separation may be exercised on a trial basis in order for a couple to determine whether to reconcile or dissolve the marriage. A separation can also be an alternative or a precursor to divorce. There are couples who decide to separate for a period of time in order to maintain health or social security benefits for a spouse. By the time a legal separation occurs, the couple has usually decided to enter into formal agreement about the property division, child custody arrangement, child support, and alimony. A formal separation is marked by written agreement, which becomes a judgment of legal separation entered by a court.

It is important to know the state rules concerning separation for clients who are not sure whether they truly want to dissolve their marriage. A separation can affect the financial responsibilities of the spouses before the divorce, as well as the property division during the divorce. In some states, living apart can change the property rights between a couple if they separate with the intent not to reconcile. The assets and debts they acquire during the separation remain their

---

[10] WILLIAM J. DOHERTY AND LEAH WARD SEARS, SECOND CHANCES: A PROPOSAL TO REDUCE UNNECESSARY DIVORCE 23–24 (2011).

separate property. However, in other states, property is treated the same during separation as it is during the marriage itself. In most states that allow for legal separation, once a couple permanently separates, spousal debt is no longer joint, and any property or income acquired or earned by one spouse is not jointly acquired.

Temporary Orders

Many clients may need or wish to obtain temporary orders contemporaneously with the divorce petition. In some states, temporary orders are a basic part of the divorce process and are issued routinely to govern how the court expects the couple to relate to one another and their children during the court proceeding. Temporary orders can compel a respondent party to appear in court and furnish information, like tax returns or a financial statement of assets. They may also be used to order the parties to behave appropriately with respect to maintaining their property and records, incurring debts, spending funds, and withdrawing resources from the marital estate. Temporary orders typically set forth which spouse is awarded use of the residence and/or car(s), custody of the children, as well as which spouse is obligated to pay child support and health insurance for the children, and/or spousal maintenance while the case is pending. They can set forth restrictions for travel, communication, and access to the children. The court can also use temporary orders to order social studies on the homes of any person requesting custody or access to the children, psychological or psychiatric evaluations, and parent education courses. If there is family violence within the home, temporary orders can provide strict boundaries for access and communication, so as to offer protection for the spouse and/or other family members in danger. Finally, the court can use temporary orders to appoint guardians ad litem for the children and/or a parenting coordinators or facilitators.

It is important to know how temporary orders are used in your county so that you can speak to your client about this during the first consultation. There may be a standard form that your client can review that requires each side to identify the issue(s) they wish the court to rule upon while the matter is pending before the court. Temporary orders are addressed in more detail in Chapter Three (Intimate Partner Violence), Chapter Five (Child Custody and Visitation), and Chapter Eight (Property Distribution and Alimony).

Therapy for Couples and Children

Many courts require divorcing couples who share children to attend couples counseling and to obtain therapy for their children, depending on the ages. Typically, these courts have the local resources and referrals to mental health professionals who offer these services to couples and children at a low cost or on a sliding fee scale. The use of mental health professionals for family members during the divorce process has been shown to be very effective for establishing a peaceful transition for divorcing couples and their children.

The Respondent's Answer

After a Petition to Divorce is filed, the spouse who has been sued is the respondent, and as in any other lawsuit, he or she has a limited time to file a written answer with the court. The range of respondent's answers vary, but the most common answer is a General Answer and Denial, which is usually a short pleading. Even if both parties agree, a general denial is necessary so that there will not be a default judgment. A *pro se* respondent may be able to answer a petition for divorce with a signed letter to the court if it identifies the parties, acknowledges receipt of the petition, and contains a valid return address. In some cases, spouses do not care about a default judgment because they agree with everything the petitioner is requesting. Filing no paperwork is cheaper and less hassle for the agreeable spouse.

On the other hand, if the petition for divorce is for cause and/or there are matters in dispute, the respondent's answer may need to include affirmative defenses, specific denials, special exceptions, and/or verified pleas. There may also be other responsive pleadings or motions that need to be filed to address jurisdiction or venue disputes.

III. CONFLICTS OF INTEREST

All attorneys must be aware of conflicts of interest that arise within their specific practice. It is important to understand the types of legal service payment arrangements allowed for family law matters pursuant to the ethical rules. A contingency payment agreement is unethical because it could incentivize an outcome at odds with the public policy of the family court. Some family law attorneys accept flat fees for simple matters, but most require retainer fees to secure legal representation.

Representing couples in probate court matters or termination of parental rights cases is an example of a situation where a family law lawyer may be prohibited from representing both parties. One of the more common situations is the friendly "uncontested divorce." Consider this scenario:

Gary and Heather have been married for seven years and now wish to go their separate ways. They simply grew apart. Both want to live their lives in a much different way after having matured since their marriage in their early twenties. They do not have a lot of money. They have asked you to represent them in a uncontested divorce. Heather is a schoolteacher. Gary is a maintenance worker for an airline company. They have agreed on splitting all their property and debt. They have no children but do have two dogs. They have agreed to share joint custody of both dogs. They have reduced their agreement to writing and have presented it to you at the first consultation.

Research the Law: Can you represent them both in a divorce? Why or why not? Research your state ethical rules to answer this question.

Ethical Considerations: A common ethical issue for attorneys who advertise via a firm website is the online collection of information from potential clients. What are the Model Rules that apply to this issue? Identify the rules and relevant comments so that you are aware of your ethical responsibilities as a family law attorney.

What information do you need to do a conflict of interest check on a potential family law client? What, if any, ethical obligations do you have in dealing with a prospective client? How can you avoid establishing an attorney-client relationship with a prospective client before the necessary conflict checks has occurred and the formal retainer agreement has been executed? Discuss the answers to these questions in class.

IV. LEGAL SEPARATION: CASE FILE—GABRIELLA SMITH

A. SIMULATION ROADMAP

In this simulation, you will interview a new client. You will also draft a formal separation agreement for this client after your interview. When you consult with a potential client about legal representation, there is a great deal of information you need to gather before you can decide how to handle the case, such as:

a) whether the case will be contested or uncontested;

b) whether the divorce should be filed as a no-fault or fault divorce; and

c) if there are other matters that you need to consider, such as child custody and support, protection against family violence, or temporary maintenance or alimony.

Most family law attorneys use questionnaires or online tools to collect initial information from their clients to help them identify which family law matters are relevant. For a client seeking separation or divorce, the questionnaire should be a more in-depth, multi-page document that requests the client to list specific information such as jurisdictional facts, details about the parent-child relationship, employment history, any history of family violence, and all financial information, including debt, retirement funds, and where and how assets are held.

The client information sheet for a separating or divorcing client should include a "Relationship Timeline" and a "Client's Day in the Life List." The relationship timeline should highlight significant dates in the client's relationship. It serves as a guideline for a deposition or direct examination of the opposing spouse, if the matter proceeds to trial. The client's "Day in the Life List" portrays a typical day between the client and the opposing party. It usually indicates the level of care and time each party puts into the home, the workday, each other, and the care of family members (if there are children or elderly relatives involved in the matter).

B. INITIAL CONSULTATION NOTES AND CLIENT FILE

Gabriella (30) and Sean (32) Smith live in New York and got married right after college at ages 22 and 24, respectively. They both have high-powered jobs and decided at the beginning of their marriage not to have children to advance their careers and travel. Gabriella just made partner at her prestigious law firm, and Sean is a Vice-President at a large brokerage firm. Gabriella has changed her mind about having children and would like to slow down her pace at work to have at least two children. Sean does not want to compromise his jetsetter lifestyle by having children. He and Gabriella are at a crossroads. Gabriella is anxious to move forward with finding a new partner and conceiving soon if she and Sean cannot move forward together. She has just placed a down payment on a townhome in New Jersey with her annual bonus in anticipation of the divorce. She has come to your family law practice to start divorce proceedings.

Client File for Gabriella Smith

Relationship Timeline for Gabriella Smith

10/YR-10	Met Sean at an undergrad party when I was a sophomore. He was a junior.
12/YR-10	Started dating Sean exclusively.
5/YR-09	Sean graduated from undergrad and moved to New York. Began working for large brokerage firm. Long distance relationship.
8/YR-09	Broke up with Sean over his cheating with a sorority sister.
1/YR-08	Got back together with Sean.
2/YR-08	Sean proposed. We got engaged. Sean worked remotely and lived with me.
5/YR-08	I graduated from undergrad, moved to New York, and lived with Sean.
8/YR-08	I began law school in New York.
12/YR-08	We got married.
7/YR-07	I got pregnant unintentionally.
9/YR-07	I had a miscarriage. I went to counseling by myself.
1/YR-06	Sean got promoted to Vice-President. He started to travel a lot and was gone 2 weeks out of every month.
3/YR-06	We had a big fight about Sean's work traveling schedule and his extra weekend trips to Vegas with his fraternity brothers.
2/YR-05	Sean's grandmother died. He went through a small bout of depression.
5/YR-05	I graduated from law school.
8/YR-05	I took the bar. Sean and I went on a 2nd honeymoon. We had a huge fight about his friendship with a female work colleague.
9/YR-05	I began working at a large law firm. I bought my first new car.
12/YR-05	Sean told me he's jealous of two of the men in my law associate class because they communicate with me via text outside of work.
6/YR-04	I found pictures of Sean's female work colleague on his phone. She had on sexy bathing suits. In one photo, she was topless. I confronted him and we had a huge argument.
7/YR-04	Sean refused to go to counseling to discuss his infidelity, which he never actually admitted.
5/YR-03	I had an affair with one of the junior partners at my firm. He was married and just had a baby.
7/YR-03	Sean and I discussed when we want to have children. He told me he wants to wait until we get to our thirties to start thinking about children. Says we are too young and should save up our money and travel first.
10/YR-03	I ended the affair with the junior partner. I moved to a different law firm.
12/YR-03	Sean surprised me with a two-week vacation to Europe.
10/YR-02	Sean got promoted to President. He got a big bonus and spent most of it on a 1-month trip to China. He got an offer to take a short-term position with his firm in Beijing.

12/YR-02	I found out Sean took the short-term position for one year without telling me. I was mad because he did not take into consideration my work schedule when he said yes.
5/YR-02	I got promoted to junior partner at my firm. Did not see Sean for six months.
12/YR-02	Sean moved back to New York permanently. Things were tense between us.
2/YR-01	Second Valentine's day we did not spend together. We had a big argument over the phone. He was in California supposedly visiting his college friend and his family.
6/YR-01	I noticed Sean leaving the room to text and pick up calls. He stayed at work later and sometimes came home at 2 a.m. during the week. His secretary sent me a birthday gift addressed to "Nikki." We had a big argument. He claimed that she got him mixed up with another colleague and that Nikki is his colleague's girlfriend.
9/YR-01	I made partner at my law firm. Sean took me out for a celebration with my friends and our family. Most of the toasts involved being happy that Sean and I have both accomplished our professional goals so now we can move on to having children.
9/YR-00	Sean and I had a blow-out argument. He moved out to stay at a hotel. He said he did not want to have kids right now.

Wife's Day in the Life List (before spouse moved out)

5:30 am	Wake up; Sean still in bed.
6:00 am	Go exercise @ gym
7:00 am	Grab breakfast & coffee w/ best friend Kamryn
8:00 am	Arrive at work
11:30 am	Lunch with co-workers or girlfriends
1:00 pm	Return to work
6:00 pm	Networking (2–3 days each week)
7:00 pm	Leave work
7:30 pm	Meet Sean for dinner (or not)
10:00 pm	Wine @ home with or without Sean
10:30 pm	Check email and social media
11:00 pm	Go to sleep

Client Financial Information

Employer: Coles & Donahue Law Firm

Position: Partner

Income: $750,000

Additional Compensation: $200,000

Bank Accounts & Balances:

Checking: $150,000

Savings: $350,000

Assets: Townhome in New Jersey (Market Value, $2.5M)

Loans: Mortgage = $7700/month

Law School Loans = $2500/month

Car payment = $1700/month

Credit Card Debts:

AAdvantage Citibank Visa = -$10,000

American Express = -$5000

JP Morgan Chase = -$7500

Monthly Expenses: $30,000 total per month, including above loans, credit card payments, current apartment rent ($5500/month), half of all utilities, gym membership ($650/month), personal trainer, club fees, monthly parking, money paid to parents ($2000/month), charitable giving ($2000/month), chef service, vacations, car maintenance, dry cleaning, self-care maintenance (facials, hair, nails, massages, waxing) ($1200/month)

C. RELEVANT STATUTORY LAWS AND PRACTICE GUIDANCE

You are a family law attorney practicing in New York State. Your research locates the following statutory law from your jurisdiction and secondary sources to help inform your work on Gabriella Smith's behalf.

1. New York State Statutes

DOMESTIC RELATIONS LAW

§ 170. Action for divorce

An action for divorce may be maintained by a husband or wife to procure a judgment divorcing the parties and dissolving the marriage on any of the following grounds:

(1) The cruel and inhuman treatment of the plaintiff by the defendant such that the conduct of the defendant so endangers the physical or mental well-being of the plaintiff as renders it unsafe or improper for the plaintiff to cohabit with the defendant.

(2) The abandonment of the plaintiff by the defendant for a period of one or more years.

(3) The confinement of the defendant in prison for a period of three or more consecutive years after the marriage of plaintiff and defendant.

(4) The commission of an act of adultery, provided that adultery for the purposes of articles ten, eleven, and eleven-A of this chapter, is hereby defined as the commission of an act of vaginal sexual contact, oral sexual contact or anal sexual contact, voluntarily performed by the defendant, with a person other than the plaintiff after the marriage of plaintiff and defendant. Oral sexual contact and anal sexual contact include, but are not limited to, sexual conduct as defined in subdivision two of section 130.00 and subdivision four of section 130.20 of the penal law.

(5) The husband and wife have lived apart pursuant to a decree or judgment of separation for a period of one or more years after the granting of such decree or judgment, and satisfactory proof has been submitted by the plaintiff that he or she has substantially performed all the terms and conditions of such decree or judgment.

(6) The husband and wife have lived separate and apart pursuant to a written agreement of separation, subscribed by the parties thereto and acknowledged or proved in the form required to entitle a deed to be recorded, for a period of one or more years after the execution of such agreement and satisfactory proof has been submitted by the plaintiff that he or she has substantially performed all the terms and conditions of such agreement. Such agreement shall be filed in the office of the clerk of the county wherein either party resides. In lieu of filing such agreement, either party to such agreement may file a memorandum of such agreement, which memorandum shall be similarly subscribed and acknowledged or proved as was the agreement of separation and shall contain the following information: (a) the names and addresses of each of the parties, (b) the date of marriage of the parties, (c) the date of the agreement of separation and (d) the date of this subscription and acknowledgment or proof of such agreement of separation.

(7) The relationship between husband and wife has broken down irretrievably for a period of at least six months, provided that one party has so stated under oath. No judgment of divorce shall be granted under this subdivision unless and until the economic issues of equitable distribution of marital property, the payment or waiver of spousal support, the payment of child support, the payment of counsel and experts' fees and expenses as well as the custody and visitation with the infant children of the marriage have been resolved by the parties, or determined by the court and incorporated into the judgment of divorce.

* * *

§ 200. Action for separation

An action may be maintained by a husband or wife against the other party to the marriage to procure a judgment separating the parties from bed and board, forever, or for a limited time, for any of the following causes:

1. The cruel and inhuman treatment of the plaintiff by the defendant such that the conduct of the defendant so endangers the physical or mental well-being of the plaintiff as renders it unsafe or improper for the plaintiff to cohabit with the defendant.

2. The abandonment of the plaintiff by the defendant.

3. The neglect or refusal of the defendant-spouse to provide for the support of the plaintiff-spouse where the defendant-spouse is chargeable with such support under the provisions of section thirty-two of this chapter or of section four hundred twelve of the family court act.

4. The commission of an act of adultery by the defendant; except where such offense is committed by the procurement or with the connivance of the plaintiff or where there is voluntary cohabitation of the parties with the knowledge of the offense or where action was not commenced within five years after the discovery by the plaintiff of the offense charged or where the plaintiff has also been guilty of adultery under such circumstances that the defendant would have been entitled, if innocent, to a divorce, provided that adultery for the purposes of this subdivision is hereby defined as the commission of an act of vaginal sexual contact, oral sexual contact or anal sexual contact, voluntarily performed by the defendant, with a person other than the plaintiff after the marriage of plaintiff and defendant. Oral sexual contact and anal sexual contact include, but are not limited to, sexual contact as defined in subdivision two of section 130.00 and subdivision four of section 130.20 of the penal law.

5. The confinement of the defendant in prison for a period of three or more consecutive years after the marriage of plaintiff and defendant.

* * *

§ 202. Defense of justification

The defendant in an action for separation from bed and board may set up, in justification, the misconduct of the plaintiff; and if that defense is established to the satisfaction of the court, the defendant is entitled to judgment.

§ 203. Judgment for separation revocable

Upon the joint application of the parties, accompanied with satisfactory evidence of their reconciliation, a judgment for a separation, forever, or for a limited period, rendered as prescribed in this article, may be revoked at any time by the court which rendered it, subject to such regulations and restrictions as the court thinks fit to impose.

* * *

§ 210. Limitations on actions for divorce and separation

No action for divorce or separation may be maintained on a ground which arose more than five years before the date of the commencement of that action for divorce or separation except where:

(a) In an action for divorce, the grounds therefor are one of those specified in subdivision (2), (4), (5) or (6) of section one hundred seventy of this chapter, or

(b) In an action for separation, the grounds therefor are one of those specified in subdivision 2 or 4 of section two hundred of this chapter.

2. American Jurisprudence—Alimony and Separation Agreements

1B AM. JUR. LEGAL FORMS 2D *Alimony and Separation Agreements*

(Internal citations omitted)

§ 17:137. Form drafting guide

A husband and wife may legally contract with each other, as part of a separation agreement, for the division of property and the settlement of property rights between them. Voluntary property settlement agreements, in the case of separating spouses, are favored in the law. Where state statutes exist that specify the formal requirements of such agreements, they should, of course, be complied with.

A property settlement agreement must be free from fraud, duress and other similar infirmities. It should determine and settle the rights of the spouses in property owned together, provide for the release by each spouse of his or her rights in the property that is apportioned to the other party, and provide for the surrender by each party of rights of inheritance and of administration in the estate of the other.

Tax Notes:

Federal tax aspects of a property settlement agreement and its particular provisions should be carefully considered in the preparation of the instrument.

§ 17:138. Form drafting guide—Checklist—Matters to be considered in drafting property settlement agreement

Checklist of matters that should be considered in drafting a separation agreement providing for the division of property and settlement of property rights:

- Full name and current address of each spouse.
- Identification of spouses as husband and as wife.
- Date and place of marriage.
- Date or approximate date of the parties' separation.
  - — Reason for separation.
- Purpose of the agreement.
- Independent legal representation of the parties.
- Statement of the consideration for the agreement.
- Name and age of each surviving child born to the marriage.
- Emancipation of any child.
  - — Approximate date of and event causing emancipation.
- Support and maintenance of one spouse by other spouse.
- Custody of minor children.
- Support of minor children.
- List and description of all property owned.
  - — By husband.
  - — By wife.
  - — By both parties.

- Dividing and apportioning property.
  - — To wife.
  - — To husband.
- Waiver and release by each party respecting property apportioned to other.
- Evaluating and stating value of property apportioned.
  - — To wife.
  - — To husband.
- Provision for payment of difference in value of apportioned property.
  - — To wife by husband.
  - — To husband by wife.
  - — Waiver of claim for difference in value where minimal.
- Encumbrances and other obligations relating to specific items of property.
  - — To be assumed by party taking items.
  - — Not to be assumed by party.
- Release and quitclaim by each party of all right and claim in property assigned to other.
- Release by each party of right to take estate or other party by statute or under will.
- Release and waiver by each party of right to administer estate of other.
- Full disclosure by each party of all property interests owned.
  - — Declaration and covenant of full disclosure.
- Provision for payment of existing debts.
  - — Of wife.
  - — Of husband.
  - — Of both parties.
- Covenant by each party to pay future debts.
- Casualty insurance coupled with property interests.
  - — Assignment with property.
- Special provisions concerning life insurance.
  - — On life of husband.
  - — On life of wife.
- After-discovered property.
  - — Provision for manner of holding and disposition.
- Special provisions regarding family residence.
  - — Occupation by husband or wife until remarriage.
- Arbitration of disputes.
- Effect on agreement of divorce or dissolution of marriage.

- Stipulation for preparation and delivery of all instruments necessary to effectuate agreement.
- Income tax matters. Gift tax matters.
    - — Effect of cash payment by one party to other as part of property settlement.
- Date of agreement.
- Number of counterparts (originals) of agreement.
- Signatures of parties.
- Approvals of counsel.
- Acknowledgments by parties, if desired or necessary.

§ 17:139. Separation and property settlement agreement

SEPARATION AND PROPERTY SETTLEMENT AGREEMENT

This agreement is made *[date of agreement]*, between *[name of husband]*, residing at *[address of husband]* ("husband"), and *[name of wife]*, residing at *[address of wife]* ("wife").

RECITALS

A. The parties were married on *[date of marriage]*, in *[name of city]*, *[name of county]*, *[name of state]*, and ever since have been and now are husband and wife.

B. Husband and wife have *[no children born of their marriage and now living/the following listed children born of their marriage and now living: [names of children] and [ages of children]]*.

C. As the result of disputes and unhappy differences between the parties, they *[separated on or about [date of separation]/have agreed to an immediate and permanent separation]*.

D. Husband and wife intend and it is the purpose of this agreement to make a complete and final settlement of all claims that *[husband/wife]* may have against *[wife/husband]* for alimony, support and maintenance, to provide fairly and adequately for *[his/her]* support and maintenance, to memorialize the separation of the parties and their agreement to remain separated, to finalize their agreements as to the division of the property, both real and personal, owned by them or either of them *[OPTIONAL: and to provide for the custody, support and maintenance of their minor [child/children]]*.

E. In order to ensure the full information and advice of both husband and wife, each has retained and has been represented by independent legal counsel in connection with the negotiations for and the drafting of this agreement in the consideration of the respective rights, duties, and obligations of the parties.

[Name of wife's attorney], of *[address of wife's attorney]*, has represented wife, and *[name of husband's attorney]*, of *[address of husband's attorney]*, has represented husband.

F. *[OPTIONAL: [An action/A proceeding] for [divorce/dissolution of marriage/separate maintenance] is [now pending/will shortly be filed by [name of plaintiff/petitioner]] in [name of court] at [address of court].]*

In consideration of the matters described above, and of the mutual benefits and obligations set forth in this agreement, the parties agree as follows:

SECTION ONE. LIVING SEPARATE AND APART

Husband and wife may and shall live separate and apart, each free from all dominion, restraint and control by the other, whether direct or indirect, as fully as if unmarried.

Each party may reside at such place or places as he or she may select.

SECTION TWO. NO MOLESTATION OR INTERFERENCE

Neither party shall molest or interfere with the other or compel or attempt to compel the other to cohabit or dwell with him or her, by any means, by legal action or otherwise.

SECTION THREE. LIST OF PROPERTY OWNED BY HUSBAND

The following property is owned by husband alone:

Item One: Real property situated in *[name of county]*, *[name of state]*, and more specifically described as follows: *[description of real property]*.

Item Two: *[Number of shares]* shares of common stock of *[name of corporation]*, a *[name of state]* corporation.

Item Three: One *[make and model of automobile]* automobile, serial number *[serial number of automobile]*, title certificate number *[title certificate number of automobile]*, registered in *[name of state]*.

Item Four: *[Description of personal property]*.

SECTION FOUR. LIST OF PROPERTY OWNED BY WIFE

The following property is owned by wife alone:

Item One: Real property situated in *[name of county]*, *[name of state]*, and more specifically described as follows: *[description of real property]*.

Item Two: $*[Dollar amount of savings account]* in a savings account, number *[specification of savings account number]*, on deposit with *[name of bank]* at *[address of bank]*.

Item Three: Savings bonds of the United States government, series *[list of series numbers]*, the present value of which is $*[dollar amount of value of savings bonds]*.

Item Four: *[Description of personal property]*.

SECTION FIVE. LIST OF PROPERTY OWNED BY HUSBAND AND WIFE

The following property is owned by husband and wife together *[in community/as joint tenants with right of survivorship/as tenants in common]*:

Item One: The premises known as *[street address of premises]*, in *[name of city]*, *[name of county]*, *[name of state]*, the former family residence of the parties, subject to a *[mortgage/deed of trust]*, of which the balance is approximately $*[dollar amount of mortgage balance]*.

Item Two: One *[make and model of automobile]* automobile, serial number *[serial number of automobile]*, title certificate number *[title certificate number of automobile]*, registered in *[name of state]*.

Item Three: $*[Dollar amount of joint checking account balance]* in a joint checking account, number *[specification of checking account number]*, on deposit with *[name of bank]*, at *[address of bank]*.

Item Four: $*[Dollar amount of joint savings account balance]* in a joint savings account, number *[specification of savings account number]*, on deposit with *[name of bank]*, at *[address of bank]*.

Item Five: *[Description of personal property]*.

SECTION SIX. PROPERTY APPORTIONED TO WIFE

There is apportioned and set aside to wife, free of all claim and demand of husband, the following items as numbered and described in SECTION THREE, FOUR and FIVE of this agreement: Item

Two of SECTION THREE, Items Two and Three OF SECTION FOUR, and Items One, Two and Three of SECTION FIVE.

Each item of property set aside and transferred to wife is assigned to and taken by her with all encumbrances and other obligations to which such items may be subject.

Wife shall pay and discharge all such encumbrances and obligations and hold husband free and harmless from the same *[OPTIONAL: except the balance of the [mortgage/deed of trust] standing against Item One of SECTION FIVE, the family residence, which husband shall pay as the same becomes due]*.

SECTION SEVEN. PROPERTY APPORTIONED TO HUSBAND

There is apportioned and set aside to husband, free of all claim and demand of wife, the following Items as numbered and described in SECTION THREE, FOUR and FIVE of this agreement: Items One and Three of SECTION THREE, Item One of SECTION FOUR, and Item Four of SECTION FIVE.

Each item of property set aside and transferred to husband is assigned to and taken by him with all encumbrances and other obligations to which such items may be subject.

Husband shall pay and discharge all such encumbrances and obligations and hold wife free and harmless from the same.

SECTION EIGHT. VALUE OF PROPERTY APPORTIONED

The present net value of all items apportioned to wife under Section Six, after deducting all encumbrances and obligations outstanding against such property and assumed by wife, but including the equity and interest of wife in such property prior to the apportionment and transfer to her, is $*[dollar amount of net value of items apportioned to wife]*.

The present net value of all items apportioned to husband under Section Seven, after deducting all encumbrances and obligations outstanding against such property and assumed by husband, but including the equity and interest of husband in such property prior to the apportionment and transfer to him, is $*[dollar amount of net value of items apportioned to husband]*.

SECTION NINE. DIFFERENCE IN VALUES OF PROPERTY APPORTIONED; PAYMENT OF DIFFERENCE

The difference between the net value of the property apportioned to wife and the net value of the property apportioned to husband, as set forth in SECTION EIGHT, is $*[dollar amount of sum]*, in favor of *[husband/wife]*.

[[Husband/Wife] shall pay to [wife/husband] the amount of the difference in net values in equal monthly installments of $[dollar amount of monthly installment payment] commencing [date of first installment payment]/The amount of the difference in net values being minimal, [husband/wife] waives and releases all claim arising from such difference].

SECTION TEN. DIVISION OF PROPERTY—EXECUTION OF INSTRUMENTS

Each party shall promptly execute and deliver to the other party or any nominee or nominees of the other party, all instruments that may be necessary, convenient or appropriate to carry into effect, fully and fairly, all the provisions of this agreement for division and confirmation of property, and mutual releases of the same.

SECTION ELEVEN. DIVISION OF PROPERTY—RELEASE OF PROPERTY RIGHTS

Each party releases, quitclaims and assigns to the other party all his or her right, title and interest, present and prospective, in each item of property in this agreement apportioned and set aside to the other party *[OPTIONAL: [including, but not limited to, all rights of dower or curtesy, choate or inchoate, homestead and family rights on probate/including, but not limited to, all community rights and rights as joint tenant]].*

SECTION TWELVE. DIVISION OF PROPERTY—FULL DISCLOSURE OF PROPERTY INTERESTS

Each party warrants that he or she has made a full disclosure of all his or her property, and that neither has knowledge of any other property of any kind in which the party so representing has any beneficial interest.

SECTION THIRTEEN. RELEASE OF ESTATE RIGHTS

Each party releases all right to share in the estate of the other, or to serve as personal representative of the estate of the other, except only as provided by will or codicil to will executed subsequent to the date of this agreement.

SECTION FOURTEEN. DEBTS AND OBLIGATIONS

Each of the parties shall pay all debts incurred by him or her after the date of this agreement and indemnify the other party against liability for the same.

[Husband/Wife] shall pay debts incurred by *[him/her]* or by *[wife/husband]* or by the parties jointly prior to the date of this agreement, including the following: *[description of debts].*

SECTION FIFTEEN. SUPPORT AND MAINTENANCE OF SPOUSE

[Husband/Wife] shall pay to *[wife/husband]* as and for *[his/her]* necessary support and maintenance, $*[dollar amount of monthly spousal support]* per month, on or before the *[ordinal number of day of month]* day of each month, and continuing until the remarriage of *[wife/husband]*, the death of husband, or the death of wife, whichever event shall first occur.

All payments by *[husband/wife]* for the support and maintenance of *[wife/husband]* shall be separate from any other obligation of *[husband/wife]* under the terms of this agreement to make payments to *[wife/husband].*

SECTION SIXTEEN. ATTORNEYS' FEES OF SPOUSE

[Husband/Wife] shall pay to *[name of attorney]*, attorney for *[wife/husband]*, on the execution of this agreement, $*[dollar amount of legal fee]* for services rendered to *[wife/husband]* in all matters relating to the separation of the parties and the negotiations for and preparation of this agreement.

[Wife/Husband] waives and releases all other and further right to reimbursement by *[husband/wife]* for attorneys' fees previously incurred or to be incurred in the future.

SECTION SEVENTEEN. MODIFICATION; BINDING EFFECT

The provisions of this agreement shall not be modified or changed except by mutual consent and agreement of the parties, expressed in writing.

This agreement shall be binding on the parties and their respective heirs, personal representatives and assigns.

Executed at *[place of execution]* the day and year first above written.

[Name of husband]

[Name of wife]

[Acknowledgments]

Approved *[OPTIONAL: as to form]* on *[date of approval by husband's attorney]*

[Name of husband's attorney]

[Address of husband's attorney]

Approved *[OPTIONAL: as to form]* on *[date of approval by wife's attorney]*

[Name of wife's attorney]

[Address of wife's attorney]

D. THE SIMULATION

1. Interviewing the Client

After reviewing the New York State statute, the Initial Consultation, and the Client's case file, draft questions to interview Gabriella Smith so that you can obtain the necessary information to draft a separation agreement. In conducting this interview, be sensitive to the cultural competency considerations you explored in Chapter One.

2. Drafting a Separation Agreement

Draft a formal separation agreement for Gabriella Smith. You will need to review the client's interview prior to drafting the agreement. A sample agreement and a checklist for preparing an agreement was provided in the preceding American Jurisprudence source to help you get started.

V. DISSOLUTION OF A MARRIAGE: CASE FILE—ADRIENNE SCOTT

A. SIMULATION ROADMAP

Before drafting a dissolution petition, you will need to interview your client to understand their objectives. Building on your prior work preparing for Gabriella's client interview, your next client is ready to petition for divorce. In this simulation, the client intake interview has already taken place, and you will review the notes recorded by your firm's paralegal.

You should first determine whether the prior interview adequately explored the reason(s) Adrienne wants to divorce, her children's needs, and her own needs after the divorce. What are the grounds for divorce that your client wants to pursue? Is there other information that you need, aside from what was collected during the initial interview to file a petition for divorce? Once you have compiled the necessary information for a pleading, use the interview notes to draft a *Petition for Divorce and Suit Affecting Parent Child Relationship*.

B. CLIENT INTERVIEW NOTES

Preliminary Facts re: Reasons for Seeking Divorce

Adrienne and Brandon Scott have been married for eight years. Brandon is a systems administrator for a small start-up company. Adrienne is a pediatric nurse. They live in Dallas, Texas. Adrienne is African-American and Brandon is Caucasian. They have two biological children, Joshua (6) and Ava (3). They have recently discussed separation because Brandon has been having an affair for the last two years with Lauren. Lauren is a single White woman who is now pregnant, presumably with Brandon's child. This is the last straw for Adrienne, and she has come to you to discuss next steps for proceeding with the separation and divorce.

Interview Notes for Client Adrienne Scott

Q: Can you describe the first four years of your marriage.

A: The first four years of the marriage were great. We got married in YR-08. Brandon was twenty-eight, and I was twenty-seven when we got married. We knew each other for four years before we got married. His parents were initially not supportive of the marriage because of my race. We had two pretty good years before our son was born, but Brandon did not see or speak to his parents that much. We traveled together and spent time with my family and our friends from college. Both of us had good jobs that we liked.

When I got pregnant with Joshua, we were both excited about having our first child together. Brandon was elated to have a son. His parents even came around to accepting me as his wife because Joshua was their first grandchild. I had a good pregnancy and problem-free delivery. The first two years with Joshua were an adjustment—like with any other couple who has a child. We got very little sleep, but we were happy. We purchased our first house when Joshua was one-year-old. We did not have a lot of debt except for student loans from college and one car note for Brandon's car. Our families grew very supportive of us. They helped out with Joshua whenever they could. Both of our parents live in the city. I took off some time from work after Joshua was born, but I went back to work after three months of unpaid maternity leave.

Q: How have the last several years compared to your first four years of marriage?

A: The last three years have been awful. The year that I was pregnant with Ava was difficult. I was constantly sick and lost time on my job. Our finances were affected when I had to take family medical leave because my doctor put me on bedrest. Both of our parents have been encouraging me to quit my job and stay home with the kids, but I don't want to be totally dependent on Brandon for money.

Q: Earlier in our consultation, you stated the reason you want to divorce your husband is because of his affair with a woman named Lauren. Can you tell me how you came to know about this affair?

A: I read some text messages between Brandon and Lauren. It was clear that they were hooking up and spending time together.

Q: How do you know that they were having sex?

A: Some of the texts referred graphically to things they did together that were sexual in nature. Several messages from Lauren had chili peppers emojis along with "Meeting tonight?" In response, Brandon would give a time and place, usually a hotel name like "Hyatt" or "Omni." The next day after these messages, Lauren would send several texts that said things like "last night" followed by a fire emoji, or "Miss you" followed by a puckered lips emoji. I took screenshots of the texts. I can send them to you.

Q: Do you know how long the affair has been going on?

A: At least two years.

Q: How do you know this?

A: When I searched his computer and checked our phone records, I saw that this one number, which I think is her cell phone number, dates back to YR-02.

Q: Has your husband admitted to this affair?

A: He denied the affair at first. Recently, he just says he is done with the issue—he does not deny it anymore. He just deflects when I ask him questions about her. One of our mutual friends told me Lauren was pregnant, so I definitely suspected that it might be his child.

Q: How did you confirm that Lauren was pregnant?

A: Lauren called me and told me she was pregnant with Brandon's son.

Q: What does Brandon say about the pregnancy?

A: He says that the baby could not possibly be his child.

Q: Did you continue to have sex with Brandon after you found out about Lauren?

A: Yes—initially when he denied it, I thought he was telling the truth. After she called and told me she was pregnant, I have not slept with him. That was about four weeks ago.

Q: Have you and your husband ever had marriage counseling?

A: No.

Q: If the court orders you and Brandon to go to counseling before you can proceed with the divorce, are you willing to make a good-faith effort to try and reconcile with him?

A: That would be really difficult for me at this point. I don't trust him at all! Unless he admits what he has done, marriage counseling would be pointless. If that baby is his, I don't see how our marriage could make it. I won't be able to really know if he is the father for another six months when the baby is born.

Q: Did you ask Brandon to do DNA testing once the child is born?

A: Yes, but he said no, it was not necessary. He won't do genetic testing unless a court orders him to do it.

Q: Have you told him that you want a divorce?

A: Yes, he knows that I want to end the marriage.

Q: Did you all talk about child custody and child support?

A: He said that he did not want to split up our children. He does not want to live separately. He said he wanted joint custody and was not interested in paying child support. He knows that having joint legal and physical custody means that he would not have to pay child support. Plus, if that child is his, he will have another child to take care of and will likely have to pay her child support.

Q: Who does most of the caretaking of the children?

A: Me, of course. I mean, he picks them up from daycare and school, but I do most of the cooking, cleaning, grocery shopping, lunch packing, clothes shopping, teacher-parent conferences, etc.

Q: Do either of your children have any special needs?

A: Yes. Ava was just diagnosed with autism, and we are awaiting further test results to understand more about what her individual developmental needs are. I may need to reduce my work schedule to stay home and help her before she enters elementary school. Joshua and Ava are otherwise healthy and happy kids.

Q: You have two options in filing for a divorce. You can seek a no-fault or a fault-based divorce. The no-fault divorce essentially ends the marriage, but it's no one spouse's legal fault. The fault-based divorce puts the marital fault squarely on one person. Do you have a sense of whether you want to file a no-fault or a fault-based divorce?

A: Fault. It is his fault! I did not have an affair—he ruined our marriage by knocking up this Lauren woman!

Q: All right. If the court finds that it was his fault, you may have some advantage as far as the property division.

A: Will the court just force us to sell the house and divide up the debt?

Q: It depends. You may be able to come to some agreement about the house if he is willing to concede and admit his affair. You may also be able to agree on division of debt if both of you have enough savings or future income to pay it off. Do you think you need any temporary alimony to get on your feet after the divorce?

A: Maybe. I need some time to save up enough money to get my own place with the kids. I have some savings in a separate account that he does not know about and another credit card that I got just in case I decided to leave him over this whole affair. I have about $1500 in savings.

Q: Alimony or spousal maintenance may be feasible for you under certain circumstances. It will depend on whether you have enough property after the divorce to take care of your minimum reasonable needs and if Ava's developmental needs require you to stop working and stay at home with her. The Texas Family Code provides certain requirements must be met in order for a spouse to qualify for alimony. You ordinarily would not meet these requirements because you have not been married for ten years and you work full-time at a good job. However, there are exceptions, and being unable to work because you need to provide substantial care and personal supervision of a child with a physical or mental disability is one of them.

A: Okay, well I just want what is fair. I can let you know the outcome of Ava's testing in two weeks.

Q: Do either of you have any other assets or debts other than what you have already mentioned (the student loans and the one car note)?

A: We both have two credit cards each—I am not sure what the total balances are on all of them. My balances are around $3000 on a Citibank Visa and $1000 on a Macy's card. He has a Chase Mastercard and an American Express. There is no telling what the balances are by now. He stopped showing me those statements years ago.

Q: What are each of your incomes?

A: I make $75,000 a year, and he makes $110,000. We both have retirement accounts. I am not sure about the balances, but his is probably $30,000–$50,000 higher than mine. He may have some stock options with the new company, but it hasn't gone public yet, so I am not sure how much they are worth right now.

Q: Okay—I may have to follow up on all of the property assets and debt particulars later. Is there any reason that you would want or need a temporary restraining order?

A: Yes. I am afraid he is going to try to move some money around and hide it from me. He has two saving accounts that I am sure have a good deal of money in them. I don't want him to try and take my money either. I would like to freeze everything as it is. I also want to stop Lauren from calling our home or my phone.

C. RELEVANT STATUTORY LAWS AND PRACTICE GUIDANCE

You are a family law attorney practicing in Texas. Your research locates these Texas statutory provisions and secondary sources to help inform your work on Adrienne Scott's behalf.

1. Texas Family Code

Title 1—Chapter 6. Suit for Dissolution of Marriage

Subchapter A. Grounds for Divorce and Defenses

§ 6.001. Insupportability

On the petition of either party to a marriage, the court may grant a divorce without regard to fault if the marriage has become insupportable because of discord or conflict of personalities that destroys the legitimate ends of the marital relationship and prevents any reasonable expectation of reconciliation.

* * *

§ 6.003. Adultery

The court may grant a divorce in favor of one spouse if the other spouse has committed adultery.

* * *

§ 6.008. Defenses

(a) The defenses to a suit for divorce of recrimination and adultery are abolished.

(b) Condonation is a defense to a suit for divorce only if the court finds that there is a reasonable expectation of reconciliation.

Subchapter D. Jurisdiction, Venue, and Residence Qualifications

§ 6.301. General Residency Rule for Divorce Suit

A suit for divorce may not be maintained in this state unless at the time the suit is filed either the petitioner or the respondent has been:

(1) a domiciliary of this state for the preceding six-month period; and

(2) a resident of the county in which the suit is filed for the preceding 90-day period.

Subchapter E. Filing Suit

§ 6.401. Caption

(a) Pleadings in a suit for divorce or annulment shall be styled "In the Matter of the Marriage of ______ and ________."

(b) Pleadings in a suit to declare a marriage void shall be styled "A Suit to Declare Void the Marriage of ________ and ________."

§ 6.402. Pleadings

(a) A petition in a suit for dissolution of a marriage is sufficient without the necessity of specifying the underlying evidentiary facts if the petition alleges the grounds relied on substantially in the language of the statute.

(b) Allegations of grounds for relief, matters of defense, or facts relied on for a temporary order that are stated in short and plain terms are not subject to special exceptions because of form or sufficiency.

(c) The court shall strike an allegation of evidentiary fact from the pleadings on the motion of a party or on the court's own motion.

* * *

§ 6.404. Information Regarding Protective Orders

At any time while a suit for dissolution of a marriage is pending, if the court believes, on the basis of any information received by the court, that a party to the suit or a member of the party's family or household may be a victim of family violence, the court shall inform that party of the party's right to apply for a protective order under Title 4.

* * *

§ 6.406. Mandatory Joinder of Suit Affecting Parent-Child Relationship

(a) The petition in a suit for dissolution of a marriage shall state whether there are children born or adopted of the marriage who are under 18 years of age or who are otherwise entitled to support as provided by Chapter 154.

(a–1) If the parties to a suit for dissolution of a marriage are the intended parents under a gestational agreement that is in effect and that establishes a parent-child relationship between the parties as intended parents and an unborn child on the birth of the child, the petition in the suit for dissolution of a marriage shall state:

(1) that the parties to the marriage have entered into a gestational agreement establishing a parent-child relationship between the parties as intended parents and an unborn child on the birth of the child;

(2) whether the gestational mother under the agreement is pregnant or a child who is the subject of the agreement has been born; and

(3) whether the agreement has been validated under Section 160.756.

(b) If the parties are parents of a child, as defined by Section 101.003, and the child is not under the continuing jurisdiction of another court as provided by Chapter 155, the suit for dissolution of a marriage must include a suit affecting the parent-child relationship under Title 5.

Subchapter F. Temporary Orders

§ 6.501. Temporary Restraining Order

(a) After the filing of a suit for dissolution of a marriage, on the motion of a party or on the court's own motion, the court may grant a temporary restraining order without notice to the adverse party for the preservation of the property and for the protection of the parties as necessary, including an order prohibiting one or both parties from:

(1) intentionally communicating in person or in any other manner, including by telephone or another electronic voice transmission, video chat, in writing, or electronic messaging, with the other party by use of vulgar, profane, obscene, or indecent language or in a coarse or offensive manner, with intent to annoy or alarm the other party;

(2) threatening the other party in person or in any other manner, including by telephone or another electronic voice transmission, video chat, in writing, or electronic messaging, to take unlawful action against any person, intending by this action to annoy or alarm the other party;

(3) placing a telephone call, anonymously, at an unreasonable hour, in an offensive and repetitious manner, or without a legitimate purpose of communication with the intent to annoy or alarm the other party;

(4) intentionally, knowingly, or recklessly causing bodily injury to the other party or to a child of either party;

(5) threatening the other party or a child of either party with imminent bodily injury;

(6) intentionally, knowingly, or recklessly destroying, removing, concealing, encumbering, transferring, or otherwise harming or reducing the value of the property of the parties or either party with intent to obstruct the authority of the court to order a division of the estate of the parties in a manner that the court deems just and right, having due regard for the rights of each party and any children of the marriage;

(7) intentionally falsifying a writing or record, including an electronic record, relating to the property of either party;

(8) intentionally misrepresenting or refusing to disclose to the other party or to the court, on proper request, the existence, amount, or location of any tangible or intellectual property of the parties or either party, including electronically stored or recorded information;

(9) intentionally or knowingly damaging or destroying the tangible or intellectual property of the parties or either party, including electronically stored or recorded information;

(10) intentionally or knowingly tampering with the tangible or intellectual property of the parties or either party, including electronically stored or recorded information, and causing pecuniary loss or substantial inconvenience to the other party;

(11) except as specifically authorized by the court:

(A) selling, transferring, assigning, mortgaging, encumbering, or in any other manner alienating any of the property of the parties or either party, regardless of whether the property is:

(i) personal property, real property, or intellectual property; or

(ii) separate or community property;

(B) incurring any debt, other than legal expenses in connection with the suit for dissolution of marriage;

(C) withdrawing money from any checking or savings account in a financial institution for any purpose;

(D) spending any money in either party's possession or subject to either party's control for any purpose;

(E) withdrawing or borrowing money in any manner for any purpose from a retirement, profit sharing, pension, death, or other employee benefit plan, employee savings plan, individual retirement account, or Keogh account of either party; or

(F) withdrawing or borrowing in any manner all or any part of the cash surrender value of a life insurance policy on the life of either party or a child of the parties;

(12) entering any safe deposit box in the name of or subject to the control of the parties or either party, whether individually or jointly with others;

(13) changing or in any manner altering the beneficiary designation on any life insurance policy on the life of either party or a child of the parties;

(14) canceling, altering, failing to renew or pay premiums on, or in any manner affecting the level of coverage that existed at the time the suit was filed of, any life, casualty, automobile, or health insurance policy insuring the parties' property or persons, including a child of the parties;

(15) opening or diverting mail or e-mail or any other electronic communication addressed to the other party;

(16) signing or endorsing the other party's name on any negotiable instrument, check, or draft, including a tax refund, insurance payment, and dividend, or attempting to negotiate any negotiable instrument payable to the other party without the personal signature of the other party;

(17) taking any action to terminate or limit credit or charge credit cards in the name of the other party;

(18) discontinuing or reducing the withholding for federal income taxes from either party's wages or salary;

(19) destroying, disposing of, or altering any financial records of the parties, including a canceled check, deposit slip, and other records from a financial institution, a record of credit purchases or cash advances, a tax return, and a financial statement;

(20) destroying, disposing of, or altering any e-mail, text message, video message, or chat message or other electronic data or electronically stored information relevant to the subject matter of the suit for dissolution of marriage, regardless of whether the information is stored on a hard drive, in a removable storage device, in cloud storage, or in another electronic storage medium;

(21) modifying, changing, or altering the native format or metadata of any electronic data or electronically stored information relevant to the subject matter of the suit for dissolution of marriage, regardless of whether the information is stored on a hard drive, in a removable storage device, in cloud storage, or in another electronic storage medium;

(22) deleting any data or content from any social network profile used or created by either party or a child of the parties;

(23) using any password or personal identification number to gain access to the other party's e-mail account, bank account, social media account, or any other electronic account;

(24) terminating or in any manner affecting the service of water, electricity, gas, telephone, cable television, or any other contractual service, including security, pest control, landscaping, or yard maintenance at the residence of either party, or in any manner attempting to withdraw any deposit paid in connection with any of those services;

(25) excluding the other party from the use and enjoyment of a specifically identified residence of the other party; or

(26) entering, operating, or exercising control over a motor vehicle in the possession of the other party.

(27) tracking or monitoring personal property or a motor vehicle in the possession of a party, without that party's effective consent, including by:

(A) using a tracking application on a personal electronic device in the possession of that party or using a tracking device; or

(B) physically following that party or causing another to physically follow that party.

(b) A temporary restraining order under this subchapter may not include a provision:

(1) the subject of which is a requirement, appointment, award, or other order listed in Section 64.104, Civil Practice and Remedies Code; or

(2) that:

(A) excludes a spouse from occupancy of the residence where that spouse is living except as provided in a protective order made in accordance with Title 4;

(B) prohibits a party from spending funds for reasonable and necessary living expenses; or

(C) prohibits a party from engaging in acts reasonable and necessary to conduct that party's usual business and occupation.

§ 6.502. Temporary Injunction & Other Temporary Orders

(a) While a suit for dissolution of a marriage is pending and on the motion of a party or on the court's own motion after notice and hearing, the court may render an appropriate order, including the granting of a temporary injunction for the preservation of the property and protection of the parties as deemed necessary and equitable and including an order directed to one or both parties:

(1) requiring a sworn inventory and appraisement of the real and personal property owned or claimed by the parties and specifying the form, manner, and substance of the inventory and appraisal and list of debts and liabilities;

(2) requiring payments to be made for the support of either spouse;

(3) requiring the production of books, papers, documents, and tangible things by a party;

(4) ordering payment of reasonable attorney's fees and expenses;

(5) appointing a receiver for the preservation and protection of the property of the parties;

(6) awarding one spouse exclusive occupancy of the residence during the pendency of the case;

(7) prohibiting the parties, or either party, from spending funds beyond an amount the court determines to be for reasonable and necessary living expenses;

(8) awarding one spouse exclusive control of a party's usual business or occupation; or

(9) prohibiting an act described by Section 6.501(a).

(a–1) If the court on its own motion refers to mediation a suit described by Subsection (a) in which a motion for a temporary order described by that subsection is pending, the court may not postpone the initial hearing on the pending motion to a date that is later than the 30th day after the date set for the hearing.

(b) Not later than the 30th day after the date a receiver is appointed under Subsection (a)(5), the receiver shall give notice of the appointment to each lienholder of any property under the receiver's control.

(c) Not later than the seventh day after the date a receiver is appointed under Subsection (a)(5), the court shall issue written findings of fact and conclusions of law in support of the receiver's appointment. If the court dispenses with the issuance of a bond between the spouses as provided by Section 6.503(b) in connection with the receiver's appointment, the court shall include in the court's findings an explanation of the reasons the court dispensed with the issuance of a bond.

§ 6.503. Affidavit, Verified Pleading, & Bond Not Required

(a) A temporary restraining order or temporary injunction under this subchapter:

(1) may be granted without an affidavit or a verified pleading stating specific facts showing that immediate and irreparable injury, loss, or damage will result before notice can be served and a hearing can be held; and

(2) need not:

(A) define the injury or state why it is irreparable;

(B) state why the order was granted without notice; or

(C) include an order setting the suit for trial on the merits with respect to the ultimate relief sought.

(b) In a suit for dissolution of a marriage, the court may dispense with the issuance of a bond between the spouses in connection with temporary orders for the protection of the parties and their property.

* * *

§ 6.505. Counseling

(a) While a divorce suit is pending, the court may direct the parties to counsel with a person named by the court.

(b) The person named by the court to counsel the parties shall submit a written report to the court and to the parties before the final hearing. In the report, the counselor shall give only an opinion as to whether there exists a reasonable expectation of reconciliation of the parties and, if so, whether further counseling would be beneficial. The sole purpose of the report is to aid the court in determining whether the suit for divorce should be continued pending further counseling.

(c) A copy of the report shall be furnished to each party.

(d) If the court believes that there is a reasonable expectation of the parties' reconciliation, the court may by written order continue the proceedings and direct the parties to a person named by the court for further counseling for a period fixed by the court not to exceed 60 days, subject to any terms, conditions, and limitations the court considers desirable. In ordering counseling, the court shall consider the circumstances of the parties, including the needs of the parties' family and the availability of counseling services. At the expiration of the period specified by the court, the counselor to whom the parties were directed shall report to the court whether the parties have complied with the court's order. Thereafter, the court shall proceed as in a divorce suit generally.

(e) If the court orders counseling under this section and the parties to the marriage are the parents of a child under 18 years of age born or adopted during the marriage, the counseling shall include counseling on issues that confront children who are the subject of a suit affecting the parent-child relationship.

Title I—Chapter 8. Maintenance

Subchapter B. Spousal Maintenance

§ 8.051. Eligibility for Maintenance

In a suit for dissolution of marriage or in a proceeding for maintenance in a court with personal jurisdiction over both former spouses following the dissolution of their marriage by a court that lacked personal jurisdiction over an absent spouse, the court may order maintenance for either spouse only if the spouse seeking maintenance will lack sufficient property, including the spouse's separate property, on dissolution of the marriage to provide for the spouse's minimum reasonable needs and:

(1) the spouse from whom maintenance is requested was convicted of or received deferred adjudication for a criminal offense that also constitutes an act of family violence, as defined by Section 71.004, committed during the marriage against the other spouse or the other spouse's child and the offense occurred:

(A) within two years before the date on which a suit for dissolution of marriage is filed; or

(B) while the suit is pending; or

(2) the spouse seeking maintenance:

(A) is unable to earn sufficient income to provide for the spouse's minimum reasonable needs because of an incapacitating physical or mental disability;

(B) has been married to the other spouse for 10 years or longer and lacks the ability to earn sufficient income to provide for the spouse's minimum reasonable needs; or

(C) is the custodian of a child of the marriage of any age who requires substantial care and personal supervision because of a physical or mental disability that prevents the spouse from earning sufficient income to provide for the spouse's minimum reasonable needs.

2. American Jurisprudence—Divorce and Separation

8B AM. JUR. PL. & PR. FORMS *Divorce and Separation*

(Internal citations omitted)

§ 10. Introductory comments

In the absence of special statutory provisions specifically governing pleadings in divorce actions, questions relating to them are governed by the rules applicable to pleadings in civil actions generally. As in other civil actions, the complaint, petition, or declaration in a divorce action should contain allegations of all the facts essential to the course of action and to plaintiff's right to maintain the action. At minimum, it must allege the existence of the marriage, the residence or domicile of the plaintiff, and the ground or grounds for divorce, as well as such other allegations as may be required by statute or rule of court.

A number of legislatures have enacted statutes, popularly referred to as "no-fault divorce" acts, which provide for the dissolution of a marriage on a finding that the relationship is no longer viable or is irretrievably broken. With respect to the allegations of grounds for divorce under a no-fault statute providing for the granting of a dissolution of marriage on the court's finding that the marriage is irretrievably broken, it is sufficient if the complaint simply alleges as an ultimate fact that the marriage is "irretrievably broken."

If the defendant wishes to contest the divorce action, the defendant must file an answer denying generally or specifically, according to the local practice, the alleged misconduct or grounds for divorce set forth in the complaint, or the defendant must allege any affirmative defenses he or she may have to the action. Failure to answer will generally result in plaintiff's obtaining a judgment of divorce by default. Under the prevailing view, a defendant may also countersue and seek a divorce by way of a cross-bill or counterclaim, which must set forth defendant's own ground or grounds for divorce from the plaintiff. Moreover, a defendant may, by cross-bill or counterclaim, set up a cause of action for divorce which has accrued in his or her favor subsequent to the filing of the original complaint or petition and which, at that time, was not a completed or suable cause for divorce. Furthermore, where the offense occurred after the defendant filed a cross-bill, the defendant may amend his or her cross-bill to allege the subsequent offense.

In divorce proceedings, some states may, on petition of the grandparents, grant reasonable visitation rights to either the maternal or paternal grandparents of the minor child or children.

§ 11. Checklist—Drafting complaint or petition in proceedings for divorce or separation

Checklist of matters, inter alia, that must be alleged in a complaint, petition, or declaration in an action for divorce or separation:

- Residence or domicile of plaintiff.
- Existence of marriage relation.
- Facts showing nature of statutory offense on which action is based, with time and place of commission stated with reasonable certainty. [Note: Some jurisdictions permit the grounds for divorce to be stated in the language of the statute.]

- Statistical matters such as name, age, gender, and residence of any dependent minor children, if required.
- Description of property owned by parties, either separately or jointly, if a property settlement is sought as part of decree.
- Request for relief.

D. THE SIMULATION

1. Drafting a *Petition for Divorce and Suit Affecting Parent Child Relationship*

Using the provided statutory provisions and practice guidance for drafting a divorce pleading, draft a *Petition for Divorce and Suit Affecting Parent Child Relationship* (the "Petition") for Adrienne Scott. The Texas Rules of Civil Procedure apply when drafting pleadings. The Petition should conform to the general rules that apply to all petitions filed in district and county courts in Texas.

You may find divorce forms promulgated by the Texas Supreme Court for *pro se* parties on the internet. Forms may be helpful to review the range of information you must provide to the court in this initial pleading. Remember that you should not rely solely on forms when drafting pleadings. You should always check to see if your pleading conforms to the state statute and local court rules. For this simulation, you are not to simply check the boxes on the state form, fill out the information, and submit it as your pleading draft. You are to draft your own document.

CHAPTER THREE

COHABITATION AND PREMARITAL AGREEMENTS

I. INTRODUCTION

It may seem surprising to turn to cohabitation and premarital agreements immediately after exploring divorce. Understanding the legal framework of marital dissolution helps illuminate why some couples seek to plan for economic risks—through contract—before a marriage or cohabiting relationship even begins. After learning how the state wields power over property, finances, and relationships at the point of marital breakdown, it becomes easier to understand the motivations behind negotiating terms regarding separation in advance. This chapter lays the groundwork for the next sections of the book on property division and spousal support by introducing the contractual tools some individuals use to shape—or limit—the state's role in governing their intimate and financial lives.

Learning Outcomes:

(1) Extract governing rules from statutes governing cohabitation and premarital agreements.

(2) Review and negotiate a cohabitation agreement.

(3) Draft a premarital agreement.

(4) Identify ethical issues that may arise with clients in negotiating, drafting, or challenging a cohabitation and/or premarital agreement.

II. OVERVIEW OF THE LAW

Lawyers negotiate cohabitation agreements and premarital agreements in the "shadow of the law."[1] This means that lawyers know what provisions to include and what protections to secure because of their knowledge of the range of possible outcomes should disputes require judicial

[1] *See* Robert H. Mnookin & Lewis Kornhauser, *Bargaining in the Shadow of the Law: The Case of Divorce*, 88 YALE L.J. 950, 968 (1979).

intervention. Lawyers also negotiate with a keen eye trained on what types of contract provisions are enforceable. The property law primer below provides essential context for understanding how ownership, classification, and control of assets can shape both the structure and enforceability of these agreements.

Primer on Property Distribution

Courts begin the property distribution process by distinguishing between marital property, which includes assets and debts acquired during the marriage, and separate property, which includes assets owned before marriage or received individually through inheritance or gift. Most states use one of two primary systems to divide marital property: equitable distribution or community property. In an equitable distribution regime, courts allocate assets in a fair (though not always equal) manner based on factors like the length of the marriage, contributions of each spouse, income disparities, homemaking roles, asset dissipation, and future needs. In community property states, courts equally split assets acquired during the marriage, although some community property states take fault and other circumstances into consideration.

Separate property can be transformed into marital property in most states by agreement, gift, or certain actions of the couple over time. In most cases, the purpose of cohabitation agreements and premarital agreements is to protect separate property or ownership in a family-owned business, where one party stands to lose significant assets if the couple dissolves the relationship. Couples who do not plan on marrying or who desire to maintain their separate property before marriage also seek to protect assets that they wish to pass along to their children rather than their partner or spouse.

Cohabitation Agreements

In the past, these types of pre-commitment agreements were reserved for wealthy couples, or for partners entering the relationship with many assets to protect. However, changes in the circumstances of modern coupling in America have made cohabitation and premarital agreements more common. Many couples now choose to cohabitate without marrying. The number of couples who choose to live together before marriage has also risen over the last several decades.[2] In addition, the divorce rate has almost tripled since 1990 for married couples ages 65 and older.[3]

Cohabitation agreements are written agreements that govern the rights and obligations of two people who are typically in a romantic relationship and live together in a shared residence. There is no uniform act that governs the legal treatment of cohabitation. In fact, there is no state that has formal legislation regarding the enforceability of cohabitation agreements. However, there are three general approaches: 1) permitting legal contract and equitable claims; 2) permitting status-based claims; and 3) providing no relief.[4] In the majority of states where cohabitation agreements are accepted as a valid contract, courts do enforce the express agreement of the parties as long as it complies with the basic requirements of contract law and sexual services are not the basis for consideration.[5]

Many states established laws for domestic partners before the Supreme Court decided *Obergefell v. Hodges*,[6] and those laws are still in effect for couples that opt not to marry. A few states

---

[2] Benjamin Gurrentz, *Living with an Unmarried Partner Now Common for Young Adults*, U.S. Census Bureau, November 15, 2018, https://www.census.gov/library/stories/2018/11/cohabitation-is-up-marriage-is-down-for-young-adults.html. "Among those ages 18–24, cohabitation is now more prevalent than living with a spouse" and "30 percent of young adults ages 18–34 are married, but 40 years ago, in 1978, 59 percent of young adults were married." *Id.*

[3] A.W. Geiger and Gretchen Livingston, *8 facts about love and marriage in America*, THE PEW RESEARCH CENTER, https://www.pewresearch.org/fact-tank/2019/02/13/8-facts-about-love-and-marriage/ (Feb. 13, 2019).

[4] Marsha Garrison, *Nonmarital Cohabitation: Social Revolution and Legal Regulation*, 42 FAM. L.Q. 309, 315–16 (2008).

[5] *See Marvin v. Marvin*, 557 P.2d 106 (1976).

[6] 576 U.S. 644 (2015) (ruling that the Fourteenth Amendment guarantees same-sex couples the fundamental right to marry).

allow for agreements between cohabitating adults who are not in a romantic partnership. For example, Colorado enacted the Colorado Designated Beneficiary Act in 2009 allowing unmarried couples to designate each other as intended beneficiaries in the event of death and grant other rights and protections via a Designated Beneficiary Agreement (DBA).[7] Notably, not all states recognize cohabitation agreements, and the law is changing rapidly in this area. Lawyers will have to research this question in their home state.

Premarital Agreements

There are several different legal frameworks that states have adopted governing premarital agreements. Many states have adopted the frameworks set forth in the Uniform Premarital Agreement Act (UPAA),[8] the Uniform Premarital and Marital Agreements Act of 2012 (UPMAA),[9] or the American Law Institute (ALI) Principles of the Law of Family Dissolution. These model laws primarily differ in the judicial review of substantive and procedural fairness.[10] This simulation applies the UPAA.

Under the UPAA, parties are free to negotiate specific aspects of their relationship, including financial matters and personal rights and obligations. Here is a list of the subject matters that parties can include in a premarital agreement in a UPAA state:

UPAA SECTION 3. CONTENT.

(a) Parties to a premarital agreement may contract with respect to:

(1) the rights and obligations of each of the parties in any of the property of either or both of them whenever and wherever acquired or located;

(2) the right to buy, sell, use, transfer, exchange, abandon, lease, consume, expend, assign, create a security interest in, mortgage, encumber, dispose of, or otherwise manage and control property;

(3) the disposition of property upon separation, marital dissolution, death, or the occurrence or nonoccurrence of any other event;

(4) the modification or elimination of spousal support;

(5) the making of a will, trust, or other arrangement to carry out the provisions of the agreement;

(6) the ownership rights in and disposition of the death benefit from a life insurance policy;

(7) the choice of law governing the construction of the agreement; and

(8) any other matter, including their personal rights and obligations, not in violation of public policy or a statute imposing a criminal penalty.

(b) The right of a child to support may not be adversely affected by a premarital agreement.[11]

While there is a catch-all paragraph within Section 3 of the UPAA permitting provisions governing personal rights and obligations, there are some subject matters that are not enforceable. Some states do not enforce terms governing household chores or punitive provisions for conduct like adultery. The UPAA does not enforce terms pertaining to child custody and other matters concerning children. Child support can be addressed to the extent that the agreement expands the

---

7 COLO. REV. STAT. ANN. § 15–22–106 (West 2019).

8 As of 2020, twenty-eight states and the District of Columbia have adopted all or part of the UPAA or the UPMAA.

9 Only two states, Colorado and North Dakota, have adopted the UPMAA.

10 *See e.g.*, *Commentary on Simeone v. Simeone*, *in* FEMINIST JUDGMENTS—FAMILY LAW (R. Rebouché ed., 2020) (comparing the different approaches to premarital agreements and analyzing one influential opinion considering the competing approaches).

11 Uniform Premarital Agreement Act, § 3, 9C U.L.A. 39 (2001).

support beyond the standard guidelines set by the state. For example, a couple can agree that child support will continue past the age of majority (eighteen), when it typically terminates.

A premarital agreement must be "voluntary" and not "unconscionable" when signed in order to be enforceable.[12] While the UPAA does not define unconscionability, courts have interpreted the term using the standard of unconscionability used in commercial law, where its meaning includes protection against one-sidedness, oppression, or unfair surprise. The definition of unconscionable does not mean unfair or disproportionate. The standard is designed to protect parties from overreaching, concealment of assets, and ruthless dealing not consistent with the obligations of marital partners to deal fairly with each other. In many states, it is fairly difficult for a party to prove that a premarital agreement is unconscionable.

The UPAA Section 6 sets forth the following:

UPAA SECTION 6. ENFORCEMENT.

(a) A premarital agreement is not enforceable if the party against whom enforcement is sought proves that:

(1) that party did not execute the agreement voluntarily; or

(2) the agreement was unconscionable when it was executed and, before execution of the agreement, that party:

(i) was not provided a fair and reasonable disclosure of the property or financial obligations of the other party;

(ii) did not voluntarily and expressly waive, in writing, any right to disclosure of the property or financial obligations of the other party beyond the disclosure provided; and

(iii) did not have, or reasonably could not have had, an adequate knowledge of the property or financial obligations of the other party.

(b) If a provision of a premarital agreement modifies or eliminates spousal support and that modification or elimination causes one party to the agreement to be eligible for support under a program of public assistance at the time of separation or marital dissolution, a court, notwithstanding the terms of the agreement, may require the other party to provide support to the extent necessary to avoid that eligibility.

(c) An issue of unconscionability of a premarital agreement shall be decided by the court as a matter of law.[13]

The UPAA also requires the agreement to be in writing and executed by both parties. It does not require any separate consideration. The agreement becomes effective upon the parties' marriage.

In many ways, lawyers seeking to draft a premarital agreement collect the same type of information as they would if they were interviewing a client seeking a divorce. This information includes a list of the client's property, debts, children from a previous relationship or marriage, and anything the client values as being an essential or integral part of the marriage.

---

[12] Uniform Premarital Agreement Act, § 6, 9C U.L.A. 43, 48–49 (2001).

[13] *Id.*

III. COHABITATION AGREEMENT: CASE FILE—JULIUS WALKER

A. SIMULATION ROADMAP

This simulation will develop two fundamental skills. First, you will review a client memorandum and a draft of a cohabitation agreement to determine if it meets your client's objectives. If not, you will note why the agreement should be modified and propose revisions to it. Second, you will consider carefully the ethics of working with an unrepresented party on the other side.

B. MEMORANDUM FROM CLIENT WITH ATTACHMENT

To: Attorney

From: Julius Walker

Re: Cohabitation Agreement for your Review

Hi,

Thanks again for helping me with this matter. As I explained in our initial meeting, I have been living with my partner, Sherrice, for the past eight months. Her adult daughter, Cynthia, age 29, also lives with us and my beloved elderly mother, age 94. I live in Sherrice's home in Boston, Massachusetts. Sherrice just presented me with the attached cohabitation agreement. I've been renting my home out. After executing this agreement, I will put my house on the market to sell.

As we discussed in person, I have sizeable assets from a workplace accident lawsuit several years ago. This accident has left me disabled and unable to work. The assets are in a legal trust for my care with $850,000 remaining. Sherrice knows that I live off this trust and that it is critical to my health, but she does not know how much is in it.

Sherrice and I want to live together while protecting ourselves from any messy complications of cohabitating. Particularly, Sherrice's daughter, Cynthia, receives public benefits and is developmentally disabled. We want to be sure that my assets do not complicate Cynthia's eligibility for the benefits that she needs. Sherrice also wants to continue receiving alimony and spousal support from her ex. She tells me that this agreement will protect her by ensuring that we are not treated like a married couple.

While it's not in the agreement, Sherrice also agreed that she would never seek alimony from me (or whatever its equivalent is since we are not married). I trust her. It's not in the agreement, but we have talked it over together.

Sherrice had a cousin who is a lawyer in Rhode Island help her put together the attached agreement. She says the cousin just helped her as a favor. She says she technically doesn't have a lawyer, and so you should contact her directly with any edits or suggestions to the agreement.

I appreciate your help. I may be a bit hard to reach in the coming days. My Auntie has been quite ill. She loves Sherrice like her own daughter. She has been moved to hospice care. She cares deeply for Sherrice and I both and has worked to leave her estate to us.

ATTACHMENT

Draft Cohabitation Agreement Between Sherrice Kearns and Julius Walker

VALIDITY OF AGREEMENT.

1. This Agreement is made between Sherrice Kearns, hereafter referred to as "Sherrice," and Julius Walker, hereafter referred to as "Julius."
2. All provisions of this Cohabitation Agreement between Sherrice Kearns and Julius Walker (hereinafter the "Agreement") have been negotiated by both parties at arm's length and neither party shall be deemed the scrivener of this Agreement. This Agreement shall not be construed for or against either party by reason of the authorship or alleged authorship of any provision hereof.
3. If any provision of this Agreement shall be held to be invalid, illegal or unenforceable, the validity, legality and enforceability of the remaining provisions shall in no way be affected or impaired thereby.
4. This instrument shall merge all undertakings, representations, understandings, and agreements whether oral or written, between the parties hereto with respect to the Property and the provisions of this Agreement and shall constitute the entire agreement unless otherwise hereafter modified by both parties in writing.
5. This instrument shall not become binding upon the parties until it shall have been executed and delivered by both parties.
6. This agreement shall be governed by and construed in accordance with the laws (other than conflict of laws provisions) of the jurisdiction of Massachusetts.

PURPOSES OF AGREEMENT.

7. The parties do not intend any of the marital status provisions of Massachusetts law to be applicable to any of their legal rights. As between the parties, their rights of support and property ownership—including interests in real or personal property that may be acquired by either of them whether individually or jointly, and the right to share in any earnings or accumulations of the other party—shall be governed exclusively by this Agreement.
8. The parties do not intend by this Agreement or by their cohabitation arrangement to create a form of marriage recognized by this or any other state.
9. The parties intend that this Agreement shall remain binding and in full force and effect regardless of any future change in their residence or domicile, and that it shall be terminated only as provided in this Agreement.
10. The purposes of this Agreement are to define the property rights, to create no liability between them for debts of the other—whether as necessaries of life or otherwise, and to provide for the financial arrangements, of the parties while they continue to reside together and, in the event, either of them wishes to terminate their cohabitation. Additionally, the parties wish to supersede and waive any claims or defenses either of them might otherwise assert if their relationship was to end, except as may be set forth herein or in a subsequent written Agreement between them. Such claims without limitation include verbal or implied

Agreements (and whether or not the parties hold themselves out to third parties as a married couple or otherwise engage in 'married-like' behavior or conduct).

11. No joint venture, partnership, express or implied joint pooling Agreement or arrangement relating to assets or liabilities, or support rights and obligations shall result from the fact of their cohabitation, or from any of the parties' activities, conduct, or verbal or written representations (except subsequently executed modifications to this Agreement) between them or to third parties during the period they continue to reside together or thereafter.

12. No de facto parent relationship will arise, or be deemed to arise, between Julius and Cynthia. No support obligation shall be deemed to arise between Julius and Cynthia. All future agreements between the parties must be memorialized in a writing signed by them both.

PARTIES' CIRCUMSTANCES.

13. The parties intend to begin residing together effective the first of next month, together with Sherrice's adult daughter, Cynthia. They have never previously resided together and have never previously accumulated any assets or shared any income together. They do not contemplate marriage.

14. Julius is 74 years of age and Sherrice is 57 years of age. Julius is a retired State Trooper, previously employed by the State of Massachusetts. Julius has four children from a prior marriage. His net worth is in excess of $600,000, and his income is derived from his pension, his investment portfolio, and ongoing benefits. His assets also include a sizeable settlement from a workplace injury. He has no present plan to recommence employment.

15. Sherrice is employed as a medical records manager earning $34,000 annually. She has a nominal net worth. She was formerly married and is now divorced. A court order provides that she is to receive $300 monthly in alimony from her ex. Sherrice receives $700 monthly in child support from Cynthia's father, even though she is above the age of 18, per a court order. Sherrice is in excellent physical health.

DISCLOSURE OF ASSETS.

16. Neither party requires any further disclosure of assets and liabilities from the other and each is entirely comfortable with the information set forth herein. This Agreement shall be fully enforceable between the parties despite their decision to not list assets and debts according to Exhibits that would otherwise be attached hereto.

JOINT PROPERTY RIGHTS.

17. Except as otherwise stated in a subsequently executed Agreement, all assets of either party acquired before the effective date of this Agreement are and shall remain the property of that party. All assets acquired by either party on or after the effective date of this Agreement shall likewise be the property of that party.

18. If the parties decide to acquire a particular asset together, they shall contribute funds to that acquisition in accordance with the proportionate interests they are to hold and shall take title to reflect those proportionate interests. If title is taken in the name of one party alone it shall be conclusively presumed that it was the parties' intention that only the party in whose name title is or was taken or held has, had, or shall have an interest in the property. For each joint acquisition of property, the parties shall execute a written addendum or modification to this Agreement, specifying the property that is co-owned by them and the terms of co-acquisition and co-ownership.

19. Neither party is or shall be authorized to incur any debt in the name of the other party, or on behalf of the other party, except as the parties may from time to time expressly agree in a writing separate from any debt instrument which is signed by both.

20. Hereafter, either party may retain his or her own bank accounts, or open new accounts in their name alone, but the parties agree that all such accounts shall be considered separately owned by the party whose name appears on the account. If the parties jointly open accounts in the names of both, all monies held in said accounts shall be jointly owned between them provided that if either party utilizes said monies neither will owe any reimbursements to the other.

21. Each party shall retain his or her own earnings and other funds in his or her own individual savings, checking, or other account, for disposition at will, except for funds needed for household expenses, as provided in the immediately succeeding paragraph.

22. The parties shall maintain a joint checking account as joint tenants for household expenses such as rent, food, household supplies, utilities, and Sherrice's reasonable personal expenses. Sherrice will have no obligation to contribute to said account, and all funds which Julius contributes to said account shall become the joint property of the parties provided. However, if said account is subsequently used to make mortgage payments on any property, notwithstanding any other provision of this Agreement, neither party shall acquire any interest in the ownership of said property by reason of said payments thereon whether for interest or principal. Further, neither party shall cause said account to become overdrawn or otherwise issue drafts or charges in excess of the balance of said account at any particular point in time.

NO OBLIGATION OF SUPPORT.

23. Neither party shall have any obligation to support the other party, either during the relationship or if the relationship terminates, for any period after termination of the Agreement or the cohabitation, regardless of the reasons for the termination. In no event shall any obligation for "palimony" or support arise between the parties at any time.

GIFTS AND INHERITANCES.

24. Neither party has any right to succeed to or inherit from the estate of the other after the death of the other except by a valid will or trust drawn by the respective party after the date of this Agreement. Naming the other party as beneficiary in a will or trust executed after the date of this Agreement shall not imply or include any agreement that the other party has a vested property interest in and to the will or trust or property referenced therein; such a right may only arise by joint, or joint and mutual, or mutual wills. The fact that one party might execute a will or trust, and the other party might not, is agreed to be within the parties' contemplation at this time.

25. If either party makes a gift of real or personal property to the other, in the event their cohabitation terminates then that gift shall remain the sole and separate property of the party to whom the gift is made; provided, however, that any gift made between the parties valued in excess of $5,000 at the time of the gift shall be identified as a gift in a writing signed by the party to be charged.

26. If either party receives a gift or inheritance from relatives or third parties, those funds or property shall be and shall remain the sole property of the person receiving said gift or inheritance unless and until the parties jointly execute a separate addendum or writing which clearly sets forth that the receiving party intends to make a gift of some interest in said funds or property to the other party.

SUBSEQUENT MARRIAGE.

27. This Agreement shall terminate upon the marriage of the parties to each other, or upon either party's marriage or domestic partnership to any other person.

TERMINATION OF COHABITATION.

28. The parties may separate at any time by mutual understanding or by the election of either party acting alone.

29. Upon the parties' separation, all rights under this Agreement shall terminate, except as to rights of ownership in specific items of real or personal property previously acquired. The parties may then agree to continue their ownership of any jointly held real or personal property, or may elect to have the property partitioned. The property to be partitioned shall be divided in kind where feasible and not an economic hardship to either party. In the event the property cannot be divided in kind, it shall be divided by mutual agreement assigning assets of equal or nearly equal value to each party, with an agreed cash payment as necessary to equalize the division. If the parties cannot mutually agree, the property shall be sold and the proceeds divided equally after deduction for all costs of sale. In any such division, no account shall be taken of the income tax liability of either party under federal, state or foreign law.

30. In the event the parties separate, or if this Agreement is terminated in any other manner, both parties waive any right to recover *pendente lite* attorney fees, court costs, or support in any action to enforce this Agreement. In the event of litigation to enforce the rights under this Agreement, the prevailing party shall be entitled to recover reasonable attorney fees as costs of suit.

31. In the event of any breach of this Agreement, or any action contesting the validity or seeking the enforcement of this Agreement, the prevailing party shall be entitled, in addition to any other remedy provided by law, to receive from the other party his or her reasonable attorney fees and costs resulting from the breach or incurred in connection with the action.

The foregoing is agreed to by:

Date:

____________________ Sherrice Kearns   ____________________ Witness for Sherrice Kearns

____________________ Julius Walker   ____________________ Witness for Julius Walker

Ethical Considerations: This client representation raises important ethical considerations governing an attorney's communications with unrepresented parties. What ethical rules govern your communications with Sherrice directly? You may find it helpful to revisit Chapter One, Section VII on the topic of *pro se* litigants as well. Be prepared to discuss your conclusions in class.

C. RELEVANT STATUTORY LAW AND PRACTICE GUIDANCE

Your research locates the following secondary source summarizing the law on cohabitation agreements in Massachusetts.

WILCOX V. TRAUTZ: THE RECOGNITION OF RELATIONSHIP CONTRACTS IN MASSACHUSETTS

Andrea D. Heinbach and Pierce J. Reed
43 BOSTON BAR J. 6 (Nov./Dec. 1999)

(*Internal citations omitted*)

* * * **Considerations for the Client**

Although the following is by no means an exhaustive list of potential considerations, unmarried couples must consider many issues regarding their relationships and their finances. Some of these issues can be resolved through the relationship contract, but most will require the execution of additional documents. All require thoughtful review by clients and counsel.

1. ***Property Rights.***

The client should consider to what extent, if any, she wishes to share ownership of real and personal property. If she desires to share ownership, the client should consider not only the title of the property, but also the division of any equity in the property, the physical use of the property, and the duties and obligations of each party with respect to maintenance and improvement of the property. Similarly, the client must consider whether she wishes to share the use of insurance proceeds in the event the property is damaged or destroyed.

Clients must also be advised to think about other types of property interests they may have, including cemetery plots, intellectual property, or interests in businesses and corporations. Other property interests might include professional licenses and pensions earned during the relationship.

2. ***Money.***

Like property, money is a critical consideration for many clients considering a cohabitation contract. A decision must be made as to which funds and accounts the client wants to share with her partner, and to what extent she wishes to do so. Clients must assess whether they frequently provide "loans" or gifts of money to their partners, and what each party's understanding is with respect to the use and repayment (if any) of those funds.

3. ***Life and Death Care.***

Another consideration for unmarried people in committed relationships is the need for legal documents concerning critical health care decisions and post-mortem dispositions. * * *

The client must consider, in the event of her incapacity, which person in her life should be designated as having authority over decisions ranging from whether to continue medical treatment (and if so, to what extent [and] under what circumstances) to hospital visitation. Similarly, the client must determine who may exercise control over the disposition of her remains and her estate. Special considerations may be warranted for insurance policies and the distribution of their proceeds after death.

Many domestic relations attorneys are familiar with the mechanics of trusts and estate law; those who are not should consult with attorneys more experienced with such issues. To the extent financial planning is implicated, the attorney should refer the client appropriately and work in conjunction with other professionals, including an experienced tax expert, to assist in avoiding or minimizing the unfavorable tax consequences of inheritance for unmarried partners.

Considerations for the Attorney

1. ***The Scope of the Agreement.***

There must be clear communication with the client about the scope of the agreement, the risks attendant with entering into such an agreement, and termination options. The attorney is obligated to ensure that the client understands that the agreement is not a substitution for a health care proxy, living will, or antenuptial agreement. The client should also be advised that, to the extent the agreement touches upon child custody, support or visitation, it may or may not be enforced by a court.

2. ***Drafting the Agreement.***

The agreement should be carefully drafted, taking into consideration traditional contract law principles, such as capacity to contract, unconscionability, and parol evidence. The agreement may also include provisions traditionally included in other types of contracts, such as clauses regarding waiver, alternative dispute resolution, and integration clauses.

3. ***Representation.***

It is recommended that each party be represented by individual counsel. Although one attorney may draft the agreement, each party should have the advice of his or her own counsel before execution.

4. ***Financial Disclosure.***

Because the agreement is, at its base, a financial agreement, there must be full disclosure regarding each party's finances, assets, and liabilities. Financial statements for each party should be attached as exhibits to the agreement.

5. ***Public Policy Considerations.***

The attorney must be mindful that a court may refuse to enforce a cohabitation agreement on public policy grounds, such as to prevent one of the parties from becoming a public charge. * * *

In addition, if the sole foundation of the agreement is sexual services or fidelity, the agreement is not enforceable. As a practical matter, any cohabitation agreement should exclude the topics of sex and fidelity and, more generally, the mention of services such as housekeeping, cooking, and traditional domestic roles. Rather, the agreement should frame consideration in terms of "the common welfare of both parties, combined with an effort to further their financial partnership."

D. THE SIMULATION—REVIEWING A COHABITATION AGREEMENT

You represent Julius in this cohabitation agreement matter. He has asked you to communicate with his partner directly to negotiate any changes to the Cohabitation Agreement. You have scheduled a call to talk with Sherrice later this week.

Prepare a list of concerns that you have issue-spotted from the cohabitation agreement provided. What is your 'wish list' of modifications to the proposed agreement? Consider preparing for this negotiation using the following chart.

Provision	Identified Concerns	Proposed Modifications	Prioritize Legal Significance (High–Low)

IV. PREMARITAL AGREEMENT: CASE FILE—SCOTT GRAMBLING

A. SIMULATION ROADMAP

Scott Grambling has hired you to draft a Premarital Agreement for Scott and his fiancée, Mei-Ling Huang. They both live in California. Review your initial interview notes, highlighting the pertinent language that reflects your client's objectives. You will need to determine what content should be included in the agreement.

B. CLIENT INTERVIEW NOTES

Client:	Scott Grambling (32)
Legal Service:	Draft, Negotiate, and Execute a Premarital Agreement
Client Objectives:	Scott wants to stipulate that his businesses and rental properties will remain his separate property. Any and all income from this separate property would be designated as Scott's separate property.
Factual Background:	Scott is engaged to marry Mei-Ling Huang (26). Scott works for his father and earns $275,000 per year. Scott and his father own several businesses and rental properties in California. For the last several years, the businesses and properties have generated approximately $1.5M in revenue. Since the COVID-19 pandemic, the revenue has decreased to half of that amount ($750,000). Scott's father insists that Mei-Ling and Scott sign a premarital agreement before the wedding. Scott lives with his fiancée currently. Scott purchased the home where they have resided in Los Angeles for the last two years. It is worth approximately $850,000. They each have one car; both cars were given to Mei-Ling by her parents before the parties started living together. One car is a YR-06 Lexus ES 300. The other is a YR-03 Range Rover Sport.
Opposing Party Information:	Mei-Ling Huang works part-time at the local city museum, earning $35,000 per year. She has recently gone back to business school to obtain her master's degree in business administration (MBA). She has completed her first year at UCLA. Scott is paying for her tuition and books. Mei-Ling has $30,000 saved in a separate account that was a gift from her mother as a 'rainy day account.' Mei-Ling's parents own a successful printing company in China. She stands to inherit a good deal of money, alongside her sister.
Time Sensitive Issues:	The wedding is two months away. Scott and Mei-Ling have not had the chance to discuss what they each want in the agreement. Mei-Ling is not very interested in signing a premarital agreement. She told Scott that she feels compelled to do so because the wedding date is close. She has over two hundred and fifty guests flying in. Her cousin, a bankruptcy attorney, has agreed to review the agreement because Mei-Ling has not retained a family law lawyer.
Proposed Terms:	Mei-Ling is unsure whether Scott has been forthright about his personal assets. Mei-Ling initially asked for $250,000 in alimony if she is married to Scott for at least five years, $500,000 for ten years, and $1 million for fifteen years.

C. RELEVANT STATUTORY LAW AND PRACTICE GUIDANCE

1. California Statute Adopting Uniform Premarital Agreement Act[14]

California Family Code

CHAPTER 2. Uniform Premarital Agreement Act

ARTICLE 2. Premarital Agreements

§ 1610 Definitions

As used in this chapter:

(a) "Premarital agreement" means an agreement between prospective spouses made in contemplation of marriage and to be effective upon marriage.

(b) "Property" means an interest, present or future, legal or equitable, vested or contingent, in real or personal property, including income and earnings.

§ 1611 Form and execution of agreement; consideration

A premarital agreement shall be in writing and signed by both parties. It is enforceable without consideration.

§ 1612 Subject matter of premarital agreements

(a) Parties to a premarital agreement may contract with respect to all of the following:

(1) The rights and obligations of each of the parties in any of the property of either or both of them whenever and wherever acquired or located.

(2) The right to buy, sell, use, transfer, exchange, abandon, lease, consume, expend, assign, create a security interest in, mortgage, encumber, dispose of, or otherwise manage and control property.

(3) The disposition of property upon separation, marital dissolution, death, or the occurrence or nonoccurrence of any other event.

(4) The making of a will, trust, or other arrangement to carry out the provisions of the agreement.

(5) The ownership rights in and disposition of the death benefit from a life insurance policy.

(6) The choice of law governing the construction of the agreement.

(7) Any other matter, including their personal rights and obligations, not in violation of public policy or a statute imposing a criminal penalty.

(b) The right of a child to support may not be adversely affected by a premarital agreement.

(c) Any provision in a premarital agreement regarding spousal support, including, but not limited to, a waiver of it, is not enforceable if the party against whom enforcement of the spousal support provision is sought was not represented by independent counsel at the time the agreement containing the provision was signed, or if the provision regarding spousal support is unconscionable at the time of enforcement. An otherwise unenforceable provision in a premarital agreement regarding spousal support may not become enforceable solely because the party against whom enforcement is sought was represented by independent counsel.

§ 1613 Effective date of agreements

A premarital agreement becomes effective upon marriage.

---

[14] Amberlynn Curry, *The Uniform Premarital Agreement Act and Its Variations Throughout the States*, 23 J. AM. ACAD. MATRIM. LAW. 355, 361 (2010) (noting that the California UPAA differs from the original UPAA regarding what issues can be contracted in a valid premarital agreement and when a premarital agreement is enforceable).

§ 1614 Amendment or revocation of agreements

After marriage, a premarital agreement may be amended or revoked only by a written agreement signed by the parties. The amended agreement or the revocation is enforceable without consideration.

§ 1615 Unenforceable agreements; unconscionability; voluntariness

(a) A premarital agreement is not enforceable if the party against whom enforcement is sought proves either of the following:

(1) That party did not execute the agreement voluntarily.

(2) The agreement was unconscionable when it was executed and, before execution of the agreement, all of the following applied to that party:

(A) That party was not provided a fair, reasonable, and full disclosure of the property or financial obligations of the other party.

(B) That party did not voluntarily and expressly waive, in writing, any right to disclosure of the property or financial obligations of the other party beyond the disclosure provided.

(C) That party did not have, or reasonably could not have had, an adequate knowledge of the property or financial obligations of the other party.

(b) An issue of unconscionability of a premarital agreement shall be decided by the court as a matter of law.

(c) For the purposes of subdivision (a), it shall be deemed that a premarital agreement was not executed voluntarily unless the court finds in writing or on the record all of the following:

(1) The party against whom enforcement is sought was represented by independent legal counsel at the time of signing the agreement or, after being advised to seek independent legal counsel, expressly waived, in a separate writing, representation by independent legal counsel. The advisement to seek independent legal counsel shall be made at least seven calendar days before the final agreement is signed.

(2) One of the following:

(A) For an agreement executed between January 1, 2002, and January 1, 2020, the party against whom enforcement is sought had not less than seven calendar days between the time that party was first presented with the final agreement and advised to seek independent legal counsel and the time the agreement was signed. This requirement does not apply to nonsubstantive amendments that do not change the terms of the agreement.

(B) For an agreement executed on or after January 1, 2020, the party against whom enforcement is sought had not less than seven calendar days between the time that party was first presented with the final agreement and the time the agreement was signed, regardless of whether the party is represented by legal counsel. This requirement does not apply to nonsubstantive amendments that do not change the terms of the agreement.

(3) The party against whom enforcement is sought, if unrepresented by legal counsel, was fully informed of the terms and basic effect of the agreement as well as the rights and obligations the party was giving up by signing the agreement, and was proficient in the language in which the explanation of the party's rights was conducted and in which the agreement was written. The explanation of the rights and obligations relinquished shall be memorialized in writing and delivered to the party prior to signing the agreement. The unrepresented party shall, on or before the signing of the premarital agreement, execute a document declaring that the party received the information required by this paragraph and indicating who provided that information.

(4) The agreement and the writings executed pursuant to paragraphs (1) and (3) were not executed under duress, fraud, or undue influence, and the parties did not lack capacity to enter into the agreement.

(5) Any other factors the court deems relevant.

§ 1616 Void marriage, effect on agreement

If a marriage is determined to be void, an agreement that would otherwise have been a premarital agreement is enforceable only to the extent necessary to avoid an inequitable result.

§ 1617 Limitations of actions; equitable defenses including laches and estoppel

Any statute of limitations applicable to an action asserting a claim for relief under a premarital agreement is tolled during the marriage of the parties to the agreement. However, equitable defenses limiting the time for enforcement, including laches and estoppel, are available to either party.

2. American Jurisprudence—Prenuptial Agreements

41 AM. JUR. 2d. *Husband and Wife*

(Internal citations omitted)

§ 82. Public policy

[W]hile antenuptial agreements are recognized, courts scrutinize such agreements to determine whether they are just and reasonable because of the confidential relationship of the parties. In deciding whether to enforce an antenuptial agreement, the trial court has discretion to approve the agreement in whole or in part or refuse to approve it as a whole. Courts retain broad discretion to modify or invalidate all or part of an antenuptial agreement where enforcement is unconscionable. Generally, however, where the legislature and people of a state have made the public policy determination that premarital agreements should be enforced, the agreements are presumptively enforceable.

* * *

§ 84. Enforceability of certain provisions

Specific matters controlled by statute, such as obligations of mutual respect, fidelity, and support, are not within the proper scope of an antenuptial agreement. Thus, a prenuptial agreement premised on a scheme to circumvent immigration laws is unenforceable and contrary to public policy as it purports to eliminate the essential aspects of marriage, such as spousal duties, responsibilities, and rights. On the other hand, an antenuptial agreement providing that each party must pay his or her own legal fees in the event of a contested divorce may not be lightly brushed aside.

A premarital agreement to raise children in a particular religion is not enforceable. Prenuptial property settlements or agreements also may be invalid if they attempt to circumvent the state's descent and distribution statutes concerning estates or attempt to divest the parties' children of legal rights. Indeed, the Uniform Premarital Agreement Act expressly provides that the right of a child to support may not be adversely affected by a premarital agreement.

A choice of law provision in an antenuptial agreement may be valid and enforceable.

§ 85. Enforceability of certain provisions—Support, maintenance, or alimony upon divorce

Historically, courts have taken contrasting views with respect to provisions in antenuptial agreements that set forth the division of property and other rights and interests upon the death of one of the parties (which were generally recognized as being conducive to marital tranquility and thus in harmony with public policy) and provisions that provide for, or affecting, property rights or conjugal and marital rights in the event of divorce (which historically were held to be void as against public policy).

Prior to the adoption of statutes governing the question, some jurisdictions held that a provision in a prenuptial agreement waiving alimony was void as against public policy. A statute may also provide that the right of spousal support must not be adversely affected by a premarital agreement. Indeed, it may be presumed that a state legislature purposefully excluded spousal support rights from a statutory list of enumerated subject matter upon which parties to a prenuptial agreement may legally contract.

Research the Law: The California Premarital Agreement Act does allow for spousal support or alimony to be included in a premarital agreement. There are specific conditions, however. What is the case law precedent regarding when a spousal support provision is unconscionable?

D. THE SIMULATION—DRAFTING A PREMARITAL AGREEMENT

Draft a premarital agreement for client Scott Grambling. You may use a template or sample form to guide you in composing the agreement. Besides state-specific practice manuals that often provide samples of pleadings or agreements, there are other commonly used websites that offer free sample documents, such as www.lawdepot.com or www.legaltemplates.net. You may also find document drafting resources on www.westlaw.com. Keep in mind what you learned in Chapter One, Section IV regarding using forms.

The following non-exhaustive checklist may also be helpful. If there is information that you need to draft the agreement that you do not have, make an outline of these subject matters to discuss with your client before finalizing the agreement. Based on the research you completed regarding spousal support/alimony for the preceding Research the Law question, determine whether there are any issues that need to be discussed with your client regarding Mei-Ling's proposed terms.

<u>Premarital Agreement Checklist</u>

- Parties to the agreement
- Effective date of agreement
- Ability to enter agreement
- Consideration
- Voluntariness
- Representation by counsel
- Time allotted for review and negotiation of agreement
- Process for amending or revoking agreement
- Disclosure of assets
- Separate property of each party
- Joint property of marital couple
- Alimony/spousal support
- Gifts and inheritances
- Rights and obligations of each party
- Dissolution of property upon divorce, death, or any other event
- Choice of law for agreement

CHAPTER FOUR

INTIMATE PARTNER VIOLENCE

I. INTRODUCTION

Intimate Partner Violence (IPV), often called domestic violence, is abuse that occurs within an intimate partner relationship, where one partner asserts power and control over the other in a way that is mentally and/or physically harmful. It includes physical and/or sexual violence, stalking and psychological aggression by a current or former spouse, boyfriend/girlfriend, dating partner, or ongoing sexual partner.[1] The prevalence of IPV within the United States and within the practice of family law cannot be overstated. After divorce proceedings, IPV is the next highest volume case type in family courts. Although national IPV statistics have decreased, approximately 23% of all family law cases involve domestic abuse.[2] One in four women and one in nine men have experienced contact sexual violence, physical violence, and/or stalking by an intimate partner in their lifetime and reported an IPV-related impact.[3] Nearly half of all homicides of women under the age of forty-four are caused by a current or former intimate partner.[4] IPV is also grossly underreported, so the statistics that are gathered do not encapsulate the entirety of the problem.

IPV occurs in every community and affects all people, regardless of age, socio-economic status, sexual orientation, gender, race, religion, or nationality. There are some groups that experience a higher percentage of IPV compared to other races, ethnicities and sexes. As compared to their numbers in the population, American Indian, Alaska Native, multiracial, and African American

---

1 Center for Disease Control, *Intimate Partner Violence Surveillance: Uniform Definitions and Recommended Data Elements, Version 2.0* 11 (2015).

2 *Id.*; U.S. Dept. of Justice, Office of Justice Programs, Bureau of Justice Statistics, *National Crime Victimization Survey, Concatenated File, 1992–2015* (Oct. 20, 2016), https://doi.org/10.3886/ICPSR36456.v1.

3 S.G. Smith, et al., *The National Intimate Partner and Sexual Violence Survey (NISVS): 2010–2012 State Report 2*, National Center for Injury Prevention and Control, Centers for Disease Control and Prevention (Apr. 2017). Examples of an IPV-related impact is an injury, fear, concern for safety, or a need for services, such as housing or counseling. *Id.*

4 Catherine G. Velopulos, et al, *Comparison of male and female victims of intimate partner homicide and bidirectionality—an analysis of the national violent death reporting system*, 87(2) J. TRAUMA ACUTE CARE SURG. 331, 333 (2019); Emiko Petrosky, et al, *Racial and Ethnic Differences in Homicides of Adult Women and the Role of Intimate Partner Violence—United States, 2003–2014*, 66 MORBIDITY AND MORTALITY WEEKLY REP. 741–46 (July 17, 2017).

women have proportionally higher rates as victims of domestic violence,[5] and people who self-identify as lesbian, gay, bisexual, or transgender are at an increased risk of rape, physical violence, and stalking by an intimate partner.[6] One in three Latinas experience domestic violence, and while this rate may not appear to be disproportionate, research shows that this rate is likely skewed low due to considerable underreporting.[7] The reasons for this higher rate among communities of color and LGBTQ populations are explored further in Section II.B.

Learning Outcomes:

(1) Review state family law and criminal law statutory provisions that govern civil and criminal protection orders in family violence cases.

(2) Recognize the ethical obligations that lawyers owe to clients regarding screening, community resources, and legal services offered to assist victims of domestic violence and batterers.

(3) Identify the documents necessary to obtain a restraining or protective order for a client.

(4) Draft an *Affidavit in Support of Ex Parte Relief and an Application for Protective Order.*

II. OVERVIEW OF THE LAW

Family violence is defined and governed primarily by state civil and criminal laws. Every state has laws that protect family members who are victims of intimate partner violence. Most states also include persons who are in dating relationships and other common victims of violent crimes associated with gender. It should be noted that the terms often used within family violence cases are "victim" and "batterer," which connote that the person who has been harmed is the victim and the person who commits the harm is the batterer. These terms have been normalized by past research and policy; however, modern terminology includes "survivor," "alleged perpetrator," or the legal terms in civil and criminal cases (petitioner/respondent or plaintiff/defendant).

Historically, domestic violence was allowed by law because a husband held a common law right to physically chastise or reasonably correct his wife. Coverture laws and the doctrine of non-intervention in private family law left women unprotected from violence in the home. Lenore Walker historically coined the term "cycle of abuse" to describe and depict the three-phase cycle of an abusive relationship: (1) a tension-building phase, when the batterer commits relatively minor abusive acts and the victim attempts to placate the batterer to prevent further violence; (2) an acute-violence phase, when the batterer escalates violence and may severely injure the victim; and (3) a loving-contrition phase, when the batterer becomes remorseful, pleads for forgiveness, and typically promises that he will never again abuse the victim.[8] Other scholars and advocates have critiqued this insular and cyclical framing for obscuring the more sustained and continuous behaviors of

[5] Matthew J. Breiding et al., *Prevalence and Characteristics of Sexual Violence, Stalking, and Intimate Partner Violence Victimization—National Intimate Partner and Sexual Violence Survey, United States, 2011*, 63 MORBIDITY AND MORTALITY WEEKLY REP. 8 (2014), www.cdc.gov/mmwr/pdf/ss/ss6308.pdf.

[6] Emily Waters, *Lesbian, Gay, Bisexual, Transgender, Queer, and HIV-Affected Intimate Partner Violence in 2016*, National Coalition of Anti-Violence Programs (NCAVP), 23 (2017), https://avp.org/wp-content/uploads/2017/11/NCAVP-IPV-Report-2016.pdf.

[7] *Id.*

[8] LENORE E. WALKER, THE BATTERED WOMAN 55–70 (1979).

power and control that dominate abusive relationships and for the hyper-carceral responses it generates.[9]

The primary way that states provide protection for victims/survivors[10] of intimate partner violence is through civil protection orders (CPOs). There are generally two forms of protection orders: temporary (or *ex parte*) restraining or protective orders (TROs or TPOs) granted on an emergency basis for two weeks or on a permanent basis for a set number of years.[11] Permanent CPOs are granted after an evidentiary hearing for up to two years or more. Issued by a civil or family court judge, CPOs are binding court orders that restrict contact between a batterer and the victim and her family and prevent the batterer from coming near the victim's home or place of work. They can also order batterers to leave their residence, pay temporary alimony, child support, and restitution.

The level of protection offered by CPOs or TROs depends on whether a violation of the order demands criminal arrest or civil sanctions. In most family courts, CPOs are enforced by subsequent pleadings (usually motions to enforce) and an additional hearing. A batterer could be fined and/or jailed for the violation. Federal case law has reduced the power of the CPO, holding that orders of protection do not impose any affirmative duty on state actors (law enforcement) to protect victims.[12]

Many states also offer criminal protective orders that victims may find easier to obtain because they do not require filing written pleadings, and the victim does not need to have legal representation. Criminal protective orders are issued by a magistrate or criminal court judge and are enforced by the police through arrest and imprisonment. In some instances, it is helpful for victims to have both orders in place for protection. A violation of the criminal protective order does not require another court hearing. It offers more immediate assistance from law enforcement. Police can arrest batterers who violate criminal orders.

In addition to understanding how state law offers protection to victims of intimate partner violence, understanding how federal law, specifically the Violence Against Women Act of 1994 (VAWA), impacts your client is critical. VAWA created federal programs within the Department of Justice and the Health and Human Services Department to reduce domestic violence, improve services, and protect victims. VAWA provides critical funds for state, tribal, and local governments as well as nonprofits and educational institutions that support survivors of domestic violence and work to prevent it. The Office on Violence Against Women (OVW) administers these grants.

VAWA requires Congressional reauthorization every five years. Each authorization raises additional issues and implements the objectives with new focuses and priorities. For example, the 2000 reauthorization focused on VAWA's intersections with immigration law and on the abuse of elderly and disabled women. The 2013 reauthorization specifically addressed trafficking and the intersections of VAWA and tribal law. It also included LGBTQI+-inclusive language and allowed for gender neutral statutory language so that LGBTQI+ IPV survivors can apply for CPOs. The latest reauthorization in 2022 addressed a variety of issues, including expanding prosecution of batterers of Native American victims in tribal courts, establishing discrimination claims for equal access and treatment by transgender victims, and expanding prohibitions against batterers regarding gun access and possession. Family law lawyers practicing in this area should become familiar with VAWA, its recurring reauthorizations, and other federal statutes governing domestic violence.

---

[9] *See e.g.*, LEIGH GOODMARK, DECRIMINALIZING DOMESTIC VIOLENCE (2018); Jamie R. Abrams, *Is Domestic Violence Politicized Too Narrowly? in* THE POLITICIZATION OF SAFETY (Jane Stoever ed., N.Y.U. Press 2019).

[10] The terms victim and survivor are used interchangeably in this chapter. Often, state civil and criminal court systems refer to people who have experienced intimate partner violence as victims; however, other agencies that provide support and resources in these situations use the term survivor to promote a sense of resiliency and autonomy.

[11] The name of the order will depend on the jurisdiction and local ordinances.

[12] *See Castle Rock v. Gonzales*, 545 U.S. 748, 768 (2005).

A. FAMILY VIOLENCE COURTS

Many states have developed specialized courts to handle domestic violence. These family violence courts are often part of the criminal court system, whereas domestic relations or family courts are part of the civil court system. The main difference between the two is that family violence courts are dedicated to a singular issue and are comprised of a professional team to assist the victim and prosecute the batterer. Family violence courts offer caseworkers and service coordinators who assist with securing counseling, creating a safety plan, and obtaining crime victim compensation for the victim. They can also provide investigators to assist with witness and evidence gathering. Finally, family violence courts typically do not require victims to hire a lawyer. Victims are represented *pro se* or by government attorneys at hearings. Batterers can represent themselves, hire an attorney, or are appointed an attorney in some jurisdictions.

It may be helpful to observe a family violence court to see how attorneys handle contested cases. When you go to court, locate any forms available for victims of abuse. State bar associations sometimes distribute packets or have information online to provide an understanding about what to expect at court. For example, New York State petitioners can review this website, https://www.womenslaw.org/laws/ny/restraining-orders/orders-protection/steps-obtaining-order-protection, to learn how to obtain a protection order. The District Attorney of Manhattan also has a page full of resources regarding orders of protection (https://www.manhattanda.org/order-protection).

Family civil courts have become very efficient in handling domestic violence cases through improved practices and procedures for securing restraining orders, monitoring of batterer-intervention programs, stricter enforcement of firearms-relinquishment laws and orders, and greater use of technology. There is a vested interest in helping both the victim and the batterer in family civil courts, primarily because they both will continue to co-parent long after the court case ends. Approaching IPV by involving community stakeholders, such as law enforcement and health/social service agencies, is necessary to achieve better outcomes for families and children. There is also a great deal of collaboration between child welfare agencies and domestic violence agencies, as well as other specialized courts, including drug dependency, mental health, and juvenile law courts.

Observing a TRO or CPO hearing in a family civil court will reveal how evidence is presented, how the burden of proof influences the presentation of evidence, how respondents respond to the petition or application, and how judges deal with the respective parties. The forms and orders in the criminal court and the civil court are different, and the ideal outcome for the victim in each court may also be different. Most respondents enter a general denial as the answer to an *Application for Protective Order*. Any specific evidence is presented at the hearing either through testimony or written documentation. The amount of evidence and the burden of proof may differ depending on whether the hearing for the TRO or CPO is in a criminal court or a civil court. An affidavit executed by the victim is often sufficient for a judge to sign a temporary order for two weeks. More evidence will need to be presented at the evidentiary hearing before a judge extends the temporary order for a year or enters a permanent injunction.

Family law lawyers need to take extra steps at the end of cases when they represent a victim of IPV. Protective orders must be delivered to other persons besides the respondent, such as appropriate members of law enforcement, schools, or child exchange facilities. This is a vital step that assures that notice of the legal protection provided by the order has been provided to all relevant interested entities.

B. INTIMATE PARTNER VIOLENCE AND INTERSECTIONS WITH OTHER LAWS

IPV also intersects with other legal areas, including immigration, housing discrimination, and criminal law. Understanding how IPV and cultural traditions and family norms intersect with immigration issues will be increasingly important for lawyers. Immigrant victims of domestic violence may have additional vulnerabilities in legal status that complicate their likelihood to use state resources for domestic violence protection. There are accordingly specific types of relief available to assist immigrant victims, such as U-Visas, that allow immigrants without lawful status the opportunity to be eligible for it if they have been victims of certain qualifying crimes.

Within communities of color, domestic violence is a complex issue. For example, considering just the Hispanic community, it is comprised of a variety of nationalities, ethnicities, and races. This diversity brings a host of risks and protective factors associated with domestic violence. About half of Latinas that experience intimate partner violence do not report it.[13] Underreporting exists because of language barriers among service providers, fear of police, shame, guilt, loyalty to partners, fear of deportation (for non-status immigrants), and previous experience with childhood victimization.[14] Only one in three domestic violence shelters have Spanish-speaking staff, and only half offer child-related services, a service that is very important to Latina survivors. These complexities are problematic for all communities of color in unique ways.

Domestic violence clients have likely overcome many hurdles by the time they ever reach an attorney. For Black, American Indian, or Alaskan Native women, the rate of physical violence, rape, and/or stalking by a partner is 30% higher than what is experienced by white, non-Hispanic, Hispanic, and Asian women.[15] While there is not one single explanation, there are some risk factors that seem to increase violent behavior, including experiences with discrimination, economic insecurity, cohabitation, and pregnancy. Women of color also face unique layers of complexity in how they experience and respond to domestic violence. They often fear and distrust law enforcement and the justice system, themselves victims of racism and classism. They also have strong ties and loyalty to their race, culture, and family, resulting in pressure from the community to keep family matters private.

As protections for gender-based violence have become more inclusive of LGBTQI+ relationships, there has been more attention paid to the severity of violence experienced by some LGBTQI+ couples. The LGBTQI+ community faces unique barriers to seeking help due to fear of discrimination or bias. For example, "outing" or threatening to reveal one's partner's sexual orientation or gender identity can be used as an abusive tool and may also be a barrier to victims seeking help. Transgender individuals may suffer from even greater IPV risks, such as facing threats, intimidation, harassment, and police violence. Members of the LGBTQI+ community may be denied assistance and domestic violence services because of homophobia, transphobia, biphobia, or inadequate services infrastructure.

Because physical and sexual violence is a crime, IPV intersects with criminal law. If law enforcement is called out to a home or other location because of domestic violence, there is usually a report generated, and charges filed against the perpetrator. If there is violence against children, the state child welfare agency may be called out to remove the children from the home. There can be separate court cases that are contemporaneously occurring in family and criminal courts. The facts proven in family court can also be admitted as evidence against a perpetrator in criminal court. The batterer will often assert a Fifth Amendment privilege in family court so as not to self-

---

[13] Emily Waters, *supra* note 6 at 23.

[14] *Id.*

[15] *Id.*

incriminate. Likewise, a guilty verdict or plea can result in certain restrictions and presumptions in family court regarding child custody and access.

Research the Law: Domestic violence findings might prove a cruelty fault-based ground for divorce. Locate your state's grounds for divorce statute. Does it allow for divorce based on cruelty? If so, how does cruelty alter the timing to file for divorce compared to filing a no-fault ground?

C. CLIENT RESOURCES

Lawyers should know both the law of domestic violence and the community resources available to support clients. Emergency shelters for victims and their children, housing assistance, clothing, food, support groups, and financial assistance are some of the resources that clients may need in addition to protective orders. Clients experiencing family violence often also need medical, psychological, and in some cases, psychiatric help. Connecting clients with service providers that can assist with immediate needs is a concrete way to ensure that your client can make the most of your legal services. For example, stable, safe housing and protective day care for young children may be the difference between your client being able to maintain her employment and move forward independently. Depending on where you live, there are usually some family services available to your clients through court referrals or from non-profits supporting families in crisis. As a family law attorney, you should be familiar with all these resources and have a prepared list to share with clients.

It is imperative to give serious thought to your client's safety. Unfortunately, no CPO can prevent murder if a spouse or ex-partner is intent on causing a person bodily harm or death. Almost 60% of the homicides by intimate partners are caused by guns. The prevalence of guns during IPV has proven to be a difficult hurdle in protecting victims. Eighty percent of children killed in mass shootings between 2009–2018—defined as shootings in which at least four people other than the shooter died—were shot in incidents tied to family or intimate partner violence.[16]

The Lautenberg Amendment to the 1996 Gun Control Act was passed to prevent persons who have been convicted of domestic violence crimes from owning or possessing a firearm. It also applies to persons who are under court order to refrain from harassing, stalking, or threatening an intimate partner. In 2024, the U.S. Supreme Court upheld the constitutionality of the section of the Gun Control Act that extended the prohibition of possessing firearms to anyone with a qualified court order of restraint from domestic violence.[17] This was a significant reversal of an appellate court ruling that would have allowed domestic abusers to be armed. Being mindful of what type of weapons a spouse or partner may have at their disposal is critical to recognizing a potentially lethal threat to your client and her children. A social services worker or counselor can help your client develop a safety plan preparing for worst case scenarios. An example of questions to ask to create a personalized safety plan can be found here: https://ncadv.org/personalized-safety-plan.

In addition, your safety and the safety of the people working with you may also require vigilant attention. There have been cases where disgruntled spouses or partners have sought out the lawyers or judges who they believe caused the pain in their lives. IPV cases are complex and fraught with uncertainty. Some family law lawyers accordingly opt not to handle these cases. Many lawyers find these types of cases fulfilling and essential to their practice and professional identity because of the opportunities the law provides for helping vulnerable people in critical situations.

---

[16] Madeleine Carlisle and Melissa Chan, *Here's Why Domestic Violence Kills So Many Women and Children in America*, TIME (Oct. 17, 2019).

[17] *United States v. Rahimi*, 602 U.S. 680 (2024).

There are several online resources for lawyers, judges, and other persons who assist victims and perpetrators of domestic violence. The following links provide interactive programs that allow for participants to learn about how victims encounter the legal system and the barriers they may face in trying to protect themselves and their children.

- Domestic Violence Resource Guide—https://nrcdv.org/
- Domestic Violence and Firearms—https://bwjp.org/wp-content/uploads/2024/12/for-publication.2024-Domestic-Violence-and-Firearms-Report-by-BWJP-and-NDVH-12.4.2024.pdf
- VAWnet Organizations Focused on Domestic Violence in LGBTQI+ Communities—https://vawnet.org/sc/organizations-focused-dv-lgbtq-communities

Ethical Considerations: You are representing a husband with a documented history of domestic violence against his ex-spouse. No current CPOs govern the relationship, however. In your interviews and intakes, the client has suggested that he "just can't forgive her for divorcing him" and that "she will pay for what she has done." You interpret these comments to be more than typical divorce frustrations and banter. What, if any, ethical obligations do you owe to third parties, such as his ex-spouse or any relative with whom she lives? How do you navigate your obligation to preserve confidential communications with your client if you believe that a third-party may be in danger?

D. CHILD PROTECTION ISSUES

Children who live with a parent experiencing intimate partner violence often are present in the home when violence is occurring, and they hear their parent being hit, objects being thrown, and the screams and crying that typically accompany abuse. "Exposure to intimate partner violence is considered to be a form of child maltreatment, and affected children are often also the victims of targeted child abuse."[18] Children often have trouble sleeping, performing at school, interacting with peers, and have issues with self-esteem. In some instances, children mimic the abusive behavior witnessed at home, or they act out in other destructive ways. IPV can impact custody disputes between parents in that most states have a rebuttable presumption that allows for a court to determine custody in favor of the non-offending parent if there is a history of family violence.

Many states allow for children to be included in their parent's application for a CPO filed against the parent's spouse or partner in civil or criminal court. The affidavit or evidence presented at the hearing should include any proof of violence or abuse directed toward the children or any proof that the children have been significantly affected by the violence in the home. If a client needs a permanent order to protect children from a batterer, an expert witness, such as a child psychologist or a therapist, can testify about the long-term harm or risk of harm to the children if exposed to abuse in the future. The CPO can request that the perpetrator be prohibited from going to the school or daycare facility of the children, and it could also include banning the offending parent from extracurricular activities and doctor's appointments. Other relatives living with a victim/survivor can also be included in a CPO, including parents and siblings of the victim/survivor, and the protection order can prohibit the perpetrator from going near their residence(s) and place of employment.

If there are children who are being abused or neglected in a parent's household, a government agency can initiate or file an interpleader or intervention to enter the family law case. Each state

[18] Sibylle Artz, et al, *A Comprehensive Review of the Literature on the Impact of Exposure to Intimate Partner Violence for Children and Youth*, 5(4) INTL J. OF CHILD, YOUTH, AND FAMILY STUDIES 493, 493 (2014).

has a child welfare agency that is responsible for investigating reports of suspected child abuse and neglect. Sometimes these investigations are initiated after a violent incident in a home involving a spouse with children present. Once the state becomes involved in the matter, each parent may be eligible to receive an appointed attorney. The case may extend for up to a year or longer, and depending on the circumstances, the parental rights may be permanently affected.

Ethical Considerations: If you gain knowledge through your client representation that causes you to suspect that your client's children (or any other children) are being abused or neglected, what legal reporting obligations do you have? Are lawyers in your home state mandatory reporters or are your communications privileged? Be prepared to discuss different ways that you could handle this type of situation consistent with your state reporting requirements.

The parental rights of your client may be at risk of being terminated because of child abuse or neglect. The parameters of this type of lawsuit are beyond the scope of this book, but it is important for family law lawyers to familiarize themselves with the laws and process of suits against parents by the state. A few helpful resources are as follows:

- Child Welfare Information Gateway—Grounds for Involuntary Termination of Parental Rights—https://www.childwelfare.gov/topics/systemwide/laws-policies/statutes/groundtermin/
- American Bar Association—Parent Know Your Rights Guides—https://www.americanbar.org/groups/public_interest/child_law/project-areas/parentrepresentation/parent-know-your-rights-resources/
- American Bar Association—National Alliance for Parent Representation—https://www.americanbar.org/groups/public_interest/child_law/project-areas/parentrepresentation/
- National Association of Counsel for Children—https://nacchildlaw.org/

III. CASE FILE—EILEEN THOMPSON V. ZACHERY THOMPSON

A. SIMULATION ROADMAP

In this simulation, you are preparing documentation in support of Eileen Thompson's request for a restraining order. Her husband has been abusive. Your paralegal has visited her in the hospital to gather the basic facts, and she has taken notes so that you can prepare an *Affidavit in Support of Ex Parte Relief*. This is a required filing with an *Application for Protective Order* (CPO). You will prepare the Affidavit and the CPO with the goal of protecting Eileen as well as anyone else in the family who may be at risk of harm from her spouse. You must prepare these documents to present to a judge in an ex parte hearing. Your objective is to prepare your argument and anticipate the judge's questions.

B. MEMO TO THE FILE

MEMORANDUM

Case Name: *Eileen Thompson vs. Zachery Thompson*

Legal Service: *Temporary Restraining Order*

Children: *Two; daughter (7) and son (3)*

Special Info: *Husband owns gun and used it as weapon during assault*

Basic Case Facts

Eileen Thompson (34) contacted the office to hire an attorney to get a temporary restraining order against her husband. She is also thinking about filing for divorce. She has been married to Zachery Thompson (38) for eight years. They have two children, Zoe (7) and Preston (3). Zachery has been arrested for aggravated assault because he slapped Eileen across the face with a gun. His bail was set fairly high, but he has contacted his brother to pay it so that he can get out of jail. Zachery has left voicemails for Eileen stating that he is planning on going back to the marital home when he is released from jail. Their home was purchased together after they were married.

Eileen is in the hospital after suffering a concussion from the blow to her face. This is not the first time that Zachery has hit her, but it is the first time that the police were called out to their home. All the assaults have occurred in their bedroom. Preston was in the room during this aggravated assault. He was over in the corner playing with some blocks. Eileen believes that Zachery did not realize Preston was there when he hit her with the gun. Zoe has been in the house during some of the previous verbal and physical altercations between her parents, but always in her room with the door closed. She has heard her parents arguing, and on one occasion heard household items falling and breaking during one of their fights.

Eileen says that her family has been concerned about her and the children's safety for some time now. Her parents have pressured her to file for divorce because they are afraid for her. Her mother has told her that she needs to leave Zachery before he kills her. When Zachery is particularly volatile, she often leaves the kids with her parents in the evenings and on weekends so that they will not be exposed to the escalating tensions at home.

Her parents have a very stable home and have been married for over forty years. Her mother is a retired elementary school teacher. Her father is a well-respected college basketball coach. They have raised four children. They are a prominent family in the community. They have tried to keep the marital issues between Eileen and Zachery out of the news.

After this most recent incident of violence, Eileen's parents told her that she and the children should stay with them so that they would not be financially dependent on Zachery any longer. Eileen left the workforce after she had Zoe, and Zachery is her sole source of support.

Paralegal Jackie Rivers consulted with Eileen in the hospital where she is being treated for a head contusion. After meeting with Eileen, Jackie began drafting an *Affidavit in Support of Ex Parte Relief.*

IV. RELEVANT STATUTORY LAW

Texas law governs Eileen's petition. Because domestic violence is addressed in both family courts and criminal courts, Eileen has multiple paths to explore. Your client's life could depend on your mobilization of legal and social service advocates to protect her.

A. TEXAS FAMILY CODE

Title 4—Protective Orders and Family Violence

Chapter 71. Definitions

§ 71.004. Family Violence

"Family violence" means:

(1) an act by a member of a family or household against another member of the family or household that is intended to result in physical harm, bodily injury, assault, or sexual assault or that is a threat that reasonably places the member in fear of imminent physical harm, bodily injury, assault, or sexual assault, but does not include defensive measures to protect oneself;

(2) abuse, as that term is defined by Sections 261.001(1)(C), (E), (G), (H), (I), (J), (K), and (M), by a member of a family or household toward a child of the family or household; or

(3) dating violence, as that term is defined by Section 71.0021.

Chapter 82. Applying for Protective Order

§ 82.001. Application

A proceeding under this subtitle is begun by filing "An Application for a Protective Order" with the clerk of the court.

§ 82.002. Who May File Application

(a) With regard to family violence under Section 71.004(1) or (2), an adult member of the family or household may file an application for a protective order to protect the applicant or any other member of the applicant's family or household

(b) With regard to family violence under Section 71.004(3), an application for a protective order to protect the applicant may be filed by a member of the dating relationship, regardless of whether the member is an adult or a child.

(c) With regard to family violence under Section 71.004(3), an application for a protective order to protect the applicant may be filed by:

(1) an adult member of the dating relationship; or

(2) an adult member of the marriage, if the victim is or was married as described by Section 71.0021(a)(1)(B).

(d) Any adult may apply for a protective order to protect a child from family violence. * * *

§ 82.004. Contents of Application

An application must state:

(1) the name and county of residence of each applicant;

(2) the name and county of residence of each individual alleged to have committed family violence;

(3) the relationships between the applicants and the individual alleged to have committed family violence;

(4) a request for one or more protective orders; and

(5) whether an applicant is receiving services from the Title IV-D agency in connection with a child support case and, if known, the agency case number for each open case.

§ 82.009. Application for Temporary Ex Parte Order

(a) An application that requests the issuance of a temporary ex parte order under Chapter 83 must:

(1) contain a detailed description of the facts and circumstances concerning the alleged family violence and the need for the immediate protective order; and

(2) be signed by each applicant under an oath that the facts and circumstances contained in the application are true to the best knowledge and belief of each applicant.

(b) For purposes of this section, a statement signed under oath by a child is valid if the statement otherwise complies with this chapter.

* * *

§ 82.041. Contents of Notice of Application

(a) A notice of an application for a protective order must:

(1) be styled "The State of Texas";

(2) be signed by the clerk of the court under the court's seal;

(3) contain the name and location of the court;

(4) show the date the application was filed;

(5) show the date notice of the application for a protective order was issued;

(6) show the date, time, and place of the hearing;

(7) show the file number;

(8) show the name of each applicant and each person alleged to have committed family violence;

(9) be directed to each person alleged to have committed family violence;

(10) show:

(A) the name and address of the attorney for the applicant; or

(B) if the applicant is not represented by an attorney:

(i) the mailing address of the applicant; or

(ii) if applicable, the name and mailing address of the person designated under Section 82.011; and

(11) contain the address of the clerk of the court.

(b) The notice of an application for a protective order must state: "An application for a protective order has been filed in the court stated in this notice alleging that you have committed family violence. You may employ an attorney to defend you against this allegation. You or your attorney may, but are not required to, file a written answer to the application. Any answer must be filed before the hearing on the application. If you receive this notice within 48 hours before the time set for the hearing, you may request the court to reschedule the hearing not later than 14 days after the date set for the hearing. If you do not attend the hearing, a default judgment may be taken and a protective order may be issued against you."

Chapter 83. Temporary Ex Parte Orders

§ 83.001. Requirements for Temporary Ex Parte Order

(a) If the court finds from the information contained in an application for a protective order that there is a clear and present danger of family violence, the court, without further notice to the individual alleged to have committed family violence and without a hearing, may enter a temporary ex parte order for the protection of the applicant or any other member of the family or household of the applicant.

(b) In a temporary ex parte order, the court may direct a respondent to do or refrain from doing specified acts.

§ 83.002. Duration of Order: Extension

(a) A temporary ex parte order is valid for the period specified in the order, not to exceed days.

(b) On the request of an applicant or on the court's own motion, a temporary ex parte order may be extended for additional 20-day periods.

* * *

§ 83.005. Exclusion of Party From Residence

(a) Subject to the limitations of Section 85.021(2), a person may only be excluded from the occupancy of the person's residence by a temporary ex parte order under this chapter if the applicant:

(1) files a sworn affidavit that provides a detailed description of the facts and circumstances requiring the exclusion of the person from the residence; and

(2) appears in person to testify at a temporary ex parte hearing to justify the issuance of the order without notice.

(b) Before the court may render a temporary ex parte order excluding a person from the person's residence, the court must find from the required affidavit and testimony that:

(1) the applicant requesting the excluding order either resides on the premises or has resided there within 30 days before the date the application was filed;

(2) the person to be excluded has within the 30 days before the date the application was filed committed family violence against a member of the household; and

(3) there is a clear and present danger that the person to be excluded is likely to commit family violence against a member of the household.

(c) The court may recess the hearing on a temporary ex parte order to contact the respondent by telephone and provide the respondent the opportunity to be present when the court resumes the hearing. Without regard to whether the respondent is able to be present at the hearing, the court shall resume the hearing before the end of the working day.

Chapter 85. Issuance of Protective Order

§ 85.001. Required Findings and Orders

(a) At the close of a hearing on an application for a protective order, the court shall find whether:

(1) family violence has occurred; and

(2) family violence is likely to occur in the future.

(b) If the court finds that family violence has occurred and that family violence is likely to occur in the future, the court:

(1) shall render a protective order as provided by Section 85.022 applying only to a person found to have committed family violence; and

(2) may render a protective order as provided by Section 85.021 applying to both parties that is in the best interest of the person protected by the order or member of the family or household of the person protected by the order.

(c) A protective order that requires the first applicant to do or refrain from doing an act under Section 85.022 shall include a finding that the first applicant has committed family violence and is likely to commit family violence in the future.

(d) If the court renders a protective order for a period of more than two years, the court must include in the order a finding described by Section 85.025(a–1).

§ 85.021. Requirements of Order Applying to Any Party

In a protective order, the court may:

(1) prohibit a party from:

(A) removing a child who is a member of the family or household from:

(i) the possession of a person named in the order; or

(ii) the jurisdiction of the court;

(B) transferring, encumbering, or otherwise disposing of property, other than in the ordinary course of business, that is mutually owned or leased by the parties; or

(C) removing a pet, companion animal, or assistance animal, as defined by Section 121.002, Human Resources Code, from the possession or actual or constructive care of a person named in the order;

(2) grant exclusive possession of a residence to a party and, if appropriate, direct one or more parties to vacate the residence if the residence:

(A) is jointly owned or leased by the party receiving exclusive possession and a party being denied possession;

(B) is owned or leased by the party retaining possession; or

(C) is owned or leased by the party being denied possession and that party has an obligation to support the party or a child of the party granted possession of the residence;

(3) provide for the possession of and access to a child of a party if the person receiving possession of or access to the child is a parent of the child;

(4) require the payment of support for a party or for a child of a party if the person required to make the payment has an obligation to support the other party or the child; or

(5) award to a party the use and possession of specified property that is community property or jointly owned or leased property.

§ 85.022. Requirements of Order Applying to Person Who Committed Family Violence

(a) In a protective order, the court may order the person found to have committed family violence to perform acts specified by the court that the court determines are necessary or appropriate to prevent or reduce the likelihood of family violence and may order that person to:

(1) complete a battering intervention and prevention program accredited under Article 42.141, Code of Criminal Procedure;

(2) beginning on September 1, 2008, if the referral option under Subdivision (1) is not available, complete a program or counsel with a provider that has begun the accreditation process described by Subsection (a–1); or

(3) if the referral option under Subdivision (1) or, beginning on September 1, 2008, the referral option under Subdivision (2) is not available, counsel with a social worker, family service agency, physician, psychologist, licensed therapist, or licensed professional counselor who has completed family violence intervention training that the community justice assistance division of the Texas Department of Criminal Justice has approved, after consultation with the licensing authorities

described by Chapters 152, 501, 502, 503, and 505, Occupations Code, and experts in the field of family violence.

(a–1) Beginning on September 1, 2009, a program or provider serving as a referral option for the courts under Subsection (a)(1) or (2) must be accredited under Section 4A, Article 42.141, Code of Criminal Procedure, as conforming to program guidelines under that article.

(b) In a protective order, the court may prohibit the person found to have committed family violence from:

(1) committing family violence;

(2) communicating:

(A) directly with a person protected by an order or a member of the family or household of a person protected by an order, in a threatening or harassing manner;

(B) a threat through any person to a person protected by an order or a member of the family or household of a person protected by an order; and

(C) if the court finds good cause, in any manner with a person protected by an order or a member of the family or household of a person protected by an order, except through the party's attorney or a person appointed by the court;

(3) going to or near the residence or place of employment or business of a person protected by an order or a member of the family or household of a person protected by an order;

(4) going to or near the residence, child-care facility, or school a child protected under the order normally attends or in which the child normally resides;

(5) engaging in conduct directed specifically toward a person who is a person protected by an order or a member of the family or household of a person protected by an order, including following the person, that is reasonably likely to harass, annoy, alarm, abuse, torment, or embarrass the person;

(6) possessing a firearm, unless the person is a peace officer, as defined by Section 1.07, Penal Code, actively engaged in employment as a sworn, full-time paid employee of a state agency or political subdivision; and

(7) harming, threatening, or interfering with the care, custody, or control of a pet, companion animal, or assistance animal, as defined by Section 121.002, Human Resources Code, that is possessed by or is in the actual or constructive care of a person protected by an order or by a member of the family or household of a person protected by an order.

(c) In an order under Subsection (b)(3) or (4), the court shall specifically describe each prohibited location and the minimum distances from the location, if any, that the party must maintain. This subsection does not apply to an order in which Section 85.007 applies.

(d) In a protective order, the court shall suspend a license to carry a handgun issued under Subchapter H, Chapter 411, Government Code, that is held by a person found to have committed family violence.

(e) In this section, "firearm" has the meaning assigned by Section 46.01, Penal Code.

V. THE SIMULATION

A. DRAFTING THE *AFFIDAVIT IN SUPPORT OF EX PARTE RELIEF*

Using the Memo to the File, draft the facts for the *Affidavit in Support of Ex Parte Relief.* Keep in mind your ethical obligations to represent facts accurately.

STATE OF TEXAS §
§
COUNTY OF DALLAS §

EILEEN THOMPSON'S AFFIDAVIT IN SUPPORT OF EX PARTE RELIEF

"I, Eileen Thompson, am the applicant in this *Application for a Protective Order.* I am above the age of eighteen years, and I am seeking protection for myself and my children, Zoe Thompson and Preston Thompson. I am fully competent to make this affidavit. The facts and circumstances alleged are true to the best of my knowledge and belief."

"I am the mother of two children, Zoe Thompson (hereafter "Zoe"), age seven, and Preston Thompson (hereafter "Preston"), age three. Zoe's date of birth is February 20, YR-07, and Preston's date of birth is June 6, YR-03."

"Zoe and Preston's father, Zachery Thompson (hereafter "Zachery"), is my husband, and the Respondent in this Application. We live together in the same home located at 4321 Rockport Way, Dallas, Texas 75218."

[FILL IN THE REST OF THE AFFIDAVIT WITH PERTINENT FACTS]

"Therefore, I request the Court grant my *Application for an Ex Parte Protective Order* until there can be a hearing."

____

EILEEN THOMPSON, Applicant SIGNED under oath on _________, YR-00.

State of Texas

County of _____________

Before me, a Notary Public, on this day personally appeared ___________________________ known to me to be the person whose name is subscribed to the foregoing document and, being by me first duly sworn, declared that the statements therein contained are true and correct.

____

NOTARY PUBLIC, State of Texas

(seal) **NAME PRINTED:** ______________________

COMM. EXP. __________________________

B. DRAFTING AN *APPLICATION FOR PROTECTIVE ORDER*

After drafting the *Affidavit in Support of Ex Parte Relief*, use the Texas statutory provisions in Section IV.A. to draft an *Application for Protective Order for Eileen Thompson*. There are model forms available via Westlaw. You may also find pertinent information on the Texas Judicial Branch website—https://www.txcourts.gov/rules-forms/standardized-protective-order-forms/. The forms on this website are for pro se litigants, and you should not fill out the form and submit it for this assignment. Prepare the Application for Protective Order as if you have been retained by Eileen Thompson to represent her in this matter.

CHAPTER FIVE

ESTABLISHMENT OF PARENTAGE

I. INTRODUCTION

The process of establishing parentage is a common 'bread and butter' practice skill for family law lawyers. The legal relationship between a child and parent is one of the most cherished and protected bonds in the family, so parentage issues can be highly emotive and litigated when these relationships are contested. Parentage law has become more complex over time because technology has dramatically expanded the ways to produce a child and the ease of testing genetic relationships. These innovations have compelled transformations in parentage law to meet the needs of 21st century families.

Establishing parentage is a way that many adults build a family. Research shows that approximately 32% of children are living with only one parent.[1] More couples are cohabitating and having children outside of marriage or before marriage. The rise in nonmarital children over the last forty years has resulted in a larger number of children born with only one legal parent (the birth mother). This chapter will introduce you to paternity establishment, which is the most prevalent parentage issue in family courts.

Absent first-hand experience with parentage law, what most people know about the establishment of parentage often comes from viewing popular television shows, like The Maury Povich Show, or reality shows like Paternity Court. This chapter presents a critical opportunity to debunk myths and misconceptions. It also reflects rapid changes in family law and highlights a budding practice area in ART.

From an interdisciplinary standpoint, parentage is also multi-faceted. It involves contract law, client counseling, and statutory interpretation. It reflects evolving social norms about parentage itself and the psychology of parenthood. As other disciplines grow and alter best practices related to the factors necessary for children's well-being, family laws also expand to fit the best interests of the child. Parentage is a dynamic subject matter in which all family law lawyers should develop expertise.

Learning Outcomes:

(1) Identify the various ways that men and women can establish legal parentage.

(2) Draft a *Petition to Establish Paternity.*

[1] Gretchen Livingston, *The Changing Profile of Unmarried Parents*, THE PEW RESEARCH CENTER (Apr. 2018), https://www.pewsocialtrends.org/2018/04/25/the-changing-profile-of-unmarried-parents/.

II. OVERVIEW OF THE LAW

Historic Presumptions and Discriminatory Classifications

Parentage was governed for centuries by presumptions attached to childbirth and marriage. A woman who birthed a child was presumed to be the legal mother. The man who was married to the woman who birthed the child was presumed to be the natural and legal father. A husband's parental rights were irrebuttable absent proof of impotence, sterility, or distance from his wife during the time of conception. State family law thus historically protected the marital family and the children born within the marriage, privileging this normative family structure.

While privileging marital families, family law historically discriminated against many communities. Children were historically treated as property under the law, which had sweeping racial and gendered implications. Only free men could hold property. The majority of persons of African descent in the U.S. were enslaved for the first two and a half centuries of the country's existence. Children born to enslaved parents were considered property. These parents had no legal rights to their children.

Enslaved couples also did not have the legal right to marry until after emancipation in 1865, thus the marital presumption offered no historic import. After the Reconstruction Amendments were ratified, formerly enslaved persons were encouraged to marry for a variety of reasons, one of which was to join the social order of families. Marriage was the easiest way for newly freed couples to legitimate the children born within their union.

Non-marital children also suffered discriminatory treatment under historic laws and presumptions. Children born outside of wedlock had no legal father and were considered illegitimate. An entire regime of laws supported this discriminatory differentiation of marital and non-marital children.

These historic and gendered presumptions and premises—framed around birth and marriage—are no longer effective or workable to determine parentage because of modern technologies and family diversity. These presumptions still exist in many states, often codified and often undergoing modernizations. Technological developments, such as DNA testing and ART, have further allowed us to reconceptualize family formation and genetic connections. The following sections explore these general areas of reform that have developed in the past half a century.

The Rights of Non-Marital Fathers

Significant constitutional and statutory reforms have transformed the law's treatment of non-marital fathers. Because non-marital fathers were treated differently than marital fathers and single mothers, several lawsuits argued that this differential treatment violated both the Fourteenth Amendment due process clause, protecting the right to raise and rear one's children, and the equal protection clause. A series of Supreme Court cases accordingly established a legal standard for non-marital fathers that has come to be known as 'the biology plus standard.'[2] Parental rights can be established if an unmarried man can prove a genetic tie to a child and show his intent to parent through financial support and/or the development of a substantial relationship with the child.

Around the time these constitutional law cases were winding their way up to the Supreme Court, the Uniform Parentage Act (UPA) was promulgated in 1973 by the National Conference of Commissioners of Uniform State Laws. This Act provided a uniform legal framework for states to establish paternity of minor children regardless of the parents' marital status. It has since been revised twice in 2002 and 2017 as explored in later sections. The 1973 UPA primarily sought to

[2] *Lehr v. Robertson*, 463 U.S. 248, 261–62 (1983).

define parentage for non-marital fathers for the purpose of securing the correlating rights and benefits for children (e.g., child support).

While the UPA served to decouple marriage from parentage somewhat, it surely did not promote family diversity or represent larger values of inclusion. Strong fiscal incentives drove these reforms too. Most single parents are working women with only one income, and many struggle with financial stability while caring for children. While the overarching policy of family courts is centered on the "best interests of the child" standard, federal and state law requires establishment of paternity before a single mother can access state welfare to assist with caring for her children. If a father can be found and identified as a biological parent, the state can force him to pay child support and even work to reimburse the state for public benefits already distributed. States can therefore protect expenditures of state funds on children if they can secure parentage and child support from fathers. It is helpful to understand the state's normative goals for parentage laws to analyze how family law statutes and policies are influenced by societal customs and government's fiscal choices.

Despite all the reforms and transformations that the UPA and constitutional challenges brought, non-marital parents do still face a different legal system. Most states, for example, have time limitations for unmarried men to assert their paternity, particularly if the child is born during the time the mother is married to a different man. Usually if both parents are unmarried, there is no time limitation on the father establishing legal parenthood. With the increase in cohabitation and decrease in marriage, the path to parentage for unmarried men is not always a clear road, and many prospective clients may bring a host of misconceptions to this topic.

One notable additional reform offers a possible method to establish parentage for non-marital fathers. The original 1973 UPA offered the possibility for fathers to acknowledge their paternity at birth by signing a Voluntary Acknowledgments of Paternity (VAP). Congress later mandated a fundamental change in the acknowledgment procedure that ratcheted up the significance of these legal documents tremendously. The Personal Responsibility and Work Opportunity Reconciliation Act of 1996 (the Welfare Reform Act) conditioned receipt of federal child support enforcement funds on state enactment of laws that greatly strengthen the effect of a VAP. These forms, typically signed at the hospital bedside, carry the weight of a judicial determination of parenthood. VAPs play a critical role in identifying possible fathers at the moment of birth, but many men do not fully understand the weight of what they are signing, and most do not complete genetic testing before signing the form. This can result in the establishment of legal parentage for the wrong person, if the man who executes a VAP is not in fact the biological father of the child.

Parentage for Same-Sex Couples

States have modernized their parentage laws to address the parenting rights of same-sex couples in a range of ways. Parentage issues for same-sex couples include a combination of unique issues (e.g., restrictive gendered language governing the marital presumption or VAPs) and they can overlap heavily with the issues faced by non-marital parents and by all families using reproductive technologies.

Today many states are re-aligning their parentage laws by amending their parentage codes to include same-sex marital couples in existing presumptions. Many states have come to interpret the historic marital presumption to allow same-sex marital partners presumptive parentage status consistent with opposite-sex marriage. Many states have also allowed VAPs to present a pathway to legal parentage for non-biological same-sex partners. States are also amending their codes to adopt equitable or functional doctrines to create parentage frameworks and presumptions that are not dependent on biology.

Constitutional challenges have also yielded transformative shifts in parentage laws. Since the Supreme Court's 2015 *Obergefell v. Hodges* ruling, a subsequent Supreme Court case, *Pavan v.*

Smith,[3] ruled on a parentage issue faced by same-sex married couples utilizing assisted reproduction technology. In *Pavan*, the Court ruled that the Arkansas state law regulating birth certificates was unconstitutional because it treated married same-sex couples utilizing ART differently than married heterosexual couples utilizing ART. In this case, two married women used sperm donors and artificial insemination to have two children, but after their birth, the state refused to place both mothers' names on the certificate. While states may differ regarding how parentage is determined, parentage laws and related laws are also bound by federal family law rulings compelling equal treatment under the law.

After *Obergefell*, the UPA was also significantly revised, seeking to actualize the larger principles of family equality through full family recognition that *Obergefell* represented. The 2017 UPA (a) removed gender distinctions throughout the Act; (b) provided new methods of establishing parentage for non-biological parents; (c) included a new multi-factor assessment to resolve competing parentage claims; (d) recognized the possibility of more than two legal parents; (e) clarified parentage issues for children born as a result of sexual assault; (f) revised surrogacy provisions; and (g) incorporated a comprehensive section dedicated to the rights of children born via assisted reproductive technology. Only three states have currently adopted the 2017 UPA. While the most recent iteration of the UPA has not been adopted wholesale, certain sections have been used to guide changes in state family law statutes, such as the article regarding establishment of de facto parenthood and the article that aligns with the Rape Survivor Child Custody Act. These sections of the 2017 UPA reflect the rapid evolution of family law. They acknowledge that children are often raised by a family network rather than just two parents, and that sometimes a mother should have veto power regarding who can become a legal father to her child.

Reproductive Technologies

Modern families are often more pluralistic and complex than the law reflects. Medical technology, such as ART, has opened up the possibility of more permutations of genetic material and birthing capabilities that call this historic presumption into question. The use of ART has grown exponentially since the 1970's when the first test tube baby was born. Approximately 12% of couples experience infertility and use ART medically to birth a genetic child. There are over a dozen ways that couples can use ART to have children, including artificial insemination, in vitro fertilization, a gestational carrier or surrogate. The use of donor eggs and sperm have increased the various permutations of producing a baby.

States require some form of legal documents to establish parentage for families using ART. The procedures and documents vary by state. Additional material regarding ART is available via the Teacher's Manual for this book, and a surrogacy simulation can be provided if time permits.

Third Parents

Historically, a child presumptively could only have one mother and one father. Modern families are far more complicated and pluralistic. Extended family, frequent cohabitation with different partners, and remarriage have produced a network of people who function as caregivers for children. Some states have started to move away from a two-parent restrictive framing to allow for a third legal parent. Most states have amended their codes to allow paths to step-parent adoption in order to align with the complexities of blended families. Other law reform efforts have explored the parentage rights of relatives and kinship caregivers who provide temporary or permanent custody for children when parental hardships such as incarceration, mental illness, or suicide occur.

---

[3] 582 U.S. 563 (2017).

III. ESTABLISHING PATERNITY—CASE FILE: HECTOR GONZÁLEZ

A. SIMULATION ROADMAP

In Chapter One, Hector González sought your advice regarding his status as a legal father. Hector signed an Acknowledgment of Paternity (AOP) when his son, Hector González, Jr., was born. As part of the simulation in Chapter One, you were tasked with creating an outline of questions for a follow-up interview of Hector. The following Client Interview Notes reflect the interview between Hector and your supervising attorney. After reviewing the Client Interview Notes and relevant sections of the Texas Family Code, you will draft a *Petition to Establish Paternity*.

B. CLIENT INTERVIEW NOTES

TO:	File
FROM:	Partner Attorney
RE:	Interview Notes—Hector González, Case File 56P-YR-00

Initial Consultation with Client:

Hector González had an initial consultation with our firm one month ago, when he first found out that his three-year-old son may not be biologically related to him. At that time, he expressed a desire to establish paternity for his son and brought a signed AOP with him to the consultation. He lived with the mother and the child for approximately one year. After moving out, he continued to pay an agreed amount for child support as well as providing other basic goods for the child. Hector also routinely visited his son each week up until he confronted the mother about an ex-boyfriend, Carlos Garcia, who claimed to be the father of the child. I conducted a follow-up interview with Hector on October 20, YR-00.

Interview Notes:

After checking with the State Bureau of Vital Statistics to determine the date upon which the AOP was filed, our firm paralegal learned that the document was never filed with the state agency. I asked Hector where he received the copy he brought with him to the initial consultation. Hector had actually retrieved the signed AOP from the hospital staff person on the same day his son was born, before it was faxed to the Bureau of Vital Statistics.

Hector explained further. After the birth certificate was brought to the room, Hector excused himself to grab a snack from the hospital cafeteria. He ran into Ms. Jenkins and asked her if it was too late for him to get a genetic/ DNA test to make sure that he was Hector Jr.'s father. She told him no, and that she had not yet faxed the AOP to the State Bureau of Vital Statistics. He told Ms. Jenkins that he and Samantha agreed to do DNA testing before submitting the AOP to the State of Texas, even though this was not something Samantha agreed to do. Ms. Jenkins retrieved the document from a folder labeled "FAX BY 5 PM DAILY." When she gave it back to Hector, she told him that once they all got DNA testing, he could check the box on the form and re-date it. She told him that as long as he put his initials by the new date, it would be fine. She told him he could go to the Social Security Administration Office to submit his AOP, but Hector never did so.

The birth certificate for Hector González, Jr. was not changed by the hospital staff, so Hector González's name is still listed on it as the father. After they returned home with the baby, Hector could not convince Samantha to allow him to take Hector Jr. to get the DNA testing. The fact that she so adamantly refused to get the genetic testing done was part of the reason that they broke up. His suspicions that he is not the biological father of Hector

Jr. have only increased. At this point, Hector is afraid that his ex-girlfriend's prior lover, Carlos Garcia, will file paperwork to establish himself as the biological father of Hector Jr.

Legal Guidance Offered:

I informed Hector that the AOP is not valid because it was not filed with the state vital statistics agency. The only way for him to establish paternity now is to file a petition and ask the court to order genetic testing. I told him that Ms. Jenkins should not have returned the AOP to him once he had signed it. He assumed that since his name was on the birth certificate, this meant that he was the legal father. I informed him that the birth certificate alone is not enough to establish paternity in Texas. In fact, Texas law does not allow an unmarried parent's name to be placed on the birth certificate without a fully executed AOP. The AOP is the only document equivalent to a court adjudication of parentage. I explained that Carlos could still enter the suit if he desired to have DNA testing completed also. I explained that if the DNA testing revealed that he is not the biological father of Hector Jr., he may still have an argument to try and establish paternity; however, his case would be significantly weakened without a genetic tie to his son. Texas does not allow for more than two legal parents. Typically, in a situation with unmarried parents, the biological father identified through DNA testing is presumptively the legal father once genetic testing has been ordered by the court.

C. RELEVANT STATUTORY LAW AND PRACTICE GUIDANCE

1. Texas Family Code

Chapter 102—Filing Suit

§ 102.001. Suit Authorized; Scope of Suit

(a) A suit may be filed as provided in this title.

(b) One or more matters covered by this title may be determined in the suit. The court, on its own motion, may require the parties to replead in order that any issue affecting the parent-child relationship may be determined in the suit.

§ 102.002. Commencement of Suit

An original suit begins by the filing of a petition as provided by this chapter.

§ 102.003. General Standing to File Suit

(a) An original suit may be filed at any time by:

(1) a parent of the child;

(2) the child through a representative authorized by the court;

(3) a custodian or person having the right of visitation with or access to the child appointed by an order of a court of another state or country;

(4) a guardian of the person or of the estate of the child;

(5) a governmental entity;

(6) the Department of Family and Protective Services;

(7) a licensed child placing agency;

(8) a man alleging himself to be the father of a child filing in accordance with Chapter 160, subject to the limitations of that chapter, but not otherwise;

(9) a person, other than a foster parent, who has had actual care, control, and possession of the child for at least six months ending not more than 90 days preceding the date of the filing of the petition;

(10) a person designated as the managing conservator in a revoked or unrevoked affidavit of relinquishment under Chapter 161 or to whom consent to adoption has been given in writing under Chapter 162;

(11) a person with whom the child and the child's guardian, managing conservator, or parent have resided for at least six months ending not more than 90 days preceding the date of the filing of the petition if the child's guardian, managing conservator, or parent is deceased at the time of the filing of the petition;

(12) a person who is the foster parent of a child placed by the Department of Family and Protective Services in the person's home for at least 12 months ending not more than 90 days preceding the date of the filing of the petition;

(13) a person who is a relative of the child within the third degree by consanguinity, as determined by Chapter 573, Government Code, if the child's parents are deceased at the time of the filing of the petition;

(14) a person who has been named as a prospective adoptive parent of a child by a pregnant woman or the parent of the child, in a verified written statement to confer standing executed under Section 102.0035, regardless of whether the child has been born; or

(15) subject to Subsection (d), a person who is an intended parent of a child or unborn child under a gestational agreement that complies with the requirements of Section 160.754.

(b) In computing the time necessary for standing under Subsections (a)(9), (11), and (12), the court may not require that the time be continuous and uninterrupted but shall consider the child's principal residence during the relevant time preceding the date of commencement of the suit.

(c) Notwithstanding the time requirements of Subsection (a)(12), a person who is the foster parent of a child may file a suit to adopt a child for whom the person is providing foster care at any time after the person has been approved to adopt the child. The standing to file suit under this subsection applies only to the adoption of a child who is eligible to be adopted.

(d) A person described by Subsection (a)(15) has standing to file an original suit only if:

(1) the person is filing an original suit jointly with the other intended parent under the gestational agreement; or

(2) the person is filing an original suit against the other intended parent under the gestational agreement.

* * *

§ 102.008. Contents of Petition

(a) The petition and all other documents in a proceeding filed under this title, except a suit for adoption of an adult, shall be entitled "In the interest of __________, a child." In a suit in which adoption of a child is requested, the style shall be "In the interest of a child."

(b) The petition must include:

(1) a statement that:

(A) the court in which the petition is filed has continuing, exclusive jurisdiction or that no court has continuing jurisdiction of the suit; or

(B) in a suit in which adoption of a child is requested, the court in which the petition is filed has jurisdiction of the suit under Section 103.001(b);

(2) the name and date of birth of the child, except that if adoption of a child is requested, the name of the child may be omitted;

(3) the full name of the petitioner and the petitioner's relationship to the child or the fact that no relationship exists;

(4) the names of the parents, except in a suit in which adoption is requested;

(5) the name of the managing conservator, if any, or the child's custodian, if any, appointed by order of a court of another state or country;

(6) the names of the guardians of the person and estate of the child, if any;

(7) the names of possessory conservators or other persons, if any, having possession of or access to the child under an order of the court;

(8) the name of an alleged father of the child or a statement that the identity of the father of the child is unknown;

(9) a full description and statement of value of all property owned or possessed by the child;

(10) a statement describing what action the court is requested to take concerning the child and the statutory grounds on which the request is made;

(11) a statement as to whether, in regard to a party to the suit or a child of a party to the suit:

(A) there is in effect:

(i) a protective order under Title 4;

(ii) a protective order under Subchapter A, Chapter 7B, Code of Criminal Procedure; or

(iii) an order for emergency protection under Article 17.292, Code of Criminal Procedure; or

(B) an application for an order described by Paragraph (A) is pending; and

(12) any other information required by this title.

(c) The petitioner shall attach a copy of each order described by Subsection (b)(11)(A) in which a party to the suit or a child of a party to the suit was the applicant or victim of the conduct alleged in the application or order and the other party was the respondent or defendant of an action regarding the conduct alleged in the application or order without regard to the date of the order. If a copy of the order is not available at the time of filing, the petition must state that a copy of the order will be filed with the court before any hearing.

(d) Notwithstanding any other provision of this section, if the Title IV-D agency files a petition in a suit affecting the parent-child relationship, the agency is not required to:

(1) include in the petition the statement described by Subsection (b)(11); or

(2) attach copies of the documentation described by Subsection (c).

Chapter 160—Uniform Parentage Act

§ 160.201. Establishment of Parent-Child Relationship

(a) The mother-child relationship is established between a woman and a child by:

(1) the woman giving birth to the child;

(2) an adjudication of the woman's maternity; or

(3) the adoption of the child by the woman.

(b) The father-child relationship is established between a man and a child by:

(1) an unrebutted presumption of the man's paternity of the child under Section 160.204;

(2) an effective acknowledgment of paternity by the man under Subchapter D, unless the acknowledgment has been rescinded or successfully challenged;

(3) an adjudication of the man's paternity;

(4) the adoption of the child by the man; or

(5) the man's consenting to assisted reproduction by his wife under Subchapter H, which resulted in the birth of the child.

* * *

§ 160.502. Order for Testing

(a) Except as otherwise provided by this subchapter and by Subchapter G, a court shall order a child and other designated individuals to submit to genetic testing if the request is made by a party to a proceeding to determine parentage.

(b) If a request for genetic testing of a child is made before the birth of the child, the court or support enforcement agency may not order in utero testing.

(c) If two or more men are subject to court-ordered genetic testing, the testing may be ordered concurrently or sequentially.

§ 160.503. Requirements for Genetic Testing

(a) Genetic testing must be of a type reasonably relied on by experts in the field of genetic testing. The testing must be performed in a testing laboratory accredited by:

(1) the American Association of Blood Banks, or a successor to its functions;

(2) the American Society for Histocompatibility and Immunogenetics, or a successor to its functions; or

(3) an accrediting body designated by the federal secretary of health and human services.

(b) A specimen used in genetic testing may consist of one or more samples, or a combination of samples, of blood, buccal cells, bone, hair, or other body tissue or fluid. The specimen used in the testing is not required to be of the same kind for each individual undergoing genetic testing.

(c) Based on the ethnic or racial group of an individual, the testing laboratory shall determine the databases from which to select frequencies for use in the calculation of the probability of paternity of the individual. If there is disagreement as to the testing laboratory's choice:

(1) the objecting individual may require the testing laboratory, not later than the 30th day after the date of receipt of the report of the test, to recalculate the probability of paternity using an ethnic or racial group different from that used by the laboratory;

(2) the individual objecting to the testing laboratory's initial choice shall:

(A) if the frequencies are not available to the testing laboratory for the ethnic or racial group requested, provide the requested frequencies compiled in a manner recognized by accrediting bodies; or

(B) engage another testing laboratory to perform the calculations; and

(3) the testing laboratory may use its own statistical estimate if there is a question regarding which ethnic or racial group is appropriate and, if available, shall calculate the frequencies using statistics for any other ethnic or racial group requested.

(d) If, after recalculation using a different ethnic or racial group, genetic testing does not rebuttably identify a man as the father of a child under Section 160.505, an individual who has been tested may be required to submit to additional genetic testing.

§ 160.504. Report of Genetic Testing

(a) A report of the results of genetic testing must be in a record and signed under penalty of perjury by a designee of the testing laboratory. A report made under the requirements of this subchapter is self-authenticating.

(b) Documentation from the testing laboratory is sufficient to establish a reliable chain of custody that allows the results of genetic testing to be admissible without testimony if the documentation includes:

(1) the name and photograph of each individual whose specimens have been taken;

(2) the name of each individual who collected the specimens;

(3) the places in which the specimens were collected and the date of each collection;

(4) the name of each individual who received the specimens in the testing laboratory; and

(5) the dates the specimens were received.

§ 160.505. Genetic Testing Results; Rebuttal

(a) A man is rebuttably identified as the father of a child under this chapter if the genetic testing complies with this subchapter and the results disclose:

(1) that the man has at least a 99 percent probability of paternity, using a prior probability of 0.5, as calculated by using the combined paternity index obtained in the testing; and

(2) a combined paternity index of at least 100 to 1.

(b) A man identified as the father of a child under Subsection (a) may rebut the genetic testing results only by producing other genetic testing satisfying the requirements of this subchapter that:

(1) excludes the man as a genetic father of the child; or

(2) identifies another man as the possible father of the child.

(c) Except as otherwise provided by Section 160.510, if more than one man is identified by genetic testing as the possible father of the child, the court shall order each man to submit to further genetic testing to identify the genetic father.

* * *

§ 160.601. Proceeding Authorized; Rules of Procedure

(a) A civil proceeding may be maintained to adjudicate the parentage of a child.

(b) The proceeding is governed by the Texas Rules of Civil Procedure, except as provided by Chapter 233.

§ 160.602. Standing to Maintain Proceeding

(a) Subject to Subchapter D and Sections 160.607 and 160.609 and except as provided by Subsection (b), a proceeding to adjudicate parentage may be maintained by:

(1) the child;

(2) the mother of the child;

(3) a man whose paternity of the child is to be adjudicated;

(4) the support enforcement agency or another government agency authorized by other law;

(5) an authorized adoption agency or licensed child-placing agency;

(6) a representative authorized by law to act for an individual who would otherwise be entitled to maintain a proceeding but who is deceased, is incapacitated, or is a minor;

(7) a person related within the second degree by consanguinity to the mother of the child, if the mother is deceased; or

(8) a person who is an intended parent.

(b) After the date a child having no presumed, acknowledged, or adjudicated father becomes an adult, a proceeding to adjudicate the parentage of the adult child may only be maintained by the adult child.

§ 160.603. Necessary Parties to Proceeding

The following individuals must be joined as parties in a proceeding to adjudicate parentage:

(1) the mother of the child; and

(2) a man whose paternity of the child is to be adjudicated.

§ 160.6035. Contents of Petition; Statement Relating to Certain Protective Orders Required

(a) The petition in a proceeding to adjudicate parentage must include a statement as to whether, in regard to a party to the proceeding or a child of a party to the proceeding:

(1) there is in effect:

(A) a protective order under Title 4;

(B) a protective order under Chapter 7A, Code of Criminal Procedure; or

(C) an order for emergency protection under Article 17.292, Code of Criminal Procedure; or

(2) an application for an order described by Subdivision (1) is pending.

(b) The petitioner shall attach a copy of each order described by Subsection (a)(1) in which a party to the proceeding or a child of a party to the proceeding was the applicant or victim of the conduct alleged in the application or order and the other party was the respondent or defendant of an action regarding the conduct alleged in the application or order without regard to the date of the order. If a copy of the order is not available at the time of filing, the petition must state that a copy of the order will be filed with the court before any hearing.

(c) Notwithstanding any other provision of this section, if the Title IV-D agency files a petition in a proceeding to adjudicate parentage, the agency is not required to:

(1) include in the petition the statement described by Subsection (a); or

(2) attach copies of the documentation described by Subsection (b).

§ 160.604. Personal Jurisdiction

(a) An individual may not be adjudicated to be a parent unless the court has personal jurisdiction over the individual.

(b) A court of this state having jurisdiction to adjudicate parentage may exercise personal jurisdiction over a nonresident individual or the guardian or conservator of the individual if the conditions in Section 159.201 are satisfied.

(c) It the court lacks jurisdiction over one individual, the court:

(1) is not precluded from making an adjudication of parentage binding on another individual over whom the court has personal jurisdiction; and

(2) may not delay the adjudication described by Subdivision (1) solely due to the lack of jurisdiction.

§ 160.605. Venue

Venue for a proceeding to adjudicate parentage is in the county of this state in which:

(1) the child resides or is found;

(2) the respondent resides or is found if the child does not reside in this state; or

(3) a proceeding for probate or administration of the presumed or alleged father's estate has been commenced.

§ 160.606. No Time Limitation: Child Having No Presumed, Acknowledged, or Adjudicated Father

A proceeding to adjudicate the parentage of a child having no presumed, acknowledged, or adjudicated father may be commenced at any time, including after the date:

(1) the child becomes an adult; or

(2) an earlier proceeding to adjudicate paternity has been dismissed based on the application of a statute of limitation then in effect.

§ 160.607. Time Limitation: Child Having Presumed Father

(a) Except as otherwise provided by Subsection (b), a proceeding brought by a presumed father, the mother, or another individual to adjudicate the parentage of a child having a presumed father shall be commenced not later than the fourth anniversary of the date of the birth of the child.

(b) A proceeding seeking to adjudicate the parentage of a child having a presumed father may be maintained at any time if the court determines that:

(1) the presumed father and the mother of the child did not live together or engage in sexual intercourse with each other during the probable time of conception; or

(2) the presumed father was precluded from commencing a proceeding to adjudicate the parentage of the child before the expiration of the time prescribed by Subsection (a) because of the mistaken belief that he was the child's biological father based on misrepresentations that led him to that conclusion.

§ 160.608. Authority to Deny Motion for Genetic Testing

(a) In a proceeding to adjudicate parentage, a court may deny a motion for an order for the genetic testing of the mother, the child, and the presumed father if the court determines that:

(1) the conduct of the mother or the presumed father estops that party from denying parentage; and

(2) it would be inequitable to disprove the father-child relationship between the child and the presumed father.

(b) In determining whether to deny a motion for an order for genetic testing under this section, the court shall consider the best interest of the child, including the following factors:

(1) the length of time between the date of the proceeding to adjudicate parentage and the date the presumed father was placed on notice that he might not be the genetic father;

(2) the length of time during which the presumed father has assumed the role of father of the child;

(3) the facts surrounding the presumed father's discovery of his possible nonpaternity;

(4) the nature of the relationship between the child and the presumed father;

(5) the age of the child;

(6) any harm that may result to the child if presumed paternity is successfully disproved;

(7) the nature of the relationship between the child and the alleged father;

(8) the extent to which the passage of time reduces the chances of establishing the paternity of another man and a child support obligation in favor of the child; and

(9) other factors that may affect the equities arising from the disruption of the father-child relationship between the child and the presumed father or the chance of other harm to the child.

(c) In a proceeding involving the application of this section, a child who is a minor or is incapacitated must be represented by an amicus attorney or attorney ad litem.

(d) A denial of a motion for an order for genetic testing must be based on clear and convincing evidence.

(e) If the court denies a motion for an order for genetic testing, the court shall issue an order adjudicating the presumed father to be the father of the child.

(f) This section applies to a proceeding to challenge an acknowledgment of paternity or a denial of paternity as provided by Section 160.309(d).

§ 160.609. Time Limitation: Child Having Acknowledged or Adjudicated Father

(a) If a child has an acknowledged father, a signatory to the acknowledgment or denial of paternity may commence a proceeding under this chapter to challenge the paternity of the child only within the time allowed under Section 160.308.

(b) If a child has an acknowledged father or an adjudicated father, an individual, other than the child, who is not a signatory to the acknowledgment or a party to the adjudication and who seeks an adjudication of paternity of the child must commence a proceeding not later than the fourth anniversary of the effective date of the acknowledgment or adjudication.

* * *

§ 160.621. Admissibility of Results of Genetic Testing; Expenses

(a) Except as otherwise provided by Subsection (c), a report of a genetic testing expert is admissible as evidence of the truth of the facts asserted in the report. The admissibility of the report is not affected by whether the testing was performed:

(1) voluntarily or under an order of the court or a support enforcement agency; or

(2) before or after the date of commencement of the proceeding.

(b) A party objecting to the results of genetic testing may call one or more genetic testing experts to testify in person or by telephone, videoconference, deposition, or another method approved by the court. Unless otherwise ordered by the court, the party offering the testimony bears the expense for the expert testifying.

(c) If a child has a presumed, acknowledged, or adjudicated father, the results of genetic testing are inadmissible to adjudicate parentage unless performed:

(1) with the consent of both the mother and the presumed, acknowledged, or adjudicated father; or

(2) under an order of the court under Section 160.502.

(d) Copies of bills for genetic testing and for prenatal and postnatal health care for the mother and child that are furnished to the adverse party on or before the 10th day before the date of a hearing are admissible to establish:

(1) the amount of the charges billed; and

(2) that the charges were reasonable, necessary, and customary.

* * *

§ 160.631. Rules for Adjudication of Paternity

(a) The court shall apply the rules stated in this section to adjudicate the paternity of a child.

(b) The paternity of a child having a presumed, acknowledged, or adjudicated father may be disproved only by admissible results of genetic testing excluding that man as the father of the child or identifying another man as the father of the child.

(c) Unless the results of genetic testing are admitted to rebut other results of genetic testing, the man identified as the father of a child under Section 160.505 shall be adjudicated as being the father of the child.

(d) Unless the results of genetic testing are admitted to rebut other results of genetic testing, a man excluded as the father of a child by genetic testing shall be adjudicated as not being the father of the child.

(e) If the court finds that genetic testing under Section 160.505 does not identify or exclude a man as the father of a child, the court may not dismiss the proceeding. In that event, the results of genetic testing and other evidence are admissible to adjudicate the issue of paternity.

D. THE SIMULATION—DRAFTING A *PETITION TO ESTABLISH PATERNITY*

Using the Texas Family Code provisions, draft a *Petition to Establish Paternity* for Hector González. You are free to search for form templates for your petition as a guide; however, the document you draft should be your own pleading that conforms to Tex. Fam. Code 160.6035. Be sure that the language used in your petition aligns with the statutory language.

CHAPTER SIX

CHILD CUSTODY AND VISITATION

I. INTRODUCTION

Child custody and visitation are integral parts of most family law cases. These issues can arise in the context of divorce or between unmarried couples when the parents' cohabitation ceases, or when an informal agreement breaks down. Child custody and visitation are also at the center of many requests for modification of court orders. Life circumstances change often. Substantial changes, like relocation or remarriage, often warrant a different custody arrangement or visitation schedule. Beneath the surface of the appellate child custody cases in your primary family law casebooks lie complex issues that demand interdisciplinary thinking and multifaceted lawyering. This chapter brings those underlying dynamics into focus. Students will engage in strategic case management, focusing on advancing client goals while applying both persuasive and preventative lawyering techniques.

Learning Outcomes:

(1) Interpret the best interests of the child standard and apply the statutory factors to a client's case.

(2) Analyze interdisciplinary considerations for the parents and children in a family law case to pursue client objectives.

(3) Identify the states with lawful jurisdiction to issue an initial child custody order and strategically select the jurisdiction that meets client objectives.

(4) Draft formal correspondence to inform client about child custody jurisdiction issues.

(5) Draft a *Motion for Temporary Custody and Visitation.*

(6) Develop a discovery plan to manage client resources and pursue client goals.

Attorneys must objectively prepare their clients for the discretionary nature of custody and visitation decisions. Child custody and visitation issues can be highly emotional and present difficult decisions for parents when considering the needs of their children and their desires as a parent. A lawyer's role in child custody matters involves not only anticipating potential legal roadblocks to achieving the client's objectives, but also working collaboratively with interdisciplinary professionals, such as social workers, therapists, and parenting coordinators, to identify and address underlying issues. Effective advocacy requires foresight: carefully drafting pleadings and discovery to minimize future conflict and protect the client's interests in a complex, emotionally charged landscape.

Child custody and visitation issues also reflect the multidimensional nature of family law as both a field of litigation and contract law. Litigation looms in the background as a possible path, but it presents great uncertainty and exposure for clients. Private custody agreements can minimize public exposure and the indeterminacy of a court decision, but each party will need to compromise and work within conflicting objectives to reach an agreement.

This chapter reintroduces the concept of "the shadow of the law,"[1] which was first mentioned in Chapter Three. Even when couples privately negotiate custody and parenting time, they do so in the shadows of their understanding of how a court would resolve the disputes. This theory reiterates how persuasive lawyering intersects with objective lawyering. Knowledge of the court system, reflections on public policy, and command of case precedent will influence the legal guidance presented to the client in private negotiation.

Finally, these issues also reflect the strong channeling power of the state toward certain behaviors and norms. Modern custody and visitation arrangements nudge and direct families toward the private ordering of their own parenting plans. This compels family law attorneys to understand what the starting point is for each parent involved in a custody or visitation determination. Notably, the starting points differ for child custody and visitation. As the next section explores, child custody and visitation decisions are centered on the child's best interest, while still balancing a parent's constitutional rights to raise and rear their child.

II. OVERVIEW OF THE LAW

History of Child Custody Frameworks

Child custody law has been framed using several different types of presumptions throughout history. These presumptions varied based on how state legislatures and courts viewed the interested parties to the suit. The starting point for child custody decisions initially began with gendered presumptions. Before the 20th century, courts began with a presumption that the father, as the legal head of household, would get custody of the children. Children were treated as the property of the father. The mother's legal identity was collapsed into her husband's legal identity under the doctrine of coverture. As women acquired legal rights in the 20th century, the presumption shifted toward maternal custody under gendered stereotypes portraying women as better able to care for children during their "tender years."

With respect to same-sex couples, historically only one parent, the birth or adoptive parent, could assert parental rights. The partner, on the other hand, had no parental or custodial rights to raise and rear the child. Since *Pavan v. Smith*,[2] most states have changed their legal requirements to comport with the laws that same-sex married couples have the same rights as heterosexual married couples.

Today, all states begin from a gender-neutral starting point in child custody issues. The overarching policy of family courts pivoted to ensuring that the best interest of the child was at the heart of all custody decisions. States apply variations of the best interests of the child standard to

[1] *See* Robert H. Mnookin and Lewis Kornhauser, *Bargaining in the Shadow of the Law: The Case of Divorce*, 88 YALE L.J. 950, 968 (1979).

[2] 582 U.S. 563 (2017) (holding that states may not deny married same-sex couples the benefit of having their names placed on their children's birth certificate when utilizes as a form of legal recognition of parentage).

make child custody decisions instead of gendered presumptions. This standard looks to a group of non-exhaustive factors such as the wishes of the child, the ability of the parents to care for the child, the health of the parties, the home environment, and the child's adjustment to home, school, and the community. Most states have a statute and/or case law that set forth a range of specific factors that the judge must consider determining custody.

In applying the best interests of the child standard, states espouse various substantive preferences or procedural presumptions favoring a certain outcome. Every state provides that legal parents have certain rights and duties in the care, custody, and control of their children. There are also foundational principles that courts follow regarding the above-mentioned three "C's." Courts presume that a fit parent acts in the best interest of his or her child. In custody disputes involving third parties, such as grandparents, courts must grant custody to a parent unless the state finds that the parent is unfit and placement with a parent is not in the child's best interest.

Some states presume that joint custody is in the best interest of the child (Texas, Kentucky), and others do not (California, Massachusetts, New York). A presumption of joint custody tells the court where to start substantively but gives the court the discretion to override that presumption with a strong factual showing that joint custody is not in the best interests of the child. Other states begin with a policy preference of joint custody, but this does not compel the court to start from joint custody at the outset. Finally, other states have a permissive approach by which states can conclude that joint custody is in the best interests of the child, but the state is neutral on the outcome. As you read the statute in Section III.C.1., consider which approach Florida follows.

Visitation and Parenting Plans

Terminology in child custody disputes has evolved in recent years to reflect transforming family norms. Historically, one parent—often the mother—was granted primary custody, leaving the non-custodial parent to rely on visitation or access[3] as the legal mechanism to maintain a relationship with their children. Today, most states provide standard visitation statutes that serve as a default framework. However, lawyers typically draft detailed "parenting plans" that specify how custody and visitation will be divided. These plans are essential for preserving parental relationships and minimizing future conflict. To be enforceable, parenting plans must include language with sufficient specificity and clarity. While the state's standard visitation guidelines may serve as a starting point, skilled family law attorneys often develop creative, customized arrangements tailored to the unique needs of the family.

Jurisdiction

Today, families are very mobile, and this can create an additional layer of conflict for parents in custody disputes. The Uniform Child Custody Jurisdiction and Enforcement Act (UCCJEA) was created to address jurisdictional matters among parents across the nation.[4] Each state has adopted the UCCJEA, except Massachusetts.[5] The UCCJEA is a critical statute for family law practitioners, as it determines which state has jurisdiction over child custody matters when parents live in different states. It outlines four potential bases for establishing jurisdiction, with a strong preference for the child's "home state"—defined as the state where the child has lived for at least six consecutive months. Alternatively, jurisdiction may lie in a state where the child and at least one parent have a significant connection, especially if substantial evidence exists concerning the

---

[3] Visitation and access are interchangeable terms. Some jurisdictions use one term or the other, but for purposed of this book, visitation will be used.

[4] The UCCJEA was initially designed to avoid forum shopping and prevent child kidnapping. The UCCJEA also contains emergency provisions to address abandonment and abuse. It also allows the state to exercise limited or temporary enforcement jurisdiction as needed.

[5] The District of Columbia and the U.S. territories of Guam, the U.S. Virgin Islands, and Puerto Rico, have also adopted the UCCJEA.

child's care, protection, training, or relationships. The UCCJEA also permits a court to decline jurisdiction if another state is deemed a more appropriate forum. If no state meets the other criteria, a default provision authorizes jurisdiction in the state where the case is filed.

Parenting Education and Family Stabilization Courses

The majority of states provide parent education courses to divorcing parents to help them navigate the divorce process and manage its effects on their children. The topics covered include the emotional and behavioral reactions of children to divorce, conflict management, co-parenting, and identifying stress indicators in children. The courses are offered in person and online, and the length varies among states, with a minimum of four hours. Seventeen states require all divorcing parents to attend some form of parent education class, regardless of whether the divorce is uncontested. In other states, the court typically has discretion regarding whether to order parents to complete this type of course before finalizing the dissolution of the marriage.

Discovery and Evidence

Custody and visitation involve conducting discovery and gathering evidence. Discovery is the exchange of information and documents between the parties. Each party seeks to find witnesses with relevant knowledge regarding the parents' relationship with the children, as well as written and demonstrative materials.[6] Information gathering in family law cases is a combination of standard discovery, public and private record searches and requests, as well as some private investigation. Forms of discovery include (1) requests for disclosure, (2) requests for production and inspection of documents and tangible things, (3) requests and motions for entry on and examination of real property, (4) interrogatories to a party, (5) requests for admission, (6) oral or written depositions, and (7) motions for psychological or physical examinations.

Every state and court system has discovery management protocols because of the comprehensive role of discovery in family law cases. For example, in New York there is a Preliminary Conference hearing on contested marriage dissolutions. The court records all the pertinent information about the case, including, but not limited to the grounds for the divorce, custody and financial issues, the specific timeline and scope of discovery, expert witness retention, and property valuation. Other states, like Texas, have discovery control plans that govern all civil cases for categorization and efficiency purposes. The level of discovery in a case is dependent on the type of suit, the number of parties, and the amount of money in dispute. The lower the level of complexity, the stricter the limit on the amount of discovery allowed and the time allotted for depositions. In contested family law cases, a social worker may conduct a home study on the two parents and interview the child(ren), as well as other interested parties, to determine which parent's environment is in the best interest of the child(ren).[7] Psychologists may be retained or appointed by the court to conduct a mental health evaluation on the parents and the child(ren).[8]

Often the amount of discovery completed for a case depends on the amount of money your client may want to spend on the dispute. A conversation about discovery should be had at the outset of any divorce case. Often clients do not understand the financial implications of a lawsuit and what it will cost to get them what they may seek. Typically, lawyers must counsel clients on what can be reasonably expected regarding property division, alimony, and child support, as well as custody. There are rarely clear "winners" in family court. Most parties must determine what they can live

---

[6] For example, demonstrative evidence could be photographs, social media postings, and audio recordings. Written evidence could include school records, medical records, and drug test results.

[7] A home study is a detailed evaluation of the home environment provided by both parents, including the amount of space, cleanliness, proximity to school and other community resources, etc.

[8] A mental health evaluation is a comprehensive assessment conducted by a licensed mental health professional that includes in-depth clinical interviews, standardized testing to assess cognitive, functional, and psychological functioning, behavioral observations, and collateral information from family members, friends, or other relevant parties.

with regarding a mediated settlement because a contested hearing will be decided by a judge or a jury. The amount of money that both parties spend on a contested divorce is basically a depletion of funds or debt that the parties will have to split or share. If they have children, it often takes away from the resources necessary to provide for them.

If the child custody and visitation dispute is part of a marital dissolution, the scope of discovery will depend on the contested issues. In most cases, there will be limited discovery if a couple can reach an agreement about property division but are in dispute about child custody and child support, or vice versa. It is much cheaper to have limited discovery because the subpoena and deposition costs will be lower with fewer documents to gather and fewer witnesses to depose.

Other Stakeholders

While the act of getting a divorce is relatively limited to the two parties to the marriage, child custody and visitation affect a wider range of stakeholders. The children may need their own counsel depending on the facts of the case. Other third parties, such as grandparents or other relatives, may enter the case to assert their own rights to custody and/or visitation with the children. As living arrangements change and necessitate child custody and visitation determinations, so do the individuals with whom the children interact every day. Each new living arrangement brings new questions. These issues can complicate the ethical boundaries for family law lawyers and potentially drive-up costs and case complexity.

One critical person who may participate in a custody or visitation case is a guardian ad litem. In many states it is possible for children to be appointed a guardian and/or attorney ad litem (GAL/AAL) in custody cases. If there are allegations of child abuse or neglect and the state is a party to the suit, a GAL is mandated by federal and often state law. If there is an allegation or finding of domestic violence against a spouse, the court can appoint a GAL, or a party can file a motion requesting that a GAL be appointed. This person can be an attorney or layperson with special training, like a Court Appointed Special Advocate (CASA). CASA (https://nationalcasagal.org) is a national organization that trains and provides community volunteers to assist with the social, educational, and legal needs of a child who has been removed from his/her parents because of abuse or neglect. A CASA volunteer can serve as an official GAL for a child and can often provide relevant testimony. CASA volunteers are required to complete intense training prior to being approved by the organization to serve as a child advocate.

Attorneys who serve in the role of GAL/AAL are also required to complete specific training, as recommended by the ABA and the National Association of Counsel for Children (NACC). Children's attorneys can operate in a dual role or as either GAL or AAL. As GAL, an attorney has duties to ascertain and recommend the custody arrangement and visitation schedule that is in the best interest of the child. When serving as AAL, an attorney has the obligation to represent the child's wishes and must take direction from the child client, unless the child is too young to give direction to the lawyer. In that instance, an AAL must use his or her substituted judgment to advocate for the child. In some states, a parent's attorney can request that a GAL/AAL be appointed for a child if it is a particularly difficult custody case.

Many states have statutes that provide guidelines for family members who seek temporary or permanent rights to children within their family. According to the Centers for Disease Control, three percent of children do not live with their parents and two-thirds of those children are being raised by their grandparents.[9] This results in 2.6 million grandparents as primary custodians of their grandchildren in America.[10] These caregivers are parenting grandchildren while their own adult children face great hardships such as incarceration, death, substance abuse, mental illness,

---

[9] Robin Marantz Henig, *The Age of Grandparents is Made of Many Tragedies*, THE ATLANTIC (June 1, 2018), https://www.theatlantic.com/family/archive/2018/06/this-is-the-age-of-grandparents/561527/.

[10] *Id.*

joblessness, or military deployment. Grandparents can raise complications in child custody determinations in that they might hire their own counsel to seek custody or access to the children. Each state has varying standards for how grandparents and other non-parent primary custodians may assert their rights against a lawful parent. Generally, if there is at least one fit parent, third party caregivers have limited rights.[11]

Family law attorneys must zealously advocate for their clients while remaining mindful of children as key stakeholders, adhering to ethical boundaries, and guiding clients through the complex web of individuals and institutions involved in the case. This includes counseling clients on how to manage interactions with other parties, such as opposing counsel, guardians ad litem, social workers, and the court.

Interdisciplinary Considerations

As explored in Chapter One, the successful practice of family law demands some knowledge of interrelated disciplines such as psychology, education, social science, and human development. Nowhere is that point more visible than in child custody determinations. The dynamics of family relationships and the choices that judges and fact finders must make regarding caregiving and support of children require great understanding of the intersectionality of these various professional fields. As you work through these simulation exercises, consider when you might need to utilize knowledge from the areas of psychology, health care, or child development.

III. CASE FILE—KATRINA FLETCHER

A. SIMULATION ROADMAP

In this simulation, you will begin a custody case on behalf of Katrina Fletcher. She is married and has four children with her spouse. You will use a comprehensive client intake, along with the relevant law and practice guidance, to complete three tasks.

First, you will draft a letter documenting client counseling related to child custody jurisdiction. Second, you will prepare a temporary motion for child custody during the pendency of the proceedings. What does a shared custody parenting plan look like for two parents living in geographically remote places? Third, you will prepare for discovery in a disputed custody case using the client intake interview, identifying parties who have knowledge of the case and evidence relating to what is in the best interests of the child. How deep should you go in uncovering facts to support your client's preferred custody outcome?

B. INTAKE INTERVIEW

The following is a memorandum documenting the Client Intake Interview of Katrina Fletcher, who is seeking a divorce and child custody.

---

[11] *Troxel v. Granville*, 530 U.S. 57 (2000) (striking down a Washington state law that allowed any third party, including grandparents, to petition the court for visitation rights over a parent's objections. The court held that parents have a fundamental right under the Fourteenth Amendment to the care, custody, and control of their children).

OFFICE MEMORANDUM

To: Law Partner

From: Associate

Re: Katrina Fletcher Intake (Case File 20CM65)

Today I met with our new client, Katrina Fletcher. During our initial interview, Katrina relayed the following facts.

Katrina Fletcher and Michelle Santos were married in YR-05 in New York. Both women come from large families, and they desired to raise children of their own. After years of Katrina trying to conceive using her ova and her ex-husband's sperm, they entered into a gestational surrogacy agreement with a carrier.

Over a period of three years, they have used a surrogate to have four children, two sets of twins. The first set of twins was born in New York, and the second set of twins was born in Florida. One set of girl twins (Kaitlyn and Kassidy, age 2) is biologically related to Katrina (via her ova), and the other set of boy twins (Mason and Monte, age 6 months) is biologically related to Michelle (via her ova). All four children are biologically related to each other because Katrina and Michelle used the same sperm donor, and they all share the same hyphenated last name (Fletcher-Santos).

After Kaitlyn and Kassidy were born, both Katrina and Michelle shared in the caregiving of the children. Katrina is a law firm partner netting $300,000 per year as a firm attorney. When Kaitlyn and Kassidy were born, Katrina took three months off work and cared for the children primarily. She transitioned back to work part-time when the three months ended, and the couple relied on a full-time nanny, Vanessa Wooten, while they were at work. The couple initially managed parenting with relative ease. Katrina would get up early with the twins and feed and dress them. Michelle would put them to bed while Katrina often worked late. The women shared the responsibilities of feeding, bathing, reading books, and playing with the children. Katrina's biological children refer to Michelle as Momma. Katrina acknowledges that Michelle is very important to them and wants Michelle to remain in their lives.

The couple had a few parenting disagreements early on that Katrina revealed in the intake interview. Katrina would get upset with Michelle for smoking occasionally. Vanessa witnessed one such argument when Katrina threw a carton of cigarettes in the trash out of frustration with Michelle. This angered Katrina particularly because Kaitlyn has chronic respiratory infections. The family's pediatrician, Alexandra Roveh, recommended that the parents avoid exposing the twins to any smoke and refrain from day care as long as possible because of Kaitlyn's vulnerabilities. Katrina believed that Michelle was being selfish and irresponsible by continuing to smoke, knowing that it compromised Kaitlyn's health.

The couple also experienced tension over Michelle's wish to baptize the children in the Catholic Church. Katrina has managed to avoid committing to baptism so far, but she knows that the issue is important to Michelle. Michelle regularly took the kids to St. Mary's Church outside of New York and attended bible study with Pastor Wanda Nobles. Katrina vehemently declined to attend. Katrina's parents, in consultation with her childhood minister, had sent her to "conversion camp," as a youth when they first understood that Katrina was gay. Katrina found the "therapy" to be traumatic and still meets with a counselor today about these difficult childhood experiences that destroyed her relationship with her parents and her faith community. The experienced soured her on organized religion. Michelle had been patiently trying to help Katrina through it. Katrina pursued other wellness and spirituality paths through meditation and yoga.

Michelle's biological children, Mason and Monte, are just six months old now. Katrina candidly admits that she does not have as strong a bond with the boys as Michelle has with the girls. The caregiving arrangement for Mason and Monte has been hard for Katrina, and it is not her preference at all. She also candidly admits that her behavior in the weeks leading up to Mason and Monte's birth destroyed her marriage.

Michelle previously netted $80,000 per year as a fashion consultant. The fashion industry suffered great financial disruption. After working fewer and fewer hours, Michelle left her job six weeks before the twins were born. The couple agreed that Katrina would work full-time, they would terminate their nanny, and Michelle would stay home to care for all the children.

In the final month before the youngest twins were born six months ago, Katrina was gearing up for a major trial scheduled for the week before Michelle's inducement date. She was working full time and extremely stressed. Katrina admits that the extreme pressures of work combined with the new single-income path they had chosen led to her having a shorter fuse and snapping easily at Michelle and the kids. Katrina had to travel to Boston every week in the month before the twins were scheduled to be induced. Katrina worked more than eighty hours a week in the critical stretch of the pregnancy and barely had time to check in on Michelle.

During these several weeks, Katrina would return home to New York on Fridays around 11 p.m. and leave again Sunday afternoon around 4:00 p.m. to return to Boston. During that time, Michelle was alone with the older twins and extremely physically uncomfortable in her final weeks of pregnancy.

In the final weeks of Michelle's pregnancy, Michelle also grew to suspect that Katrina was having an affair with one of her co-workers who was also active on the Boston trial team. After noticing several sexually explicit social media posts between Katrina and her co-worker, Leila, on Instagram, Michelle hired a private investigator. The private investigator took photos of Katrina and the co-worker having lunch, where they held hands, shared an extended hug, and talked playfully. The private investigator also took photos of the two of them checking out of the hotel together the next morning. The private investigator could not confirm whether they were checking out of separate rooms or one room.

The week before the twins were born, Michelle confronted Katrina with the pictures that the private investigator had taken a few days earlier. They had a huge fight. Katrina never admitted to having an affair. Michelle lashed out at Katrina physically and hit her repeatedly in the face. This was the first time there had been any physical altercation between the two of them. While the children were both asleep when the altercation started, Kassidy was crying at the end of it. Katrina gave her some warm milk, and she went back to sleep.

Michelle's suspicions and accusations led to tremendous tension between the couple in those final days before the twins were born. Katrina was quite distraught recalling a fight that she got into with Michelle at Antonio and Billy's home a few days before the twins were born. Antonio and Billy were good friends of Michelle and Katrina, and they knew the couple was going through a very difficult time. They threw a small baby shower to celebrate the twins' arrival trying to lift their friends' spirits. Katrina and Michelle had a huge fight at the gathering.

Katrina drove off in a fit of rage, leaving Michelle behind at Antonio and Billy's. She recounted how Michelle had called the police worried that Katrina had been drinking for several hours before this occurred. The 911 operator said that an officer would be on the lookout for a car matching Katrina's description, but no police encounter ever took place after Michelle placed the call.

Katrina was particularly distraught about this occurrence because she learned later from her friend, Sasha, that Michelle posted an inquiry on Facebook about whether anyone knew of any local resources to talk to loved ones about excessive alcohol abuse. Michelle's post never said why she was asking, but Katrina felt like this was an inflammatory and inappropriate thing to post. Katrina admitted that her alcohol consumption has risen somewhat but described her drinking as "consistent with every other stressed out trial lawyer I know."

The baby shower was the breaking point for the couple. Antonio and Billy helped Michelle pack a few things that evening and they drove her to Florida where the children were born a few days later. Katrina was not there for the birth. Michelle has stayed in Florida since Mason and Monte were born. She brought the kids into her parents' three-bedroom house in Miami. Michelle's parents and brother do not have legal status. Michelle has the oldest twins co-sleeping with her and the youngest sharing a crib in her room. Michelle's younger brother, Sammy (age 24), also lives with their parents. He works in the entertainment sector promoting clubs and performers. He works long hours, often coming home in the early hours of the morning, sometimes smelling of marijuana, sometimes with a girl he met at the clubs.

She allowed Katrina to see the children for a few weekends here and there early on. She has removed Katrina from social media accounts to keep her from even seeing pictures of the kids. It has been six weeks since she has seen the kids. Katrina described it as "soul crushing" not having any access to the kids.

Michelle has vowed to stay in Florida with the kids. She had been homesick for years living in New York City. She came from a large extended family in Guatemala and Miami. Michelle's mother brought her to the United States as a young child, and they had enjoyed a great life of family gatherings with a robust Catholic faith and a love for Guatemalan culture and music.

Michelle petitioned for divorce and custody of all four children in Florida this week. Michelle seeks temporary custody while the proceeding is pending. Katrina is prepared to divorce. She wants to retain sole custody of her biological twins, Kaitlyn and Kassidy. She also wants to retain reasonable visitation rights with Mason and Monte, allowing Michelle the same for Kaitlyn and Kassidy. She wants to have custody of Kaitlyn and Kassidy during the court proceedings with reasonable visitation with Mason and Monte. The hearing is late next week.

You have been hired as the attorney to represent Katrina as the Defendant/Respondent in the Florida case. You are licensed to practice in Florida only.

Research the Law: You and your supervisor now realize from your intake interview that Katrina and Michelle's different levels of religiosity are likely to be a key issue in their custody case. Your supervising attorney asked you to pull Florida case law on this topic. Recall the strategies you studied in Legal Research and Writing to find cases citing to a statute. You could start with the statute itself and then focus or narrow your citing authority results down to relevant cases. Even seasoned family law attorneys who are well-versed in the best interests of the child standard need to refine their case law selection to be responsive to the client's case.

C. RELEVANT STATUTORY LAW AND PRACTICE GUIDANCE

Your legal research reveals the following statutory provisions governing child custody determinations and parenting time agreements.

1. Florida Statute—Initial Child Custody Jurisdiction

Chapter 61. Dissolution of Marriage; Support; Time-Sharing

61.503. Definitions

(3) "Child custody determination" means a judgment, decree, or other order of a court providing for the legal custody, physical custody, residential care, or visitation with respect to a child. The term includes a permanent, temporary, initial, and modification order. The term does not include an order relating to child support or other monetary obligation of an individual. * * *

(7) "Home state" means the state in which a child lived with a parent or a person acting as a parent for at least 6 consecutive months immediately before the commencement of a child custody proceeding. In the case of a child younger than 6 months of age, the term means the state in which the child lived from birth with any of the persons mentioned. A period of temporary absence of any of the mentioned persons is part of the period.

* * *

61.507. Effect of child custody determination

A child custody determination made by a court of this state which had jurisdiction under this part binds all persons who have been served in accordance with the laws of this state or notified in accordance with s. 61.509 or who have submitted to the jurisdiction of the court, and who have been given an opportunity to be heard. As to those persons, the determination is conclusive as to all decided issues of law and fact except to the extent the determination is modified.

61.508. Priority

If a question of existence or exercise of jurisdiction under this part is raised in a child custody proceeding, the question, upon request of a party, must be given priority on the calendar and handled expeditiously.

* * *

61.514. Initial child custody jurisdiction

(1) Except as otherwise provided in s. 61.517, a court of this state has jurisdiction to make an initial child custody determination only if:

(a) This state is the home state of the child on the date of the commencement of the proceeding, or was the home state of the child within 6 months before the commencement of the proceeding and the child is absent from this state but a parent or person acting as a parent continues to live in this state;

(b) A court of another state does not have jurisdiction under paragraph (a), or a court of the home state of the child has declined to exercise jurisdiction on the grounds that this state is the more appropriate forum under s. 61.520 or s. 61.521, and:

1. The child and the child's parents, or the child and at least one parent or a person acting as a parent, have a significant connection with this state other than mere physical presence; and

2. Substantial evidence is available in this state concerning the child's care, protection, training, and personal relationships;

(c) All courts having jurisdiction under paragraph (a) or paragraph (b) have declined to exercise jurisdiction on the grounds that a court of this state is the more appropriate forum to determine the custody of the child under s. 61.520 or s. 61.521; or

(d) No court of any other state would have jurisdiction under the criteria specified in paragraph (a), paragraph (b), or paragraph (c).

(2) Subsection (1) is the exclusive jurisdictional basis for making a child custody determination by a court of this state.

(3) Physical presence of, or personal jurisdiction over, a party or a child is not necessary or sufficient to make a child custody determination.

Chapter 61. Dissolution of Marriage; Support; Time-Sharing

61.13. Support of children; parenting and time-sharing; powers of court

* * *

(2)(a) The court may approve, grant, or modify a parenting plan, notwithstanding that the child is not physically present in this state at the time of filing any proceeding under this chapter, if it appears to the court that the child was removed from this state for the primary purpose of removing the child from the court's jurisdiction in an attempt to avoid the court's approval, creation, or modification of a parenting plan.

(b) A parenting plan approved by the court must, at a minimum:

1. Describe in adequate detail how the parents will share and be responsible for the daily tasks associated with the upbringing of the child;

2. Include the time-sharing schedule arrangements that specify the time that the minor child will spend with each parent;

3. Designate who will be responsible for:

a. Any and all forms of health care. If the court orders shared parental responsibility over health care decisions, the parenting plan must provide that either parent may consent to mental health treatment for the child.

b. School-related matters, including the address to be used for school-boundary determination and registration.

c. Other activities; and

4. Describe in adequate detail the methods and technologies that the parents will use to communicate with the child.

(c) The court shall determine all matters relating to parenting and time-sharing of each minor child of the parties in accordance with the best interests of the child and in accordance with the Uniform Child Custody Jurisdiction and Enforcement Act, except that modification of a parenting plan and time-sharing schedule requires a showing of a substantial and material change of circumstances.

1. It is the public policy of this state that each minor child has frequent and continuing contact with both parents after the parents separate or the marriage of the parties is dissolved and to encourage parents to share the rights and responsibilities, and joys, of childrearing. Unless otherwise provided in this section or agreed to by the parties, there is a rebuttable presumption that equal time-sharing of a minor child is in the best interests of the minor child. To rebut this presumption, a party must prove by a preponderance of the evidence that equal time-sharing is not in the best interests of the minor child. Except when a time-sharing schedule is agreed to by the parties and approved by the court, the court must evaluate all of the factors set forth in subsection (3) and make specific written findings of fact when creating or modifying a time-sharing schedule.

2. The court shall order that the parental responsibility for a minor child be shared by both parents unless the court finds that shared parental responsibility would be detrimental to the child.

* * *

4. In ordering shared parental responsibility, the court may consider the expressed desires of the parents and may grant to one party the ultimate responsibility over specific aspects of the child's welfare or may divide those responsibilities between the parties based on the best interests of the child. Areas of responsibility may include education, health care, and any other responsibilities that the court finds unique to a particular family.

5. The court shall order sole parental responsibility for a minor child to one parent, with or without time-sharing with the other parent if it is in the best interests of the minor child.

* * *

7. Access to records and information pertaining to a minor child, including, but not limited to, medical, dental, and school records, may not be denied to either parent. Full rights under this subparagraph apply to either parent unless a court order specifically revokes these rights, including any restrictions on these rights as provided in a domestic violence injunction. A parent having rights under this subparagraph has the same rights upon request as to form, substance, and manner of access as are available to the other parent of a child, including, without limitation, the right to in-person communication with medical, dental, and education providers.

(d) The circuit court in the county in which either parent and the child reside or the circuit court in which the original order approving or creating the parenting plan was entered may modify the parenting plan. The court may change the venue in accordance with s. 47.122.

(3) For purposes of establishing or modifying parental responsibility and creating, developing, approving, or modifying a parenting plan, including a time-sharing schedule, which governs each parent's relationship with his or her minor child and the relationship between each parent with regard to his or her minor child, the best interest of the child shall be the primary consideration. A determination of parental responsibility, a parenting plan, or a time-sharing schedule may not be modified without a showing of a substantial, material, and unanticipated change in circumstances and a determination that the modification is in the best interests of the child. If the parents of a child are residing greater than 50 miles apart at the time of the entry of the last order establishing time-sharing and a parent moves within 50 miles of the other parent, then that move may be considered a substantial and material change in circumstances for the purpose of a modification to the time-sharing schedule, so long as there is a determination that the modification is in the best interests of the child. Determination of the best interests of the child shall be made by evaluating all of the factors affecting the welfare and interests of the particular minor child and the circumstances of that family, including, but not limited to:

(a) The demonstrated capacity and disposition of each parent to facilitate and encourage a close and continuing parent-child relationship, to honor the time-sharing schedule, and to be reasonable when changes are required.

(b) The anticipated division of parental responsibilities after the litigation, including the extent to which parental responsibilities will be delegated to third parties.

(c) The demonstrated capacity and disposition of each parent to determine, consider, and act upon the needs of the child as opposed to the needs or desires of the parent.

(d) The length of time the child has lived in a stable, satisfactory environment and the desirability of maintaining continuity.

(e) The geographic viability of the parenting plan, with special attention paid to the needs of school-age children and the amount of time to be spent traveling to effectuate the parenting plan. This factor does not create a presumption for or against relocation of either parent with a child.

(f) The moral fitness of the parents.

(g) The mental and physical health of the parents.

(h) The home, school, and community record of the child.

(i) The reasonable preference of the child, if the court deems the child to be of sufficient intelligence, understanding, and experience to express a preference.

(j) The demonstrated knowledge, capacity, and disposition of each parent to be informed of the circumstances of the minor child, including, but not limited to, the child's friends, teachers, medical care providers, daily activities, and favorite things.

(k) The demonstrated capacity and disposition of each parent to provide a consistent routine for the child, such as discipline, and daily schedules for homework, meals, and bedtime.

(*l*) The demonstrated capacity of each parent to communicate with and keep the other parent informed of issues and activities regarding the minor child, and the willingness of each parent to adopt a unified front on all major issues when dealing with the child.

(m) Evidence of domestic violence, sexual violence, child abuse, child abandonment, or child neglect, regardless of whether a prior or pending action relating to those issues has been brought. If the court accepts evidence of prior or pending actions regarding domestic violence, sexual violence, child abuse, child abandonment, or child neglect, the court must specifically acknowledge in writing that such evidence was considered when evaluating the best interests of the child.

(n) Evidence that either parent has knowingly provided false information to the court regarding any prior or pending action regarding domestic violence, sexual violence, child abuse, child abandonment, or child neglect.

(*o*) The particular parenting tasks customarily performed by each parent and the division of parental responsibilities before the institution of litigation and during the pending litigation, including the extent to which parenting responsibilities were undertaken by third parties.

(p) The demonstrated capacity and disposition of each parent to participate and be involved in the child's school and extracurricular activities.

(q) The demonstrated capacity and disposition of each parent to maintain an environment for the child which is free from substance abuse.

(r) The capacity and disposition of each parent to protect the child from the ongoing litigation as demonstrated by not discussing the litigation with the child, not sharing documents or electronic media related to the litigation with the child, and refraining from disparaging comments about the other parent to the child.

(s) The developmental stages and needs of the child and the demonstrated capacity and disposition of each parent to meet the child's developmental needs.

(t) Any other factor that is relevant to the determination of a specific parenting plan, including the time-sharing schedule. * * *

(b) When a parent refuses to honor the other parent's rights under the time-sharing schedule, the parent whose time-sharing rights were violated shall continue to pay any ordered child support or alimony.

(c) When a parent refuses to honor the time-sharing schedule in the parenting plan without proper cause, the court:

1. Shall, after calculating the amount of time-sharing improperly denied, award the parent denied time a sufficient amount of extra time-sharing to compensate for the time-sharing missed, and such time-sharing shall be ordered as expeditiously as possible in a manner consistent with the best interests of the child and scheduled in a manner that is convenient for the parent deprived of time-sharing. In ordering any makeup time-sharing, the court shall schedule such time-sharing in a manner that is consistent with the best interests of the child or children and that is convenient for the nonoffending parent and at the expense of the noncompliant parent.

2. May order the parent who did not provide time-sharing or did not properly exercise time-sharing under the time-sharing schedule to pay reasonable court costs and attorney's fees incurred by the nonoffending parent to enforce the time-sharing schedule.

3. May order the parent who did not provide time-sharing or did not properly exercise time-sharing under the time-sharing schedule to attend a parenting course approved by the judicial circuit.

4. May order the parent who did not provide time-sharing or did not properly exercise time-sharing under the time-sharing schedule to do community service if the order will not interfere with the welfare of the child.

5. May order the parent who did not provide time-sharing or did not properly exercise time-sharing under the time-sharing schedule to have the financial burden of promoting frequent and continuing contact when that parent and child reside further than 60 miles from the other parent.

6. May, upon the request of the parent who did not violate the time-sharing schedule, modify the parenting plan if modification is in the best interests of the child.

7. May impose any other reasonable sanction as a result of noncompliance.

(d) A person who violates this subsection may be punished by contempt of court or other remedies as the court deems appropriate.

(5) The court may make specific orders regarding the parenting plan and time-sharing schedule as such orders relate to the circumstances of the parties and the nature of the case and are equitable and provide for child support in accordance with the guidelines schedule in s. 61.30. An order for equal time-sharing for a minor child does not preclude the court from entering an order for child support of the child. * * *

2. Practice Guidance

As a practicing family law lawyer, you will regularly give careful thought to your client's objectives, limitations, and disposition. You will spend some time researching the context of child custody lawyering to strategize carefully. The following reading will help you prepare a discovery plan that is comprehensive, coordinated, and cost-conscious. It describes the possible fee structures and discovery tools available to family law lawyers, preparing you to make an effective discovery plan.

American Jurisprudence: Trials
Edward J. Winter, Jr. and Brian R. Hersh

Child Custody Litigation

IV. Investigating the Case; Interviewing and Preparing Lay Witnesses

*** * * § 28. Contacting and interviewing witnesses**

A lawyer who has personally interviewed the witnesses will come to the trial far better prepared than one who has delegated the job to someone else; he will be able to present his case with greater ease, assurance, and effectiveness.

All friendly potential witnesses should be contacted. This should be done informally, and not by way of deposition, so that witnesses can be placed in a relaxed and cooperative mood, and the presence of the adversary avoided. It is often advisable to interview the witnesses in the privacy of their own homes. This may afford a more reliable impression of a person's credibility, mannerisms, and habits. * * *

The attorney should use [their] imagination in selecting potential witnesses, and should not limit himself to next door neighbors. Baby-sitters, maids, school bus drivers, teachers, coaches, waitresses, camp counselors, scoutmasters, and deliverymen,—in short, anyone who has had significant contacts with the child or the parties can be helpful. * * *

§ 39. The professional expert—Criteria for selection

The professional expert—the psychiatrist, psychologist, social worker, and others—should be selected on the basis of ability and integrity. [They] must be sufficiently objective that [they] will not minimize the weak points of the client's case. [They] can then be helpful to counsel in planning strategy, in presenting favorable findings, and in preparing a response to adverse findings. Ideally, [their] qualifications should include impressive academic attainments, membership in professional societies, participation in professional meetings and seminars, significant writings, and much actual experience in the field.

* * * It is obvious, too, that other experts such as the children's teachers, the members of the clergy with whom the family has been associated, and the medical doctor who has served the family are

all necessarily pre-selected. The family doctor in particular may have encountered physical manifestations of the stormy home situation, in treating the parents and the children. * * *

§ 40. The professional expert—Psychiatrists and psychologists

If a psychiatrist or psychologist has already seen the parties, and his findings are favorable to your client, his testimony can be a real asset. However, the fact that such a mental health professional has arrived at conclusions unfavorable to your client should not be cause for despair. * * * If, therefore, counsel anticipates that psychiatric testimony unfavorable to his client will be presented to the court, [they] should obtain another expert whose diagnosis and prognosis of [their] client's condition will differ from that of the opposing expert, and will impeach the latter's opinion. * * *

XIII. Discovery

* * * § 88. Request for admissions

The discovery device of request for admissions is most effectively used to establish or develop certain facts that are apt to be conceded, or, if they are unreasonably denied, to establish the foundation for assessing as costs the expense of proving those facts at the trial. In the former category would be such matters as the dates of the parties' marriage and separation, the names and dates of birth of the children, and the residence of the parties. In the latter category might fall the nature and extent of the financial resources of the parties, and acts of which the opposing party might have been guilty, such as drunkenness or immoral conduct, which would indicate the opposing party's unfitness to have custody. * * *

§ 89. Inspection of books, documents, and household premises

* * * Aside from inspection of such records, the motion for production and inspection can be used to gain entry into the opposing party's home, to determine the suitability of the environment in which the adverse party proposes to rear the children. The opportunity for taking photographs, afforded by such an inspection, should not be overlooked. Sometimes these inspections can be carried out by informal agreement between counsel. * * *

§ 91. Depositions

Oral depositions serve four basic purposes: (1) To assist the lawyer in the investigation and preparation of the case for trial; (2) to assist the lawyer in evaluating the case for the purpose of settlement, and to provide information for use in settlement negotiations; (3) to provide substantive proof and admissions for use during the trial; and (4) to provide a basis for impeachment of the deponent during the trial.

Depositions are especially useful in child custody cases, because they provide the attorney with an opportunity to evaluate the habits and personality of the adverse party, an all-important factor in the determination of the custody issue. Does he or she make a positive impression, have a pleasant appearance, testify honestly and frankly, or does he or she testify cunningly and evasively, distort the truth, anger easily under cross-examination, and make a generally poor impression? Counsel should be attuned to these factors and be prepared at the trial to capitalize on what he has learned concerning the opposing party's weaknesses.

Though very useful, oral depositions are quite expensive, and the financial limitations of the parties may dictate that other modes of discovery be employed. * * *

§ 98. Physical or mental examination of children or opposing party

* * * It is also important to note that § 402 of the Uniform Marriage and Divorce Act includes, among the factors upon which the determination as to custody is to be made, "the mental and physical health of all individuals involved." Moreover, § 405 of the Act authorizes the court-appointed investigator, upon order of the court, to refer the child to professional personnel for diagnosis.

Physical and mental examinations can be a very vital tool in child custody cases.

IV. THE SIMULATION

A. DRAFTING A CLIENT LETTER

While the client is surely most anxious to get to work on the substance of her custody case, the lawyer must pause and first confirm that the case is in the right jurisdiction appropriate for your representation. Review the provisions of the Florida statute in Section III.C.1. to identify the rules that govern child custody jurisdiction. The chapter introduction also previewed the UCCJEA. Is the UCCJEA the governing law that Florida has adopted? Does Florida have jurisdiction to resolve custody? Under what specific statutory provision? Do other states also have jurisdiction over this child custody dispute?

Katrina has represented to you that she "doesn't want to fight Michelle on jurisdiction." She "just wants to get her kids back and see them regularly." You discussed the counter arguments with Katrina in your initial client interview communicating why New York might be an alternate jurisdiction. Katrina privately revealed that she has been plagued with guilt for her transgressions in Boston, and she is willing to litigate this matter in Florida to appease Michelle.

You can only represent Katrina in Florida. You know that many witnesses are likely to reside in New York. You want to be sure that you protect your legal guidance carefully on this point and document this jurisdictional decision carefully for your records. Draft a letter to Katrina documenting this decision to accept jurisdiction in Florida. Explain to Katrina in writing what the pros and cons are of this decision.

B. DRAFTING A *MOTION FOR TEMPORARY CUSTODY*

Arguing for child custody is one of the most important lawyering tasks for a family law lawyer. Assuming that the client has agreed to accept Florida's jurisdiction, prepare a motion for temporary custody. This is more complex than a typical temporary custody hearing because of the geographic separation, the differences in biological parenthood, and your client's preference for sibling separation.

Katrina is currently without access to her children. Katrina cannot wait until the matter progresses to seek temporary custody and parenting time with the children. While discovery will develop further facts and refine the arguments considerably, Katrina is frantic to secure a temporary arrangement throughout the proceedings. This is likely also important to the children's development as well.

Your argument will be informed by the procedural context governing child custody set forth in Section III.C.1. and the substantive standards governing the "best interests of the child" as set forth in the permanent custody statute in Section III.C.1. Prepare a written argument tethering the facts of your client intake to the legal standards governing the best interests of the child. Be precise and specific in your request to the court. Be compelling and persuasive in advocating your case.

Once you draft the motion, you will need to send it to a supervising attorney for review. Write a cover email to your supervisor that communicates any concerns that you have regarding custody issues that the supervising attorney will need to address defensively on Katrina's behalf. Identify the primary arguments you anticipate Michelle's counsel making in support of her custody petition.

C. PREPARING A DISCOVERY STRATEGY

Your client intake with Katrina is captured in Section III.B. This gives you a big picture overview of the kinds of evidence and issues that might shape an ultimate custody determination.

As currently presented, you only have your client's side of the story with no corroboration or support. It is now your job as the lawyer to develop a thoughtful strategic plan to build a strong argument to achieve Katrina's custody goals.

The statute revealed the factors that govern child custody. The practice guidance revealed evidentiary considerations that shape a lawyer's case strategy. What documents might support your child custody argument? Which witnesses might testify? What factors are strongest for our client?

For this simulation exercise, prepare a discovery strategy that manages your client's resources and objectives effectively. Your supervising attorney wants you to prepare a list of the witnesses that the firm should contact, any experts that might be necessary, any documents you need to obtain, any admissions you might secure, and any interrogatories you might prepare.

You might use a chart like the following one to prepare your plan. Extract possible witness names from the client intake interview. What parties might have relevant information? What discovery tool would most efficiently and effectively secure the information you need for your case? You might consider interrogatories, admissions, production of documents, depositions, informal interviews, and expert witnesses. Consider costs carefully and distinguish between high dollar items and low dollar discovery strategies. Use the substantive best interests of the child statutory factors to shape your discovery strategy because that directs you to the most relevant material.

Type of Discovery	Witness	Relevance to Best Interests of the Child Analysis	Cost ($, $$, $$$)

CHAPTER SEVEN

CHILD SUPPORT

I. INTRODUCTION

Child support is an essential topic for family law practitioners to master. Child support law uses the power of the state to compel parents to pay monthly awards to support their children. The purpose of child support is to provide financial resources to the custodial parent for food, clothing, and essentials. Child support holds both parents responsible for the care of a child so that the state can conserve fiscal outlays for children most in need. It dictates strong state values that are strictly applied across all family structures and geographies. The dominant goal of the government is to ensure that parents are held accountable for the cost of raising a child, rather than the state bearing the brunt of this cost via public benefits.

The study of child support stands in stark contrast to topics like spousal support and property distribution, which are governed by state law. Child support is governed by a complex web of federal and state statutes and involves multiple government and private actors. It is also fraught with important policy critiques. While the value of state compelled private child support for children sounds benevolent, many parents fall crushingly behind on child support because of an inability to pay, and they face strict civil and criminal penalties. For children receiving public benefits, the payments by the parent might actually reimburse the state coffers and not, as a practical matter, improve the child's quality of life. These outcomes have meaningful effects on all parties involved. As you study this chapter, rigorously scrutinize the work of the state and the strengths and weaknesses of existing approaches.

Learning Outcomes:

(1) Extract standard child support award calculations from state guidelines.

(2) Distinguish between mandatory calculations and discretionary deviations in child support client counseling.

(3) Prepare a *Petition for Child Support* and provide strategic guidance for an evidentiary hearing on the petition.

(4) Communicate with client regarding effective legal strategies to balance family relationships while achieving legal objectives.

To assist in learning these four objectives, it can be helpful to think of child support through the analytical framework of the 5Ws and H:

- **What** is child support? What approach governs it?
- **Who** gets/pays child support?
- **When** does child support start/end?
- **Where** does one go to get child support?
- **Why** calculate child support in this approach?
- **How** to calculate child support?

In this simulation assignment, you will help advise a client on all these child support questions.

II. OVERVIEW OF THE LAW

Understanding *what* child support is requires historic and modern context. While there are several different models and all states differ in the details, state models for child support today are driven by a federally mandated structure. This should catch your attention given how much of family law has been grounded in state law. This federal framework demands mathematically calculable awards that create consistency and efficiency across courtrooms, judges, and families. These guidelines apply in a gender-neutral manner and without regard to marital status. Ultimately, this federal structure provides an equitable method to relieve states from bearing the fiscal burden of supporting single parent families that fall near the federal poverty line.

In the past, family law judges had great discretion to fashion orders on a case-by-case basis seeking results that were 'just' or 'reasonable.' These discretionary models created inconsistency and uncertainty, both of which undermined settlement and increased conflict. These historic models also encouraged forum-shopping whereby litigants could shop for different courts or different judges seeking better results. Past child support standards were also gendered, presuming that the duty of support rested with the father alone. Traditionally, the duty of support was only imposed on married fathers. When child support was inadequate or non-existent, the caregiver would likely then need support from public benefits programs. Harsh and discriminatory bastardy laws then held non-marital parents financially liable, including racialized and classed models of indentured servitude. Laws that discriminated between marital and nonmarital children were later challenged and reforms changed the law's treatment of non-custodial parents.

The federal government intervened to transform state child support frameworks. The Child Support Enforcement Amendments of 1984 required states to develop child support guidelines and provided federal grants for compliance. Under this law, there were no particular guideline requirements established, and so variability persisted. While the law required that the guidelines be made available to judges, they were not binding. The 1984 law imposed some early enforcement mechanisms (such as wage withholding), paternity establishment procedures, reporting and data collection procedures, and incentives for state recoupment efforts.

The Family Support Act of 1988 strengthened enforcement mechanisms, further mandated wage withholding, and set up collection programs through the Office of Child Support Enforcement. The law required states to develop guidelines for consistent mathematical awards that would be presumptive awards. Judges could only deviate from the presumptive award by justifying a deviation with written findings of fact that the presumptive award would be unjust or inappropriate. This framework reveals *why* the child support system exists as it does, both to provide for the basic needs of children and to hold parents accountable for state expenditures.

Child support lawyering involves many stakeholders. Parents, children, the federal government, and the state government all comprise the *who* of child support systems. The legal system often separates suits concerning children born to unmarried parents and children who are parties to divorce. Historically, the law treated children born out of wedlock differently than children born within marriage. As mentioned in Chapter Five, the Supreme Court has since ruled that these two groups of children cannot be treated differently.

Due to a federal law requiring that states establish paternity before mothers can receive public benefits though,[1] often there is still a separate court where a government attorney brings suits establishing parentage for nonmarital children. These types of suits, along with child welfare and juvenile law cases, are often referred to as 'public family law,' because the state or government is the party initiating these legal matters.

This reveals differences in the *where* lens of child support. Depending on whether you reside in a city or a small town, child support for these two different groups may be handled in two separate courts. In small towns, the civil courts hear every civil matter, including family law matters. In larger geographies there are often specialized courts, with family district courts handling private family law matters and specialized state district courts handling public family matters.

Often these different court systems have different demographic characteristics. Most of the families in the family district courts are comprised of marital, middle and high income, college-educated parents. Most of the families in the specialized state district court systems are comprised of nonmarital, low-income, high school educated (or less) parents. From a cultural perspective, there may be a higher percentage of Caucasian and Asian families in private family courts and a higher percentage of African American and Latino families in public family courts. The reasons for this separation are complex and beyond the scope of this book, but worthy of deep and meaningful exploration for practitioners understanding the systems within which they work.[2]

Title IV-D of the Social Security Act ("SSA") governs the enforcement of child support orders by the state office of the attorney general, and the courts are named for this section of the SSA. Title IV-D courts are specialized courts that provide assistance to the obligee parent in locating the obligor parent and/or enforcing a child support order. Parents seeking legal help in IV-D courts are typically low-income parents who have sought state aid through the Temporary Assistance for Needy Families (TANF) program. TANF is a federal-state cash assistance program for low-income

---

[1] The Personal Responsibility and Work Opportunity Reconciliation Act of 1996 (PRWORA) is a federal law that created the Temporary Assistance for Needy Families (TANF) program for families with children and expectant mothers. One restriction on the use of federal TANF funds is that persons must cooperate with child support requirements, including paternity establishment, or they will receive a reduced benefit or lose the benefit entirely.

[2] For further discussion on this topic, *see* Tianna N. Gibbs, *Paper Courts and Parental Rights: Balancing Access, Agency and Due Process*, 54 HARVARD CIVIL RIGHTS-CIVIL LIBERTIES L. REV. 549 (2019); Tonya Brito, et al., *"I Do for My Kids": Negotiating Race and Racial Inequality in Family Court*, 83 FORDHAM L. REV. 3027 (2015); Jessica Dixon Weaver, *Overstepping Ethical Boundaries? Limitations on State Efforts to Provide Access to Justice in Family Courts*, 82 FORDHAM L. REV. 2705 (2014); Shani King, *The Family Law Canon in a (Post?) Racial Era*, 72 OHIO STATE L. J. 575 (2011); Angela Onwuachi-Willig, *The Return of the Ring*, 83 CALIF. L. REV. 1647 (2009); Jill Hasday, *Parenthood Divided: A Legal History of the Bifurcated Law of Parental Relations*, 90 GEORGETOWN L. J. 299 (2001).

families with children. TANF provides temporary financial assistance to help pay for food, shelter, utilities, and expenses (other than medical).

Regardless of whether children are born within or outside of marriage, the duty of support for parents is the same. Parents are obligated to financially support their children until they reach the age of 18 years old or *when* they graduate from high school. Child support can cease if a child dies, is emancipated, enlists in the military, or if the parents' rights are terminated. If a child is disabled, a court may order child support to continue indefinitely, if the child is unable to be self-supporting.

The question of *how* to calculate child support depends on the approach adopted in your home state. State guidelines can differ in what counts as income. For example, states vary on whether disability payments or personal injury awards are qualifying income. States may impute income to those who are voluntarily unemployed or under-employed. States do not impose $0 awards, instead setting a higher minimum. Jurisdictions do not ordinarily apply the guidelines beyond an upper income bound of the guidelines. Income exceeding the guidelines may instead be the basis for a deviation from the presumptive award.

A minority of states apply a "Flat Percentage of Income" model where a set percentage of a parent's net income is paid for child support. The percentage is based on the number of children the parent is obligated to support in the household. It is adjusted if the obligor parent has different children residing in more than one household. There is a cap on the number of children and the number of households within the statutory guidelines. Only one parent receives child support—the parent who has primary physical custody of the children. When parents maintain joint physical custody of children in these states, neither parent owes child support.

The majority of states apply an "Income Shares" model to their child support guidelines. Students will likewise apply this approach in the simulation assignment. This model treats the two parents as one economic unit and calculates their gross monthly income. Gross monthly income is broadly defined to include all income from all sources, except means-tested government assistance. States can include "offsets," which are reductions in gross monthly income for prior family support awards.

The Income Shares model attempts to approximate the standard of living that existed as an economic unit, but it also applies to non-marital families who may never have actually functioned as a singular economic unit. It then identifies what percentage each parent contributes to the total gross monthly income. The state publishes a standardized chart denoting exactly how much the state has determined is the proper award amount for the number of kids in a household with that combined gross monthly income. The state then allocates the award payments at the same percentage of the parents' respective contributions to the monthly income. Thus, if one parent earns 70% of the combined gross monthly income and the second parent earns 30%, for a child support award of 1,000 monthly, parent 1 would owe $700 and parent 2 would owe $300 of the total presumptive award.

There is a statutory mechanism to deviate from the presumptive award if the judge concludes that the presumptive award would be unjust or inappropriate. Deviations are often based on extraordinary medical, dental, or educational needs or the independent wealth of the child. This discretionary function of child support heavily shapes our client's goals in this simulation assignment. These calculation models are also backed up by a robust child support enforcement system including stiff criminal, civil, and administrative penalties for non-payment.

III. CASE FILE—MARLENE GOMEZ

A. SIMULATION ROADMAP

In this simulation exercise, you will prepare a *Petition for Child Support* and prepare for an evidentiary hearing on the petition. Your client seeks child support from the father of their child. Your client also seeks to understand her likelihood of obtaining child support. She wants to know whether she will need to go to court to secure support or whether she can reliably obtain support through informal means.

B. CLIENT INTAKE MEMORANDUM

Internal Office Memorandum

To: Marlene Gomez Child Support Case File No. 872–19

From: Attorney

Date: June 1, YR-00

Re: Client Intake

This memorandum is attorney work product and subject to the attorney-client privilege.

Today I met with our new client, Marlene Gomez. Marlene has a child with Ryan Juarez. She is currently unemployed. Ryan signed a voluntary acknowledgment of paternity at Veronica's birth, which holds the weight of a judicial determination of parentage.

Veronica, their daughter, just finished second grade. Veronica has autism. Marlene and Ryan were dating when Veronica was born. They dated off and on until recently. Marlene and Veronica have always lived in New York. Ryan moved to Kentucky two years ago with the U.S. Army. Ryan has been active-duty military for a decade. Marlene worried that the cross-country move would be too disruptive to Veronica and so she stayed in New York. Marlene's formal relationship with Ryan slowly dissipated after that move two years ago, although the two remain close.

Two years ago, Marlene asked Ryan for child support to care for Veronica. Ryan began paying $175 a week for Veronica's care informally.

That arrangement worked well until his family members started facing deep financial challenges during the global health pandemic. Beginning in February, Ryan stopped sending money for Veronica's care. He has not paid any child support since January. He recently told Marlene that he was supporting family members through their unemployment—however long that might last—and he could not presently pay child support.

Marlene herself is struggling too. She used to work as a medical records specialist for an orthopedic doctor making $24,000 a year. She was laid off six months ago. She is worried about her financial stability without Ryan's support for Veronica.

Marlene is especially worried about Veronica's needs. Veronica has struggled at school in both her academics and her behaviors. She requires intensive and specialized care. Marlene needs to secure more stable child support from Ryan without risks of disruptions. She also needs to request additional funds for Veronica's specialized care. Marlene does not think that the public school alone can meet Veronica's needs.

Marlene hired us to prepare a petition for child support. She has some hesitation about the formality of a court order because she has been on and off again with Ryan. She fears that this formal move will ruin any prospect of reconciliation with Ryan. She worries that a litigation approach will be the "nuclear option." We discussed how a private order might be entered in court. She wants to discuss this with us further.

C. MEMORANDUM FROM PARALEGAL

MEMORANDUM

To: Attorney

From: Paralegal

Date: July 5, YR-00

Re: Marlene Gomez Child Support (Case No. 872–19)

Attorney Work Product

You asked me to research Ryan Juarez's income for the purposes of calculating child support. This memorandum summarizes the file I have compiled in anticipation of the petition. I reviewed Mr. Juarez's Leave and Earnings Statement (LES) from the United States Military showing his military pay and allowances from YR-00.

His total monthly income is $4,608.33. This monthly income total is based on his current status as Sgt. 1st Class U.S. Army, his ten years of enlistment, his housing allowance, his imminent danger pay, and his per diems while deployed. I have prepared the primary source materials to support a petition for child support. They are in a file in the law firm's case room.

Please note that military pay is materially higher during deployment. Ryan is currently deployed. If we wait to file for child support until after he returns home, the calculation will likely be lower.

Please also note that I did a quick Internet search of our new client, consistent with our standard client intake practices. I found an Etsy website selling "Marlene's Macrame." The picture and seller location seem to match our client. There are dozens of different products for sale ranging from $20–$200. I flag this for your follow-up and attention.

Please let me know if you need any further documentation for this petition.

D. CLIENT'S FORWARDED EMAIL

Email

To: veronica.gomez7814@hotmail.com

From: rangerryan908@aol.com

Date: May 1, YR-00

Subject: Ver-Bear

Marlene,

Pls. give Veronica a big hug from her Papa. I miss her so much. It is so lonely out here. I would give anything to be playing at home with my little Ver-Bear.

I got your message. I'm sorry that I have not sent any $$ to help with Veronica lately. My family is really feeling the hurt of the economy right now. It is tearing me up knowing how hard things are for them and how far away I am from them. I've been sending $$$ to my parents and my abuelita to help them make rent and pay bills.

I know you understand how hard things are for them now. I know you care for them like your own family. Thanks for your understanding.

I'll send what I can, when I can for Veronica. Thx. for understanding how hard this is for me.

Love,
Ryan

P.S.: Tell Ver-Bear we had a crazy sandstorm here this week. It reminded me of being at Coney Island with her right before that storm on her birthday! ☺

E. SCHOOL CORRESPONDENCE

Sylvia Campos
Guidance Counselor
P.S. 890
700-b 95th Street
New York, NY

Re: Veronica's IEP Meeting Recap

Dear Ms. Gomez,

As we discussed in our meeting today, I have enjoyed working with Veronica since she began kindergarten here at P.S. 890. We have worked together to meet Veronica's individualized educational objectives each year of her studies. It has been my pleasure working with Veronica to support her learning needs and to help her flourish to her fullest potential.

Veronica's needs are complex and multifaceted. As we discussed, we will continue making every possible service available to Veronica. In addition, Veronica would benefit from intensive speech therapy and behavioral therapy interventions outside of school. It is my strong recommendation that you and Veronica's father consider working with Chrysalis Care to secure outside support. Based on my prior referrals, I anticipate that these interventions would cost approximately $1,000 monthly.

In my experience, for children with autism, effective and supportive interventions during these early years are critical to building strong educational roots. Her disciplinary record, however, particularly reveals to me the depths of the frustrations Veronica is experiencing daily in a traditional educational environment. Intensive behavioral therapy could help Veronica dramatically.

Veronica has tremendous potential. As we discussed, we will still deploy our full range of special education resources to support Veronica. This is our legal obligation and our mission. As a public institution, however, we are lacking some of the more intensive therapeutic interventions that Chrysalis Care could provide.

Please let me know if you need any further documentation of this recommendation. We are here to support you and Veronica on this educational journey.

Warm regards,

Sylvia Campos

Sylvia Campos
Guidance Counselor

F. RELEVANT STATUTORY LAW AND PRACTICE GUIDANCE

1. New York State Child Support Chart

Every state has standard child support guidelines consistent with federal mandates. These guidelines are intended to determine a predictable and equitable amount of child support based on the income of the obligor parent. The child support guidelines are presumed to be reasonable and an order of support conforming to the guidelines is presumed to be in the best interest of the child. Here is an excerpt of the child support guidelines from the N.Y.S. website. The full guidelines are updated and available at https://childsupport.ny.gov/dcse/pdfs/CSSA.pdf.

THE CHILD SUPPORT STANDARDS CHART

INCOME RANGE
50,000 -59,999

ANNUAL INCOME		NUMBER OF CHILDREN				
		1	2	3	4	5+
FROM	THRU	ANNUAL OBLIGATION AMOUNT				
50,000	50,099	8,500	12,500	14,500	15,500	17,500
50,100	50,199	8,517	12,525	14,529	15,531	17,535
50,200	50,299	8,534	12,550	14,558	15,562	17,570
50,300	50,399	8,551	12,575	14,587	15,593	17,605
50,400	50,499	8,568	12,600	14,616	15,624	17,640
50,500	50,599	8,585	12,625	14,645	15,655	17,675
50,600	50,699	8,602	12,650	14,674	15,686	17,710
50,700	50,799	8,619	12,675	14,703	15,717	17,745
50,800	50,899	8,636	12,700	14,732	15,748	17,780
50,900	50,999	8,653	12,725	14,761	15,779	17,815

ANNUAL INCOME		NUMBER OF CHILDREN				
		1	2	3	4	5+
FROM	THRU	ANNUAL OBLIGATION AMOUNT				
55,000	55,099	9,350	13,750	15,950	17,050	19,250
55,100	55,199	9,367	13,775	15,979	17,081	19,285
55,200	55,299	9,384	13,800	16,008	17,112	19,320
55,300	55,399	9,401	13,825	16,037	17,143	19,355
55,400	55,499	9,418	13,850	16,066	17,174	19,390
55,500	55,599	9,435	13,875	16,095	17,205	19,425
55,600	55,699	9,452	13,900	16,124	17,236	19,460
55,700	55,799	9,469	13,925	16,153	17,267	19,495
55,800	55,899	9,486	13,950	16,182	17,298	19,530
55,900	55,999	9,503	13,975	16,211	17,329	19,565

ANNUAL INCOME		NUMBER OF CHILDREN				
		1	2	3	4	5+
FROM	THRU	ANNUAL OBLIGATION AMOUNT				
51,000	51,099	8,670	12,750	14,790	15,810	17,850
51,100	51,199	8,687	12,775	14,819	15,841	17,885
51,200	51,299	8,704	12,800	14,848	15,872	17,920
51,300	51,399	8,721	12,825	14,877	15,903	17,955
51,400	51,499	8,738	12,850	14,906	15,934	17,990
51,500	51,599	8,755	12,875	14,935	15,965	18,025
51,600	51,699	8,772	12,900	14,964	15,996	18,060
51,700	51,799	8,789	12,925	14,993	16,027	18,095
51,800	51,899	8,806	12,950	15,022	16,058	18,130
51,900	51,999	8,823	12,975	15,051	16,089	18,165

ANNUAL INCOME		NUMBER OF CHILDREN				
		1	2	3	4	5+
FROM	THRU	ANNUAL OBLIGATION AMOUNT				
56,000	56,099	9,520	14,000	16,240	17,360	19,600
56,100	56,199	9,537	14,025	16,269	17,391	19,635
56,200	56,299	9,554	14,050	16,298	17,422	19,670
56,300	56,399	9,571	14,075	16,327	17,453	19,705
56,400	56,499	9,588	14,100	16,356	17,484	19,740
56,500	56,599	9,605	14,125	16,385	17,515	19,775
56,600	56,699	9,622	14,150	16,414	17,546	19,810
56,700	56,799	9,639	14,175	16,443	17,577	19,845
56,800	56,899	9,656	14,200	16,472	17,608	19,880
56,900	56,999	9,673	14,225	16,501	17,639	19,915

2. New York State Child Support Worksheet

Most states provide online calculators and guidelines for child support calculations. Here is a New York worksheet for assessing the non-custodial parent's child support obligation. The "basic child support obligation" comes from the state guidelines excerpted from the N.Y.S. Child Support Chart and provided in Section F.1.

BASIC CHILD SUPPORT GUIDELINES WORKSHEET

The following calculations refer to noncustodial parents only:

1 Annual Income* 1. ______________

2 Approximate Basic Child Support Obligation** 2. ______________

3 Subtract line 2 from line 1. 3. ______________

a. If line 3 is greater than or equal to $21,128 (the 2025 self-support reserve), enter the line 2 amount on line 7 below. No further calculations are necessary.

b. If line 3 is less than $21,128 (the 2025 self-support reserve) but greater than or equal to $15,650 (the 2025 poverty income guidelines amount for a single person), proceed to step 4.

c. If line 3 is less than $15,650 (the 2025 poverty income guidelines amount for a single person), enter $300 on line 7 below. No further calculations are necessary.

4 Annual Income (copy from line 1) 4. ______________

5 Self-Support Reserve 5. ______________

6 Subtract line 5 from line 4. 6. ______________

Enter on line 7 below the greater of $600 or the amount on line 6.

7 APPROXIMATE BASIC CHILD SUPPORT OBLIGATION** 7. ______________

NOTE:

* See Family Court Act § 413 (1)(b)(5) for the complete definition of "income" under the Child Support Guidelines. Income includes gross total income as should have been or should be reported in the most recent federal income tax return. Income may also include amounts imputed by the court. To the extent not already included in gross income, add investment income (minus the sums expended in connection with such investment), voluntarily deferred income or compensation and income received from the following sources: workers' compensation, disability benefits, unemployment insurance benefits, social security benefits, veterans benefits, pensions and retirement benefits, fellowships and stipends, and annuity payments. Income deductions include certain self-employment deductions, certain unreimbursed employee business expenses, except to the extent these allowances reduce personal expenditures, certain alimony or maintenance or child support actually paid to a spouse or on behalf of a child not a party to the instant action, public assistance, supplemental security income, New York City or Yonkers income or earnings taxes actually paid, and Federal Insurance Contributions Act (FICA) taxes actually paid.

** The Basic Child Support Obligation is defined by Family Court Act § 413(1)(b)(1). The noncustodial parent's portion of the Basic Child Support Obligation includes the amount resulting from multiplying the noncustodial parent's income by the appropriate child support percentage, then adding the noncustodial parent's share of cash medical support obligations, educational, and child care expenses where appropriate.

3. New York State Child Support Statute

This statutory excerpt from the N.Y.S. Family Court Act explains how the court might deviate from the presumptive award calculation.

§ 413–a. Review and cost of living adjustment of child support orders

(f) The court shall calculate the basic child support obligation, and the non-custodial parent's pro rata share of the basic child support obligation. Unless the court finds that the non-custodial parents' pro-rata share of the basic child support obligation is unjust or inappropriate, which finding shall be based upon consideration of the following factors:

(1) The financial resources of the custodial and non-custodial parent, and those of the child;

(2) The physical and emotional health of the child and his/her special needs and aptitudes;

(3) The standard of living the child would have enjoyed had the marriage or household not been dissolved;

(4) The tax consequences to the parties;

(5) The non-monetary contributions that the parents will make toward the care and well-being of the child;

(6) The educational needs of either parent;

(7) A determination that the gross income of one parent is substantially less than the other parent's gross income; * * *

(10) Any other factors the court determines are relevant in each case, the court shall order the non-custodial parent to pay his or her pro rata share of the basic child support obligation, and may order the non-custodial parent to pay an amount pursuant to paragraph (e) of this subdivision.

(g) Where the court finds that the non-custodial parent's pro rata share of the basic child support obligation is unjust or inappropriate, the court shall order the non-custodial parent to pay such amount of child support as the court finds just and appropriate, and the court shall set forth, in a written order, the factors it considered; the amount of each party's pro rata share of the basic child support obligation; and the reasons that the court did not order the basic child support obligation. Such written order may not be waived by either party or counsel; provided, however, and notwithstanding any other provision of law, including but not limited to section four hundred fifteen of this part, the court shall not find that the non-custodial parent's pro rata share of such obligation is unjust or inappropriate on the basis that such share exceeds the portion of a public assistance grant which is attributable to a child or children. Where the non-custodial parent's income is less than or equal to the poverty income guidelines amount for a single person as reported by the federal department of health and human services, unpaid child support arrears in excess of five hundred dollars shall not accrue.

4. U.S. Army Regulation 608–99

Your research also reveals the following excerpted Army regulation governing child support.

1–7. Management of personal affairs

a. The Army recognizes the transient nature of military duty. This regulation, however, prohibits the use of a Soldier's military status or assignment to deny financial support to Family members or to evade court orders on financial support, child custody and visitation, paternity, and related matters.

b. Soldiers are required to manage their personal affairs in a manner that does not bring discredit upon themselves or the U. S. Army. This responsibility includes—

(1) Maintaining reasonable contact with family members so that their financial needs and welfare do not become official matters of concern for the Army (see para 2–1).

(2) Conducting themselves in an honorable manner with regard to parental commitments and responsibilities (see chap 2).

(3) Providing adequate financial support to family members (see paras 2–3 through 2–9).

(4) Complying with all court orders (see paras 2–2, 2–4, and 2–11).

Section II: Obligations to Provide Financial Support to Family Members

2–3. Financial support by agreement

a. *Oral financial support agreement.* It is not the Army's policy to become involved in disputes over the terms or enforcement of oral financial support agreements. Where an oral agreement exists and is being followed, the Army will not interfere. When a dispute arises over the terms of an oral agreement, the parties are not in agreement, and there is no agreement for the purposes of this paragraph (see para 2–6 and para B–2). * * *

(b) A soldier is not required to provide financial support to his or her children beyond the amount required in paragraph 2–6, unless required to do so by court order (see also para 2–14).

(4) With regard to a written financial support agreement that has not been approved, ratified, incorporated within a divorce decree, or continued by its specific language, a family member may, depending on the applicable rules of law, seek a court judgment for arrearages resulting from a soldier's breach of the agreement or specific performance of the agreement with regard to future payments due.

2–4. Financial support required by court or Child Support Enforcement Agency order

a. *Domestic orders.* Soldiers will comply with the financial support provisions of all state court or CSEA orders (see para 2–5 and para B–3). Failure of a Soldier to comply with a financial support or related provision of a state court or CSEA order (for example, provision of a court order directing a division of property or payment of a particular expense) may also be the basis for a lawful order from a commander to comply with such provision. * * *

2–5. Punitive provisions regarding financial support

a. Soldiers will not violate any of the following:

(1) The financial support provision of a state court or CSEA order, or a foreign court order enforceable under paragraph 2–4*b*.

(2) The financial support provision of a written financial support agreement as described in paragraph 2–3 in the absence of a court order.

(3) The financial support requirements of paragraph 2–6 in the absence of a written financial support agreement or a court order containing a financial support provision.

b. This paragraph is punitive in nature (see para 1–6). Commanders are responsible for the enforcement of this paragraph (see para 3–8).

c. A Soldier cannot fall into arrears without violating this regulation. Although the collection of arrearages based on violations of subparagraphs 2–5*a*(1) and 2–5*a*(2) may be enforced in court, there is no legal means to collect arrearages based on violations of subparagraph 2–5*a*(3). Nevertheless, in all cases, Soldiers should be encouraged, but not ordered, to pay arrearages. Additionally, a Soldier who falls into arrears may be punished under the provisions of UCMJ, Art. 92 for failing to make the support payment required by subparagraphs 2–5*a*(1), 2–5*a*(2), or 2–5*a*(3) at the time that the support obligation was originally due. Punishment in such instances is based on failure to provide financial support when due, not for failure to pay arrearages.

2–6. Financial support required in the absence of a financial support agreement or court order

a. Application. This paragraph establishes requirements for interim financial support (paras 2–6*d* and 2–6*e*) and enhanced interim financial support for spouses (para 2–6*f*). Both types of support only apply in the absence of a financial support agreement or a court order containing a financial support provision and until such an agreement is signed or such an order is issued. Allegations or even proof of desertion, adultery, or other marital misconduct, or criminal acts on the part of a spouse will not excuse a Soldier's obligation to comply with the provisions of this regulation unless a battalion-level commander, or higher, has released the Soldier under the provisions of paragraphs 2–12 through 2–14. The interim financial support required to be paid by this paragraph does not constitute an "alimony or separate maintenance payment" under Sections 71 or 215 of the Internal Revenue Code (26 USC).

b. Pro-rata share. Under this paragraph, when the term "pro-rata share" is used with regard to BAH RC/T–WITH, the amount of each such share of BAH RC/T–WITH is calculated using the equation in figure 2–1. * * *

2–9. Form and timing of financial support payments

a. Unless otherwise required by court order or by a written financial support agreement, a financial support payment may be made in any of the ways listed in subparagraphs 2–9*a*(1) through 2–9*a*(7) as long as the payment reaches the adult Family member concerned, or the adult having custody of the child concerned, by the date required in paragraphs 2–9*b* and 2–9*c*. A Soldier seeking to make payment by allotment must make payments by alternative means until the allotment takes effect.

(1) Cash.

(2) Check.

(3) Money order.

(4) Electronic fund transfer.

(5) Voluntary allotment.

(6) Involuntary allotment.

(7) Garnishment (or wage assignment).

b. Unless otherwise required by a court order or by a written financial support agreement, a financial support payment made in cash, check, or money order will be personally delivered to the individual identified in paragraph 2–9*a*, not later than the first day of the month following the month to which the financial support payment pertains. Soldiers making cash payments may have to prove that the payment was made and should obtain a receipt or other proof that the payments were made (see para 3–4*a*(2)).

Source: Army Regulation, Army Regulation 608–99, https://armypubs.army.mil/epubs/DR_pubs/DR_a/ARN30639-AR_608-99-000-WEB-1.pdf.

IV. THE SIMULATION

You represent Marlene Gomez, the mother of Veronica Gomez (age 10). Using the materials provided in Sections III and IV, you have three (3) tasks to complete on your client's behalf.

A. Prepare a *Petition for Child Support*.

B. Hearing Preparation—i) identify witnesses to be called; ii) draft direct examination outline for questioning witnesses; and iii) develop persuasive arguments for deviations to the presumptive award.

C. Email Marlene to update her on your completed legal services and to set her expectations for a support award.

A. PETITIONING FOR CHILD SUPPORT

Section III.B. reveals that Marlene wants to explore formalizing Ryan's support obligations to Veronica. To do this, we need to commence a child support petition. Your supervising attorney has first asked you to prepare a petition on Marlene's behalf to begin this client representation. This form gives the Family Court jurisdiction to begin the proceeding. Chapter 1.II.C. previously explored how standard forms can save attorneys valuable time and resources. The following sample form will inform your independent drafting. Prepare a petition seeking child support, including a justification to meet Veronica's educational and therapeutic needs.

FAMILY COURT OF THE STATE OF NEW YORK COUNTY OF

____

In the Matter of a Proceeding for Support

Under Article 4 of the Family Court Act

Petitioner,

-against-

Respondent. ______________________________

TO THE FAMILY COURT:

The undersigned Petitioner respectfully alleges that:

1. a. I reside at [specify]:[3]

 b. Respondent resides at [specify]:[4]

2. I am authorized to originate this proceeding because [check applicable box(es)]:

□ Respondent and I were married at on

[3] Unless the Court has ordered the address to be confidential on the ground that disclosure would pose an unreasonable health or safety risk. *See* Family Court Act § 154–b; Form 21 (available at www.nycourts.gov).

[4] Unless the Court has ordered the address to be confidential on the ground that disclosure would pose an unreasonable health or safety risk. *See* Family Court Act § 154–b; Form 21 (available at www.nycourts.gov).

□ Respondent and I have the child(ren) named below in common

□ Other [specify Petitioner's relationship to child(ren)]:

3. Respondent is chargeable with the support of the following spouse and dependent(s):

NAME	DATE OF BIRTH
SPOUSE:	
CHILD(REN):	

4. [Check applicable box(es); if children have different fathers, include separate paragraphs]:

□ The father of the above-named child(ren) is [specify]:

□ The father was married to the child(ren)'s mother at the time of the conception or birth.

□ An order of filiation was made on [specify date and court and attach true copy]:

□ An acknowledgment of paternity was signed on [specify date]: by [specify who signed and attach a true copy]:

□ The father is deceased.

□ The father of the below-named child(ren) has not been legally established.

□ A paternity agreement or compromise was approved by the Family Court of [specify county]: County on [date], YR-00, concerning [name parties to agreement or compromise and child(ren)]:________________________. A true copy of the agreement or compromise is attached.

5. [Applicable to cases in which mother is not a party]: The name and address of the mother is [indicate if deceased or if address ordered to be kept confidential pursuant to Family Court Act § 154–b(2) or Domestic Relations Law § 254]:

6. [Check applicable box(es); if not applicable, SKIP to ¶ 7]: Respondent has an □ employer □ income payor, as defined in Civil Practice Law and Rules 5241(a), whose address is [specify]:____________ as a source of income.

7. I am hereby applying for child support services from the Support Collection Unit (the IV-D program pursuant to Title 6-A of the Social Services Law) through the filing of this Petition, unless [check a box only if applicable]:

□ I have already applied for child support services from the Support Collection Unit (the IV-D program pursuant to Title 6-A of the Social Services Law).

□ I do not need to apply now because I have continued to receive child support services after the public assistance or care case, or foster care case, for my family has closed.

□ I do not wish to apply for child support services.

□ I am not eligible to apply for child support services because I am petitioning for spousal support only.

8. No previous application has been made to any judge or court, including a Native American tribunal, or is presently pending before any judge or court, for the relief requested in this petition (except

WHEREFORE, I am requesting that this Court issue an order of support directing Respondent to pay fair and reasonable support, that Respondent be required to exercise the option of additional coverage for health insurance in favor of (his) (her) spouse and above-named child(ren), and for such other and further relief as the law provides.

NOTE: (1) A COURT ORDER OF SUPPORT RESULTING FROM A PROCEEDING COMMENCED BY THIS APPLICATION (PETITION) SHALL BE ADJUSTED BY THE APPLICATION OF A COST OF LIVING ADJUSTMENT AT THE DIRECTION OF THE SUPPORT COLLECTION UNIT NO EARLIER THAN TWENTY-FOUR MONTHS AFTER SUCH ORDER IS ISSUED, LAST MODIFIED OR LAST ADJUSTED, UPON THE REQUEST OF ANY PARTY TO THE ORDER OR PURSUANT TO PARAGRAPH (2) BELOW. SUCH COST OF LIVING ADJUSTMENT SHALL BE ON NOTICE TO BOTH PARTIES WHO, IF THEY OBJECT TO THE COST OF LIVING ADJUSTMENT, SHALL HAVE THE RIGHT TO BE HEARD BY THE COURT AND TO PRESENT EVIDENCE WHICH THE COURT WILL CONSIDER IN ADJUSTING THE CHILD SUPPORT ORDER IN ACCORDANCE WITH SECTION FOUR HUNDRED THIRTEEN OF THE FAMILY COURT ACT, KNOWN AS THE CHILD SUPPORT STANDARDS ACT.

(2) A PARTY SEEKING SUPPORT FOR ANY CHILD(REN) RECEIVING FAMILY ASSISTANCE SHALL HAVE A CHILD SUPPORT ORDER REVIEWED AND ADJUSTED AT THE DIRECTION OF THE SUPPORT COLLECTION UNIT NO EARLIER THAN TWENTY-FOUR MONTHS AFTER SUCH ORDER IS ISSUED, LAST MODIFIED OR LAST ADJUSTED BY THE SUPPORT COLLECTION UNIT, WITHOUT FURTHER APPLICATION BY ANY PARTY. ALL PARTIES WILL RECEIVE A COPY OF THE ADJUSTED ORDER.

(3) WHERE ANY PARTY FAILS TO PROVIDE, AND UPDATE UPON ANY CHANGE, THE SUPPORT COLLECTION UNIT WITH A CURRENT ADDRESS, AS REQUIRED BY SECTION FOUR HUNDRED FORTY-THREE OF THE FAMILY COURT ACT, TO WHICH AN ADJUSTED ORDER CAN BE SENT, THE SUPPORT OBLIGATION AMOUNT CONTAINED THEREIN SHALL BECOME DUE AND OWING ON THE DATE THE FIRST PAYMENT IS DUE UNDER THE TERMS OF THE ORDER OF SUPPORT WHICH WAS REVIEWED AND ADJUSTED OCCURRING ON OR AFTER THE EFFECTIVE DATE OF THE ADJUSTED ORDER, REGARDLESS OF WHETHER OR NOT THE PARTY HAS RECEIVED A COPY OF THE ADJUSTED ORDER.

Dated: ______________________________

Petitioner ______________________________

Print or type name ______________________________

Signature of Attorney, if any ______________________________

Attorney's Name (Print or Type) ______________________________

Attorney's Address and Telephone Number ______________

____

Source: https://www.nycourts.gov/LegacyPDFS/FORMS/familycourt/pdfs/4-3.pdf.

B. PREPARING FOR A HEARING

A hearing before a Support Magistrate will be scheduled next. The Magistrate will take testimony and hear evidence. Your supervisor wants you to summarize Marlene's key argument that the behavioral and speech interventions demand a deviation from the presumptive award in an outline that she can use to prepare for the hearing. Structure your outline by providing the specific statutory rule that governs child support deviations and the facts that best support a deviation in this case. Identify any witnesses who can provide factual testimony.

C. COUNSELING THE CLIENT

Finally, your supervisor wants to be sure that Marlene is apprised of the work that you are doing on her behalf. Before communicating with the client, ground yourself in your cultural competency assessment as introduced in Chapter One.

You will either draft an email or simulate a client meeting with Marlene to update her on your work. Even preparing for a live client meeting would require written notes to structure and guide the conversation. Prepare a written memorandum advising Marlene of the likely support award. Help Marlene anticipate which outcomes are highly likely and which outcomes are more discretionary. It is important to memorialize client guidance in writing. Your memo should be written such that it could be easily converted to meeting notes for the file or a follow-up client letter.

The client has some hesitation in petitioning for child support. Your communication should explain how a public order and wage withholding would work and the benefits it would provide to Marlene's stability. Counsel also located the military regulation captured in Section F.4. Help Marlene consider how this regulation might present a new path for her to secure child support. Help Marlene consider the option of privately negotiating a support award using this regulation. Consider the relative pros and cons of this alternative.

Your supervising attorney particularly wants you to address the fluctuations of military pay in your communication with Marlene. Prepare Marlene for the possibility that the award might be modified if there is a "material and substantial change in the circumstances of the child or either parent."

CHAPTER EIGHT

PROPERTY DISTRIBUTION AND ALIMONY

I. Introduction
II. Overview of the Law
III. Case File—Cody Williams v. Sarah Williams
    A. Simulation Roadmap
    B. Partner Email to Associate and Attachments
    C. Client Voice Mail
IV. Relevant Statutory Laws and Practice Guidance
    A. Ohio Statute—Property Distribution
    B. Ohio Statute—Alimony
    C. Affidavit of Income and Expenses
    D. Practice Guidance
    E. Law Firm Billable Time Sheet
V. The Simulation
    A. Drafting an Affidavit
    B. Interviewing an Expert Witness
    C. Researching Case Law
    D. Counseling the Client
    E. Tracking Attorney Time

I. INTRODUCTION

Property division is a core family law skill that typically requires lawyers to develop a solid base of knowledge beyond the state family law code. It is a dominant component of marital dissolutions, and many family law lawyers consult with professional experts to assist clients in obtaining an accurate value of the family's net worth. For most married couples who divorce, the separation of real property and other assets, like retirement and stock accounts, is one of the most impactful aspects of the family break up. Depending on the socio-economic status of clients, your ability to navigate property division will need to be constantly updated to stay abreast of the latest types of property and how it can be divided.

Studying family law through the lens of private family law practice can give you a distorted view of the field because the families who have the resources to hire a private lawyer are primarily the families who have assets to divide in the first place. This fact skews the hardships of divorce and its economic implications considerably in that families with very little property still require legal assistance analyzing the ramifications of splitting a pension or losing social security benefits.

Most family law clients are quite financially vulnerable at the moment of dissolution. The parties to the marriage are going to divide their property, and they may each also be paying their lawyer on top of that stark division of assets. Clients may not realize that in addition to losing each other, they are losing ground financially. At least one or both spouses may have to start over—building assets or trying to dig themselves out of a hole (while also paying for the cost of raising children). Divorce might necessitate a forced sale of the family home. It might mean relocating to a different school district, extending a work commute, or lost proximity to day care options. In more dire cases, divorce might mean bankruptcy. Many traditional family law casebooks leave the impression that parties are dividing up wealth, but notably they are often dividing up debt as well.

Understanding the financial dynamics of a divorce and the vulnerabilities marital separation creates is important to building your family law practice. The practice of law is not abstract; it is deeply interpersonal, community-centered, and relational. Building a family law practice will likely expand out from your own community and your social and professional circles. Clients want lawyers who understand their financial situation and their communities' norms, pressures, and dynamics. Clients experience divorce differently through varying lenses of class, race, religion, profession, immigration status, sexual orientation, and gender. Family law lawyers who understand these unique norms in their communities can build their practices within these communities as they build and sustain trust among clients. Developing cultural competence to engage effectively with various clients will continue to be an important part of your professional identity.

Learning Outcomes:

(1) Apply statutory provisions governing property distribution and alimony accurately and objectively to a client's case.

(2) Draft of an affidavit making financial disclosures to the court reporting income and assets.

(3) Prepare to interview a financial valuation expert for possible retention in valuing stocks.

(4) Research alimony case law to find factually analogous cases to anticipate legal issues.

(5) Advise client regarding likely outcomes in property distribution and alimony award.

(6) Calculate time spent on client matters in law firm billing report.

II. OVERVIEW OF THE LAW

Property Distribution

Property distribution is central to any family law practice for clients at all economic levels. The division of assets determines who gets the house, the debts, the cars, the coveted season tickets to a beloved sports team, the furniture, the family photographs, the memorabilia, and sometimes the family pet. These issues have obvious financial implications. Many of these tangible assets also carry deep emotional and nostalgic value for many people.

When two people join in marriage, they are often not thinking about how the accumulation of property will be dealt with if they divorce. Marriage trends for the last several years have illustrated that people are waiting later to get married. The average age of first marriage is at its highest in U.S. history—28.6 for women and 30.2 for men.[1] This has led to an increase in the number of couples who cohabitate before marriage, as well as an increase in the amount of assets individuals collect before marriage.

Understanding the outcomes in property division and alimony disputes in marital dissolution cases is beneficial for attorneys who draft premarital and cohabitation agreements. Attorneys acquire valuable insights regarding the best ways to protect their client's property or strategies for a fair dispute resolution in a dissolution. The topics covered in this chapter will be helpful for you to reconsider after covering Chapter Three, which covers premarital and cohabitation agreements.

[1] U.S. Census Bureau, *Historical Marital Status Tables*, Table MS-2. Estimated Median Age at First Marriage, by Sex: 1890 to Present [1.0 MB] (November 7, 2024).

The first question to consider in property distribution is the jurisdiction in which you practice and the property regime that governs division of property at divorce. Most couples marry and commingle assets and debt without even knowing what property distribution framework will govern a potential dissolution. There are generally two types of property regimes: title theory and community property.[2] Title theory maintains that the spouse who holds title to the asset is the spouse who retains ownership of it. It is also known as the separate or common law property system. Community property systems provide that each spouse has a vested one-half interest in all property acquired during the marriage. In this regime, separate property is property acquired before marriage by either spouse, and any gift, bequest, or devise acquired during the marriage by either spouse.

Though these two systems differ in how property is characterized during marriage, distribution of property at divorce leads to very similar results. Most states that utilize either regime endorse equitable distribution of property. Equitable distribution of marital property does not always result in equal distribution among spouses. Equitable distribution is grounded in the concept of marriage as a partnership to which both spouses contribute. Courts are instead tasked with weighing the labor and contributions of both spouses during marriage toward the family assets.

If you have taken a basic family law course, you will be familiar with the four-step process of property dissolution—(1) identify property, (2) classify it as marital or separate property, (3) value property, and (4) distribute the marital property. Identifying and valuing property are components of family law that are often not fully covered in family law casebooks and exam coverage. These two steps can be quite complex depending on the type of property, and some clients will need to hire an expert witness to testify about both how property should be classified and how it should be valued.

There are many categories of property, including traditional real property, business interests, social security benefits, stocks and bonds, intellectual property, employment benefits, professional degrees and licenses, and pets. The average American couple only has a few items to divide: the marital home, retirement benefits, personal property (e.g., furniture and cars), and debt acquired during the marriage. Most couples can resolve property disputes through bartering or selling property and dividing the proceeds. For those who are unable to resolve property distribution, this chapter will provide a broad overview of the key steps attorneys must master to assist their clients with both mediated settlement agreements and disputed hearings regarding property and alimony.

When reviewing the various approaches to property distribution, consider how each system classifies and allocates property at the end of a marriage. The state's most significant role is exercised at the time of dissolution. One way to conceptualize equitable distribution is as a big 'bucketing' exercise: each piece of property is sorted into one of three buckets: spouse 1's separate property, spouse 2's separate property, or marital property. State statutes govern how this sorting is done. For example, in a community property regime, there is a presumption that all property acquired during the marriage is marital property. Typically, property acquired before the marriage or after legal separation is separate property, unless a spouse can prove that a statutory exception applies to specific property such that it should be placed in a separate property bucket. using the statutory exceptions. In a title theory system, the state also plays a role in classification of property. At the time of dissolution, courts classify property acquired during the marriage as marital—regardless of title—unless it falls within a statutory exception. These exceptions may include premarital agreements, gifts or inheritances, property traceable to a spouse's separate assets, or passive appreciation of separate property. After classification and distribution, each spouse exits

[2] There is a third concept known as the "kitchen sink" or "all property" method used in eleven states. This model provides that all assets, regardless of their classification or which spouse owns them are thrown into the pot and available for taking by either spouse.

the marriage with their separate property bucket and a share of the marital bucket, as determined by the court.

The states use a series of factors to distribute the marital property bucket. The judge has great discretion in matters of property division, informed by case law precedent developed in your home state. The court might look to the length of the marriage, the age and health of the spouses, the relative economic position of the spouses, and other factors. Most states do this division seeking an "equitable distribution," which is fair and just, not necessarily equal. Some states begin from a presumptive starting point of "equal," but then allow persuasive arguments that equal is not necessarily equitable under the facts of the case.

A minority of states use a community property approach to property distribution at dissolution. Community property states presume that any property acquired *during* the marriage is marital property owned 50% by spouse 1 and 50% by spouse 2. This puts aside title theory during the marriage and positions the marital couple as equal partners, regardless of economic or non-economic contributions. There are some narrow exceptions to the community property presumption, such as inheritances and personal injury awards or settlements. There are also some persuasive mechanisms by which a spouse can petition for disproportionate division of property in the court's discretion.

The distribution in community property states is more fixed, consistent, and predictable. Accordingly, community property might promote settlement better than the more indeterminate task of distributing marital property in equitable distribution. In equitable distribution, the court applies factors to determine the division of marital property seeking to yield a just and equitable distribution in each case.[3] Consider carefully the pros and cons of the different approaches. You will read an Ohio statute in Section IV.A. and then identify whether Ohio is governed by equitable distribution, community property, or another format entirely. Understanding a state's property distribution scheme is vital in order to properly advise and advocate for divorcing clients.

Alimony

Alimony, alternatively known as spousal support or maintenance depending on your jurisdiction, goes hand in hand with property distribution. As you study alimony in your home state, consider carefully what policies alimony serves and what values it reflects. Historically, alimony addressed a critical economic disparity between husbands and wives created by title theory. Title theory granted property at dissolution to the spouse to whom the property was titled, nearly always the husband historically. Absent additional legal mechanisms, this would leave wives unable to support themselves without property and without market earning power through employment outside of the home. Alimony filled this void by creating a mechanism for one spouse (usually the husband) to support the other spouse. Over time those rules transformed to gender-neutral statutes, as equality for women was established by federal and state law, and they were able to hold property and earn income.

The question that faces courts today is what theory supports the ongoing use of alimony in family law? Is it a contract-based theory where one spouse acted in reliance on the other? Is it a partnership-based model that considers what each spouse contributed to the marriage? Is it an equality-based model trying to position the spouses with equal standards of living at dissolution? What role should fault play in alimony? Historically, fault-based approaches yielded harsh outcomes for women. If men committed a fault-based ground for divorce and forfeited their right to alimony, this method was not pragmatically punitive to husbands who likely did not need alimony anyway. If women committed the same fault-based grounds for divorce and forfeited their right to alimony,

---

[3] Most community property states have legal standards that promote equitable rather than equal divisions of assets at divorce.

this could lead to the wife needing public benefits as support. There are continuous critiques of alimony that should influence family law practice and client counseling. Lawyers will need to study their home state statutes and case law to consider whether clients are eligible for alimony, and if so, under what grounds. Some states handle alimony in two steps, requiring petitioners to first prove that there is a need and then considering persuasive arguments looking at statutory factors, such as the age of the parties, the length of the marriage, the standard of living established during the marriage. Other states only allow courts to consider alimony if the property distribution does not allow the spouse the means to sufficiently support themselves.

Alimony reveals how our client's expectations and understanding of the law might differ starkly from the actual substance of the law. Many clients, particularly older and wealthier clients, might believe that alimony is common and expected, when in reality it is a much rarer and narrower legal outcome in modern divorce. When alimony is awarded, it is more likely to be rehabilitative or more limited in duration than the permanent awards that governed historically. You will study your state statute carefully to see whether your client can request alimony, whether fault is considered, what factors shape the award, and what events might cut off alimony (such as remarriage). Unlike other topics that are more predictable and consistent, such as child support, alimony is hard to advise clients about, particularly whether and how much alimony might be awarded, if any. It also reinforces that the practice of family law might vary in different income brackets and communities. Alimony only works if one spouse has the means to pay. If both spouses are struggling economically, this is not a viable legal tool for support.

III. CASE FILE—CODY WILLIAMS V. SARAH WILLIAMS

A. SIMULATION ROADMAP

In this simulation exercise, you will represent Cody Williams in a divorce proceeding. You have already filed divorce papers on his behalf in Ohio. You now need to get to work on developing the case. This simulation includes several different tasks. You will work to complete a mandatory court affidavit of income and expenses, prepare to retain an expert to handle a valuation dispute, research factually relevant case law governing alimony, advise the client of possible property outcomes, and complete these tasks within a tight budget of billable hours pursuant to the attorney-client relationship.

B. PARTNER EMAIL TO ASSOCIATE AND ATTACHMENTS

To:	Associate
From:	Patricia Partner
Re:	Williams Case File (Client Matter No. 143909d)

Hi,

Hope you had a great weekend! I need your help on the Cody Williams case file. We need to do three things before our upcoming meeting with him. I first met Cody last month. He and his wife, Sarah, have been separated for some time. We worked with Cody to file his petition for divorce last month. You can review our petition on the firm's server under his client matter number. He would like to finalize his divorce so that he can remarry someday in the future.

There are a few matters we need to get moving on in anticipation of property distribution. I've attached my intake notes from my meeting with Cody. Can you prepare the required Ohio Affidavit of Income and Expenses based on my notes? You can find the Affidavit on the Family Court's public website.

I know we still have some information gaps and follow-up questions for Cody. I'd like to go over any gaps with him carefully during our meeting to be sure we will be able to accurately and thoroughly complete this affidavit by the end of the month. Please complete as much of the affidavit as you can based on the intake notes and prepare a list of follow-up questions.

Second, I know we are going to have an issue with the valuation of Sarah's stock options from her family's tire business. Sarah described them to Cody as "effectively worthless," but I suspect they are actually worth a substantial amount of money. This separate property item is the most valuable resource Sarah has. The stock options themselves are squarely covered by Sarah and Cody's prenuptial agreement, so it is not a matter of distribution to Cody. The value of the stock options will be important to calculating her overall economic position as relevant to both property distribution and alimony.

I used Khaled Alted in a valuation matter years ago and thought his work was quite good. It has been some time though, so we need to vet him carefully again. I previously worked with him on a personal injury economic valuation, which was a very different matter. I'd like to interview him for this case more carefully. I've attached his online bio. Can you prepare an outline of questions for our interview discussing the possibility of our firm retaining him in this matter? I want to be sure he is the right expert for this case. To save some time, perhaps you can use AI to help you get started with some general questions that you can supplement.

Track your hours carefully. We have only a retainer fee of $3,000 in this case currently. I need to confer with the client before exceeding it. Check in with me if your billable hours (rate of $120/hour) get close to the retainer fee.

Third, I am considering how these stock options will affect Sarah's eligibility for alimony. I am wondering whether their later distribution might disrupt the finality of an alimony award. Can you research any Ohio case law on whether stock proceed distributions might constitute a change in circumstances sufficient to change an existing alimony award? This will be helpful context to know as we negotiate on alimony. I need to give Cody some guidance on how likely an alimony award is in our next meeting. Prepare a short research memorandum that explains the relevant case law.

ATTACHMENT 1 of 2
C.WilliamsIntake.doc

From the desk of Patricia Partner
CONFIDENTIAL
Attorney Work Product

I met with Cody Williams today. He has hired us to petition for divorce in Ohio from his wife, Sarah Williams. Sarah and Cody Williams were married in Ohio in August YR-10. They met as students at The Ohio State University. They got married immediately after graduation. Sarah came from a very wealthy family and she held unvested stock options in the family tire business in Ohio, valued at $200,000 in YR-10. Because of this family wealth, her parents pressured her to obtain a prenuptial agreement before marrying. The agreement stated that all of Sarah's stock or proceeds from the stocks in the family tire business would remain her separate property. Cody does not contest or challenge the prenuptial agreement's validity.

When they married, Sarah already owned a condo in the Buckeye Bungalows that her parents bought her as a gift to live in during college (a $120,000 cash purchase). Cody moved in after they married. After graduation, Cody worked as a marketing director for a Columbus medical supply company. He first made $40,000 a year, but ultimately progressed to his current salary of $70,000 with $10,000 bonuses annually. Sarah worked as a school guidance counselor making $55,000 a year. Sarah's savings account had $3,500 when they married. She currently has $145,000 in her personal savings account, all of which has come from her parents' annual cash gifts. Cody's savings account had $1,200 in savings when they married. He currently has cash assets of $78,000 spread across his personal checking account, savings account, and investment account. Cody guesses that Sarah's stocks in the family business are presently worth "millions," but she says they are "worthless."

In YR-09, Cody's grandpa bequeathed him $30,000. Cody wanted to use that money as a down payment on a larger home for the couple. Due to a poor real estate market, they sold the Buckeye Bungalow condo for $95,000. Sarah and Cody took the $95,000 from the sale and put it in an investment account in their names jointly. Cody manages this account actively. It is presently worth $195,000. Using Cody's $30,000 as the down payment, they jointly bought a four-bedroom home in Cardinal Cul-de-Sac, a trendy up and coming area of Columbus, for $185,000. Today the house is worth $240,000 and they owe $83,250 on their mortgage. Taking advantage of low interest rates, Sarah took out a home equity loan for $50,000 in YR-04 to make some improvements to the property. She used that money to install hard wood floors, redo the kitchen, and convert a half bath into a full. Sarah currently owes $3,900 on the equity line.

Their marriage was happy until YR-05-when their first child, Tate, was born. Sarah nearly died in childbirth after an emergency blood transfusion and a dramatic loss of blood pressure. This scary event, combined with the new joys of parenting, led Sarah to find "New Awakenings" church. She became a "born again" Christian. She ceased all use of alcohol and cigarettes, and she quit her job to focus on "raising Tate in Christ."

While Cody tried to attend church with Sarah, he did not experience the same transformation Sarah did. He continued to smoke cigarettes and drink alcohol regularly. He smoked pot occasionally. This created tension for the couple. Sarah could not see past what she believed to be Cody's "moral shortcomings." She worried about the effects of Cody's behavior on Tate and his upbringing. Cody found this frustrating because he used to enjoy game tailgating with Sarah and parties with friends. He felt like she changed the rules in the middle of the marriage, and they no longer had much in common.

In YR-02, Sarah became pregnant with their second child, Ruby Jane. The stress of this pregnancy was too much for them. Cody desperately wanted Sarah to terminate the pregnancy, but Sarah refused and committed to raising the child on her own. She could no longer tolerate living with someone who would even consider ending the pregnancy. Sarah moved out of the marital home on August 1, YR-02. She moved into her grandmother's home in Kentucky, which was vacant after her grandmother relocated to an assisted living facility. Cody and Sarah have lived largely separate lives since. Cody sees the kids every other weekend, and they have found a 'new normal' living apart.

In YR-00, however, Cody met his current girlfriend, Isabelle. He now wants to end his marriage so he can remarry someday. Although he and Sarah had lived apart for years, they were never formally separated legally.

Sarah's grandmother's house has four-bedrooms. Wanting to serve her community, she connected with the Holy Saints church in Kentucky. She now uses the fourth bedroom as a refuge for wayward individuals who need a place to stay based on pastoral referrals. Over the year she has lived in this house, over 30 different people have stayed in her spare room, including homeless youth, undocumented asylum-seekers, pregnant teens, and mentally ill adults. She charges $15 a night because she wants to teach accountability and responsibility. She donates all of the proceeds back to the church.

Sarah's parents continue to support her with cash gifts of $20,000 annually. This summer, Sarah was diagnosed with Lyme disease. Cody has started to see the kids more because of her fatigue and chronic pain. She mentioned at their last hand-off that her medical bills were piling up.

ATTACHMENT 2 of 2
Bio.html

Appraisal & Valuation Specialist, Khaled Alted

Mr. Khaled Alted
Alted, Amos, Rivner, Accounting Forensics & Valuations, PLLC
180 Main Street
Click here to contact me today!

Introduction

Mr. Alted renders expert testimony and consulting services in high-stakes complex business litigation and family law matters throughout Ohio. Mr. Alted is experienced in forensic accounting, economic damage claims, financial fraud matters, partner/shareholder disputes, personal injury/wrongful death suits, property division disputes, and tax litigation.

Before joining the firm and working his way to partner, Mr. Alted was an accountant at Goodyear Tires and a C.P.A. with Alted & Alted.

Mr. Alted is a licensed C.P.A., Accredited in Business Valuations (ABV), and a Certified Divorce Financial Analyst® (CDFA®). He has testified more than 40 times in courtroom proceedings and in depositions more than sixty times. He has published dozens of reports and articles on complex valuation matters. See his full list of publications here.

He brings proven results to his clients, combining financial knowledge with a warm, interpersonal demeanor.

C. CLIENT VOICE MAIL

IV. RELEVANT STATUTORY LAWS AND PRACTICE GUIDANCE

As a practicing family law attorney, you are generally familiar with your state's property distribution and alimony statutory provisions. You likely have these statutes on your desk readily accessible. You nonetheless would not work from memory recall alone. You should always have the statute handy for precise terminology and statutory provisions. They are provided here. You review the following Ohio statutes governing property distribution and alimony.

A. OHIO STATUTE—PROPERTY DISTRIBUTION

Title 31—Domestic Relations

Chapter 3105. Divorce, Alimony, Annulment, Dissolution of Marriage

§ 3105.171. Equitable division of marital and separate property—distributive award.

(A) As used in this section:

(1) "Distributive award" means any payment or payments, in real or personal property, that are payable in a lump sum or over time, in fixed amounts, that are made from separate property or income, and that are not made from marital property and do not constitute payments of spousal support, as defined in section 3105.18 of the Revised Code.

(2) "During the marriage" means whichever of the following is applicable:

(a) Except as provided in division (A)(2)(b) of this section, the period of time from the date of the marriage through the date of the final hearing in an action for divorce or in an action for legal separation;

(b) If the court determines that the use of either or both of the dates specified in division (A)(2)(a) of this section would be inequitable, the court may select dates that it considers equitable in determining marital property. If the court selects dates that it considers equitable in determining marital property, "during the marriage" means the period of time between those dates selected and specified by the court.

(3)(a) "Marital property" means, subject to division (A)(3)(b) of this section, all of the following:

(i) All real and personal property that currently is owned by either or both of the spouses, including, but not limited to, the retirement benefits of the spouses, and that was acquired by either or both of the spouses during the marriage;

(ii) All interest that either or both of the spouses currently has in any real or personal property, including, but not limited to, the retirement benefits of the spouses, and that was acquired by either or both of the spouses during the marriage;

(iii) Except as otherwise provided in this section, all income and appreciation on separate property, due to the labor, monetary, or in-kind contribution of either or both of the spouses that occurred during the marriage;

(iv) A participant account, as defined in section 148.01 of the Revised Code, of either of the spouses, to the extent of the following: the moneys that have been deferred by a continuing member or participating employee, as defined in that section, and that have been transmitted to the Ohio public employees deferred compensation board during the marriage and any income that is derived from the investment of those moneys during the marriage; the moneys that have been deferred by an officer or employee of a municipal corporation and that have been transmitted to the governing board, administrator, depository, or trustee of the deferred compensation program of the municipal corporation during the marriage and any income that is derived from the investment of those moneys during the marriage; or the moneys that have been deferred by an officer or employee of a government unit, as defined in section 148.06 of the Revised Code, and that have been transmitted to the governing board, as defined in that section, during the marriage and any income that is derived from the investment of those moneys during the marriage.

(b) "Marital property" does not include any separate property.

(4) "Passive income" means income acquired other than as a result of the labor, monetary, or in-kind contribution of either spouse.

(5) "Personal property" includes both tangible and intangible personal property.

(6)(a) "Separate property" means all real and personal property and any interest in real or personal property that is found by the court to be any of the following:

(i) An inheritance by one spouse by bequest, devise, or descent during the course of the marriage;

(ii) Any real or personal property or interest in real or personal property that was acquired by one spouse prior to the date of the marriage;

(iii) Passive income and appreciation acquired from separate property by one spouse during the marriage;

(iv) Any real or personal property or interest in real or personal property acquired by one spouse after a decree of legal separation issued under section 3105.17 of the Revised Code;

(v) Any real or personal property or interest in real or personal property that is excluded by a valid antenuptial or postnuptial agreement;

(vi) Compensation to a spouse for the spouse's personal injury, except for loss of marital earnings and compensation for expenses paid from marital assets;

(vii) Any gift of any real or personal property or of an interest in real or personal property that is made after the date of the marriage and that is proven by clear and convincing evidence to have been given to only one spouse.

(b) The commingling of separate property with other property of any type does not destroy the identity of the separate property as separate property, except when the separate property is not traceable.

(B) In divorce proceedings, the court shall, and in legal separation proceedings upon the request of either spouse, the court may, determine what constitutes marital property and what constitutes separate property. In either case, upon making such a determination, the court shall divide the marital and separate property equitably between the spouses, in accordance with this section. For purposes of this section, the court has jurisdiction over all property, excluding the social security benefits of a spouse other than as set forth in division (F)(9) of this section, in which one or both spouses have an interest.

(C)(1) Except as provided in this division or division (E) of this section, the division of marital property shall be equal. If an equal division of marital property would be inequitable, the court shall not divide the marital property equally but instead shall divide it between the spouses in the manner the court determines equitable. In making a division of marital property, the court shall consider all relevant factors, including those set forth in division (F) of this section.

(2) Each spouse shall be considered to have contributed equally to the production and acquisition of marital property.

(3) The court shall provide for an equitable division of marital property under this section prior to making any award of spousal support to either spouse under section 3105.18 of the Revised Code and without regard to any spousal support so awarded.

(4) If the marital property includes a participant account, as defined in section 148.01 of the Revised Code, the court shall not order the division or disbursement of the moneys and income described in division (A)(3)(a)(iv) of this section to occur in a manner that is inconsistent with the law, rules, or plan governing the deferred compensation program involved or prior to the time that the spouse in whose name the participant account is maintained commences receipt of the moneys and income credited to the account in accordance with that law, rules, and plan.

(D) Except as otherwise provided in division (E) of this section or by another provision of this section, the court shall disburse a spouse's separate property to that spouse. If a court does not disburse a spouse's separate property to that spouse, the court shall make written findings of fact that explain the factors that it considered in making its determination that the spouse's separate property should not be disbursed to that spouse.

(E)(1) The court may make a distributive award to facilitate, effectuate, or supplement a division of marital property. The court may require any distributive award to be secured by a lien on the payor's specific marital property or separate property.

(2) The court may make a distributive award in lieu of a division of marital property in order to achieve equity between the spouses, if the court determines that a division of the marital property in kind or in money would be impractical or burdensome.

(3) The court shall require each spouse to disclose in a full and complete manner all marital property, separate property, and other assets, debts, income, and expenses of the spouse.

(4) If a spouse has engaged in financial misconduct, including, but not limited to, the dissipation, destruction, concealment, nondisclosure, or fraudulent disposition of assets, the court may compensate the offended spouse with a distributive award or with a greater award of marital property.

(5) If a spouse has substantially and willfully failed to disclose marital property, separate property, or other assets, debts, income, or expenses as required under division (E)(3) of this section, the court may compensate the offended spouse with a distributive award or with a greater award of marital property not to exceed three times the value of the marital property, separate property, or other assets, debts, income, or expenses that are not disclosed by the other spouse.

(F) In making a division of marital property and in determining whether to make and the amount of any distributive award under this section, the court shall consider all of the following factors:

(1) The duration of the marriage;

(2) The assets and liabilities of the spouses;

(3) The desirability of awarding the family home, or the right to reside in the family home for reasonable periods of time, to the spouse with custody of the children of the marriage;

(4) The liquidity of the property to be distributed;

(5) The economic desirability of retaining intact an asset or an interest in an asset;

(6) The tax consequences of the property division upon the respective awards to be made to each spouse;

(7) The costs of sale, if it is necessary that an asset be sold to effectuate an equitable distribution of property;

(8) Any division or disbursement of property made in a separation agreement that was voluntarily entered into by the spouses;

(9) Any retirement benefits of the spouses, excluding the social security benefits of a spouse except as may be relevant for purposes of dividing a public pension;

(10) Any other factor that the court expressly finds to be relevant and equitable.

(G) In any order for the division or disbursement of property or a distributive award made pursuant to this section, the court shall make written findings of fact that support the determination that the marital property has been equitably divided and shall specify the dates it used in determining the meaning of "during the marriage."

(H) Except as otherwise provided in this section, the holding of title to property by one spouse individually or by both spouses in a form of co-ownership does not determine whether the property is marital property or separate property.

(I) A division or disbursement of property or a distributive award made under this section is not subject to future modification by the court except upon the express written consent or agreement to the modification by both spouses.

(J) The court may issue any orders under this section that it determines equitable, including, but not limited to, either of the following types of orders:

(1) An order granting a spouse the right to use the marital dwelling or any other marital property or separate property for any reasonable period of time;

(2) An order requiring the sale or encumbrancing of any real or personal property, with the proceeds from the sale and the funds from any loan secured by the encumbrance to be applied as determined by the court.

Bring it home! Statutory spotlight.

Your family law course may study law using general rules and trends or it may use your home state statutes and rules to more specifically prepare you for local practice. Compare your home state statutes with the property distribution rule in this simulation. Your professor may provide a state statutory supplement to replace the statute provided here or you may research your home state rules independently.

B. OHIO STATUTE—ALIMONY

Title 31—Domestic Relations

Chapter 3105. Divorce, Alimony, Annulment, Dissolution of Marriage

§ 3105.18. Awarding spousal support—modification of spousal support.

(A) As used in this section, "spousal support" means any payment or payments to be made to a spouse or former spouse, or to a third party for the benefit of a spouse or a former spouse, that is both for sustenance and for support of the spouse or former spouse. * * *

(B) In divorce and legal separation proceedings, upon the request of either party and after the court determines the division or disbursement of property . . . ., the court of common pleas may award reasonable spousal support to either party. During the pendency of any divorce, or legal separation proceeding, the court may award reasonable temporary spousal support to either party.

An award of spousal support may be allowed in real or personal property, or both, or by decreeing a sum of money, payable either in gross or by installments, from future income or otherwise, as the court considers equitable.

Any award of spousal support made under this section shall terminate upon the death of either party, unless the order containing the award expressly provides otherwise.

(C) (1) In determining whether spousal support is appropriate and reasonable, and in determining the nature, amount, and terms of payment, and duration of spousal support, which is payable either in gross or in installments, the court shall consider all of the following factors:

(a) The income of the parties, from all sources, including, but not limited to, income derived from property divided, disbursed, or distributed under section 3105.171 of the Revised Code;

(b) The relative earning abilities of the parties;

(c) The ages and the physical, mental, and emotional conditions of the parties;

(d) The retirement benefits of the parties;

(e) The duration of the marriage;

(f) The extent to which it would be inappropriate for a party, because that party will be custodian of a minor child of the marriage, to seek employment outside the home;

(g) The standard of living of the parties established during the marriage;

(h) The relative extent of education of the parties;

(i) The relative assets and liabilities of the parties, including but not limited to any court-ordered payments by the parties;

(j) The contribution of each party to the education, training, or earning ability of the other party, including, but not limited to, any party's contribution to the acquisition of a professional degree of the other party;

(k) The time and expense necessary for the spouse who is seeking spousal support to acquire education, training, or job experience so that the spouse will be qualified to obtain appropriate employment, provided the education, training, or job experience, and employment is, in fact, sought;

(*l*) The tax consequences, for each party, of an award of spousal support;

(m) The lost income production capacity of either party that resulted from that party's marital responsibilities;

(n) Any other factor that the court expressly finds to be relevant and equitable.

(2) In determining whether spousal support is reasonable and in determining the amount and terms of payment of spousal support, each party shall be considered to have contributed equally to the production of marital income.

(D) In an action brought solely for an order for legal separation under section 3105.17 of the Revised Code, any continuing order for periodic payments of money entered pursuant to this section is subject to further order of the court upon changed circumstances of either party.

(E) If a continuing order for periodic payments of money as alimony is entered in a divorce or dissolution of marriage action that is determined on or after May 2, 1986, and before January 1, 1991, or if a continuing order for periodic payments of money as spousal support is entered in a divorce or dissolution of marriage action that is determined on or after January 1, 1991, the court that enters the decree of divorce or dissolution of marriage does not have jurisdiction to modify the amount or terms of the alimony or spousal support unless the court determines that the circumstances of either party have changed and unless one of the following applies:

(1) In the case of a divorce, the decree or a separation agreement of the parties to the divorce that is incorporated into the decree contains a provision specifically authorizing the court to modify the amount or terms of alimony or spousal support.

(2) In the case of a dissolution of marriage, the separation agreement that is approved by the court and incorporated into the decree contains a provision specifically authorizing the court to modify the amount or terms of alimony or spousal support.

(F) (1) For purposes of divisions (D) and (E) of this section and subject to division (F)(2) of this section, a change in the circumstances of a party includes, but is not limited to, any increase or involuntary decrease in the party's wages, salary, bonuses, living expenses, or medical expenses, or other changed circumstances so long as both of the following apply:

(a) The change in circumstances is substantial and makes the existing award no longer reasonable and appropriate.

(b) The change in circumstances was not taken into account by the parties or the court as a basis for the existing award when it was established or last modified, whether or not the change in circumstances was foreseeable.

(2) In determining whether to modify an existing order for spousal support, the court shall consider any purpose expressed in the initial order or award and enforce any voluntary agreement of the parties. Absent an agreement of the parties, the court shall not modify the continuing jurisdiction of the court as contained in the original decree.

Bring it home! Statutory spotlight.

Your family law course may study law using general rules and trends or it may use your home state statutes and rules to more specifically prepare you for local practice. Compare and contrast your home state alimony statute with the rule in this simulation. Your professor may provide a state statutory supplement to replace the statute provided here or you may research your home state rules independently.

C. AFFIDAVIT OF INCOME AND EXPENSES

Your local rules require submission of the following affidavit of income and expenses. This is a court filing that you would work with your client to complete accurately and thoroughly. In this simulation exercise, you will complete a draft affidavit for your supervising attorney in anticipation of an upcoming client meeting.

This assignment reveals that the initial client intake did not capture all the details necessary to achieve the client's objective. Reflect on this situation as a new lawyer. At this moment, do you know how much money is in your bank account, what each of your monthly expenses are, and what your precise income is? Most clients do not know this precise information either, thus requiring some detailed client preparation. Many law firms send a preparation form directing clients to complete a meticulous intake questionnaire containing this information. This assignment presents an opportunity to reflect on what your comprehensive client intake methodology might be to efficiently capture all essential information from your client in your initial meeting.

IN THE COURT OF COMMON PLEAS
______________________ DIVISION
______________________ COUNTY, OHIO

______________________ Plaintiff/Petitioner 1	Case No. ______________________
vs./and	Judge ______________________
______________________ Defendant/Petitioner 2	Magistrate ______________________

Instructions: Check local court rules to determine when this form must be filed. This affidavit is used to make complete disclosure of income, expenses, and money owed. It is used to determine child and spousal support. Do not leave any category blank. For each item, if none, put "NONE." If you do not know exact figures for any item, give your best estimate, and put "EST." **If you need more space, add additional pages.**

AFFIDAVIT OF BASIC INFORMATION, INCOME, AND EXPENSES

Affidavit of ______________________
(Print Name)

Date of marriage ______________ Date of separation ______________

SECTION I – BASIC INFORMATION

Plaintiff/Petitioner 1	Defendant/Petitioner 2
Date of Birth ______________	Date of Birth ______________
Last 4 Digits of Social Security # XXX-XX-_____	Last 4 Digits of Social Security # XXX-XX-_____
Phone Number ______________	Phone Number ______________
Email Address ______________	Email Address ______________
Is an interpreter needed? ☐ Yes or ☐ No If yes, explain: ______________	Is an interpreter needed? ☐ Yes or ☐ No If yes, explain: ______________
Health: ☐ Good ☐ Fair ☐ Poor If health is not good, please explain:	Health: ☐ Good ☐ Fair ☐ Poor If health is not good, please explain:

Education: (*Check highest level achieved*) ☐ Grade School ☐ High School ☐ Associate ☐ Bachelor's ☐ Post Graduate	Education: (*Check highest level achieved*) ☐ Grade School ☐ High School ☐ Associate ☐ Bachelor's ☐ Post Graduate
Other Technical Certifications: Active Member of the U.S. Military ☐ Yes ☐ No	Other Technical Certifications: Active Member of the U.S. Military ☐ Yes ☐ No

SECTION II – INCOME

	Plaintiff/Petitioner 1	Defendant/Petitioner 2
Employed	☐ Yes ☐ No	☐ Yes ☐ No
Date of Employment	____________	____________
Name of Employer	____________	____________
Payroll Address	____________	____________
Payroll City, State, Zip	____________	____________
Scheduled Paychecks Per Year	☐ 12 ☐ 24 ☐ 26 ☐ 52	☐ 12 ☐ 24 ☐ 26 ☐ 52

A. YEARLY INCOME, OVERTIME, COMMISSIONS, AND BONUSES FOR PAST THREE YEARS

	Plaintiff/Petitioner 1		Year	Defendant/Petitioner 2
Base yearly income	$__________	3 years ago —	20___	$ __________
	$__________	2 years ago —	20___	$ __________
	$__________	Last year —	20___	$ __________
Yearly overtime, commissions, and/or bonuses	$__________	3 years ago —	20___	$__________
	$__________	2 years ago —	20___	$__________
	$__________	Last year —	20___	$__________

B. COMPUTATION OF CURRENT INCOME

	Plaintiff/Petitioner 1	Defendant/Petitioner 2
Base Yearly Income	$__________	$__________
Average yearly overtime, commissions, and/or bonuses over last 3 years (from part A)	$__________	$__________

	Plaintiff/Petitioner 1	Defendant/Petitioner 2
Unemployment Compensation	$________	$________
Disability Benefits		
Workers' Compensation	$________	$________
Social Security	$________	$________
Other: ________	$________	$________
Retirement Benefits		
Social Security	$________	$________
Other: ________	$________	$________
Spousal Support Received	$________	$________
Interest and dividend income (*source*) ________	$________	$________
Other income (*type and source*) ________	$________	$________
TOTAL YEARLY INCOME	$________	$________
Supplemental Security Income (SSI) and/or public assistance	$________	$________
Social Security or Veteran's benefits received for child(ren) ☐ Based on parent's disability ☐ Based on child's disability	$________	$________
Child support you receive from a child support enforcement agency or court order for minor and/or dependent child(ren) not of the marriage or relationship	$________	$________

SECTION III – CHILDREN AND HOUSEHOLD RESIDENTS

Minor and/or dependent child(ren) who is/are adopted or born from this marriage or relationship:

Name	Date of birth	Living with

In addition to the above child(ren):
Plaintiff/Petitioner 1 has__________other minor biological or adopted child(ren).
Defendant/Petitioner 2 has__________other minor biological or adopted child(ren).
There is/are__________adult(s) in your household.

SECTION IV – EXPENSES

List monthly expenses below for your present household.

A. MONTHLY HOUSING EXPENSES

Rent or first mortgage (including taxes and insurance)	$__________
Second mortgage/equity line of credit	$__________
Real estate taxes (if not included above)	$__________
Renter or homeowner's insurance (if not included above)	$__________
Homeowner or condominium association fee	$__________
Utilities	
° Electric	$__________
° Gas, fuel oil, propane	$__________
° Water and sewer	$__________
° Telephone and/or cell phone	$__________
° Trash collection	$__________
° Cable/satellite television	$__________
° Internet service	$__________
Cleaning	$__________
Lawn service and/or snow removal	$__________
Other: ______________________________	$__________
______________________________	$__________
TOTAL MONTHLY:	$__________

B. OTHER MONTHLY LIVING EXPENSES

Food	
° Groceries (including food, paper, cleaning products, toiletries, and other)	$__________
° Restaurant	$__________
Transportation	
° Vehicle loan, lease	$__________
° Vehicle maintenance	$__________
° Gasoline	$__________

° Parking, public transportation $________

Clothing

° Clothes (other than child(ren)'s) $________

° Dry cleaning and laundry $________

Personal grooming

° Hair and nail care $________

° Other: ____________________ $________

Other: ____________________ $________

TOTAL MONTHLY: $________

C. <u>MONTHLY MINOR CHILD-RELATED EXPENSES</u>
(for child(ren) of the marriage or relationship)

Work and/or education-related child care $________

Other child care $________

Extraordinary parenting time travel cost $________

School tuition $________

School lunches $________

School supplies $________

Extracurricular activities and lessons $________

Clothing $________

Child(ren)'s allowances $________

Special and extraordinary needs of child(ren) (not included elsewhere) $________

Other: ____________________ $________

TOTAL MONTHLY: $________

D. <u>MONTHLY INSURANCE PREMIUMS</u>

Life $________

Auto $________

Health $________

Disability $________

Other: ____________________ $________

TOTAL MONTHLY: $________

E. MONTHLY WORK AND EDUCATION EXPENSES FOR SELF

Mandatory work expenses (union dues, uniforms, or other) $__________

Additional income taxes paid (not deducted from wages) $__________

Tuition $__________

Books, fees, and other $__________

College loan $__________

Other: ______________________________ $__________

______________________________ $__________

TOTAL MONTHLY: $__________

F. MONTHLY HEALTH CARE EXPENSES
(not covered by insurance)

Physicians $__________

Dentists and orthodontists $__________

Optometrists and opticians $__________

Prescriptions $__________

Other: ______________________________ $__________

TOTAL MONTHLY: $__________

G. MISCELLANEOUS MONTHLY EXPENSES

Extraordinary obligations for other minor/handicapped child(ren) [for child(ren) who were not born of this marriage or relationship and were not adopted by these parties] $__________

Child support for child(ren) who were not born of this marriage or relationship and were not adopted by these parties $__________

Expenses paid for adult child(ren) or other dependent(s) $__________

Spousal support paid to former spouse(s) $__________

Subscriptions and books $__________

Charitable contributions $__________

Memberships (associations and clubs) $__________

Travel and vacations $__________

Pets $__________

Gifts $__________

Attorney fees $__________

Other: ______________________________ $__________

______________________________ $__________

TOTAL MONTHLY: $__________

H. <u>MONTHLY INSTALLMENT PAYMENTS INCLUDING BANKRUPTCY PAYMENTS</u>

(*Do not repeat expenses already listed.*)
Examples: car, credit card, rent-to-own, or cash advance payments

To whom paid	Purpose	Balance due	Monthly payment
			$
			$
			$
			$
			$
			$
			$
			$
			$
			$
			$
			$
		TOTAL MONTHLY:	**$**

GRAND TOTAL MONTHLY EXPENSES (Sum of A through H): $__________

OATH OR AFFIRMATION
(Do not sign until Notary Public is present)

I, (print name)______________________, swear or affirm that I have read this Affidavit and, to the best of my knowledge and belief, the facts and information stated in this Affidavit are true, accurate, and complete. I understand that if I do not tell the truth, I may be subject to penalties for perjury.

____
Your Signature

STATE OF ______________________)
) **SS**
COUNTY OF ____________________)

Sworn to or affirmed before me by______________________this______day of_____________,_______.

____
Signature of Notary Public

____
Printed Name of Notary Public

Commission Expiration Date: _____________

(Affix seal here)

D. PRACTICE GUIDANCE

You know from the case file that there are going to be valuation issues involving stock options. Here is a short practice guidance offering some context and perspective about how these issues might play out in litigation and the role that expert witnesses can play.

Massachusetts Continuing Legal Education, Inc.
Trying Divorce Cases in Massachusetts
Chapter 13

EFFECTIVE USE OF EXPERTS
Donald G. Tye, Esq., et. al.

§ 13.4.2. Selecting the Expert

No good trial attorney would employ a potential expert witness without a face-to-face meeting. You want an expert who appears honest, confident, and competent but not condescending. He or she should have a neat appearance and a respectful and dignified attitude. Good eye contact and a personable style will enhance your expert's credibility with the judge. Remember that your expert is, in some sense, a teacher who must instruct the trier of fact. Some highly qualified technical experts are poor teachers.

(a) *Prior Experience*

If you are hiring an expert to testify, qualifications are not enough. You want an expert who will make a credible and persuasive witness. Prior experience in court, reputation, and demeanor are of great significance. That does not mean that you should never consider an expert without prior experience to testify as an expert witness. Often, the "practical" expert, who qualifies to offer expert opinion testimony by virtue of his or her life experience, familiarity with the particular subject, and work in the particular field, may have greater credibility than the "theoretical" expert. * * *

(c) *Personality Factors*

An expert's communication skills are particularly important when the subject is technical or complex. Experts need to be capable of explaining their opinions in simple, clear terms—substituting plain English for technical jargon. If your expert will be testifying on a subject that the judge may well be unfamiliar with, you should take that into account. The expert's testimony should be a teaching exercise.

(d) *Special Knowledge*

Whether your expert is sufficiently qualified to be permitted to testify as an expert witness in the subject area at issue is a preliminary question of fact that must be decided by the judge. General knowledge in the field may not be enough to qualify your witness as an expert. Your expert must have specific knowledge of the particular subject matter in question. The judge's discretionary determination will not be reversed on appeal unless no evidence supports his or her conclusion. *Commonwealth v. Roy*, 2 Mass. App. Ct. 14, 22 (1974). Keep in mind that, even if a judge qualifies your expert, the weight accorded their testimony is solely in the judge's discretion.

E. LAW FIRM BILLABLE TIME SHEET

Law Firm Time Sheet

Date: ___/___/_____

Attorney's Name: ____

Case No.:__________________

Task Description	Start Time	End Time	Initials	Total Time
			Total Billable Hours	

Attorney's Signature: ____ Date: ___/___/_____

V. THE SIMULATION

This simulation brings together many real-world aspects of family law lawyering. You have a new client, Cody Williams, and you promptly filed the initial divorce papers, but now there are many steps to develop the case further. Lawyers must be proactive and think several steps ahead. Lawyers need to be versatile, preparing for both litigation and negotiated settlements. Lawyers need to objectively advise their clients about possible outcomes with restraint and caution. Lawyers need to persuasively advocate for their clients and anticipate conflicts that could arise. This simulation prompts all of these interconnected complex lawyering skills.

This simulation has five steps. These practice exercises include an important real-world ethical overlay. In every client representation, you would track your hours honestly, thoroughly, and consistently. Here, the partner is particularly concerned about exceeding the initial retainer with the client. She wants you to manage your time carefully. Thus, as you complete the first four tasks, monitor your time accurately.

A. DRAFTING AN AFFIDAVIT

The partner has asked you to begin completing the Affidavit of Income and Expenses. This is important because it is a court filing that requires careful client consultation. It involves extracting relevant financial information from our initial client intake and identifying follow-up information to obtain from our client.

B. INTERVIEWING AN EXPERT WITNESS

The partner has asked you to prepare to interview a potential expert witness. What information do you need to know about their qualifications? What questions should you ask? Think about how important it might be to understand the expert's background and experiences as well as gauging their demeanor and disposition. This expert will have one specific task—valuing Sarah's stocks in the family tire business.

Ethical Considerations: The partner suggested that you could use artificial intelligence (AI) to obtain some general questions for interviewing the expert witness. What ethical rules govern your use of AI while providing legal representation to a client? Do you need to obtain consent from your client prior to your search? The answer may depend on the local and/or state rule(s) set forth in your jurisdiction.

C. RESEARCHING CASE LAW

The partner has asked you to research cases anticipating how the stock options might affect Sarah's argument for alimony. Draft a short memorandum explaining the relevant case law. Recall how to conduct cost-effective legal research here. You are looking for cases that cite to the alimony statute, and you already have the alimony statutory cite. Thus, you have a very efficient path into relevant cases. Your partner has directed you to be cost-efficient. You do not want to sift through hundreds and hundreds of cases.

D. COUNSELING THE CLIENT

Finally, Cody has directly inquired about the status of the house. With property distribution matters, there is rarely such a thing as a discreet and quick question. Rather, the outcome on one isolated question is likely interconnected to the entirety of the property distribution analysis. Prepare to call Cody back with guidance on this question. This legal advice will require you to push against client's frequent misunderstandings of how the legal system works. Help him understand the equitable distribution framework and how the house will fit in this framework holistically.

E. TRACKING ATTORNEY TIME

Attorneys usually track their time for clients in tenths or ten-minute increments. This assists with billing clients who pay retainers for legal services. Ethically, rounding up or down should occur once you reach a threshold number or increment. For example, if you have a phone conference with opposing counsel that lasts fifteen minutes, the client is billed for 0.2 (20 minutes) of time. Once you reach a five-minute increment, you can round up, but if the number is below five, you should round down.

CHAPTER NINE

NEGOTIATION

I. INTRODUCTION

Negotiation is a critical skill for family law lawyers to develop and refine throughout their careers. The relevance of strong negotiation skills to the practice of family law cannot be overstated. Family law lawyers are negotiating daily on issues that range from the mundane to the critical. Minor issues, such as extensions for discovery deadlines and factual stipulations, are often negotiated via email correspondence or formal letter agreements. Family law lawyers also negotiate weighty and impactful matters that are central to client's lives, such as child custody and possession of the family home, through extensive phone conferences and/or mediation (which is covered in Chapter Ten).

Negotiation is rarely the subject of dramatic television and movie plotlines like adversarial litigation can be. It is not the first image that comes into many law students' minds when they envision the practice of family law. This chapter is very important to help you 'bridge to practice' because negotiations can happen daily for a family law lawyer. The ability to discern when to acquiesce, compromise, or take a hard stance on an issue is vital for all lawyers. It is particularly useful for family law lawyers because they are often working with the same opposing counsel repeatedly throughout the course of their career. Your professional identity can be tied to how well you are able to get along with other attorneys while still obtaining the best outcome for your clients.

Learning Outcomes:

(1) Identify tools and resources available to draft shared parenting plans and practice using these tools to facilitate successful negotiations.

(2) Comply with your client's objectives in achieving a negotiated parenting plan responsively and ethically.

(3) Resolve negotiation disputes with opposing counsel in a manner that meets your client's objectives while maintaining a strong professional identity.

(4) Isolate remaining unresolved parenting issues for judicial resolution.

This chapter notably could have been framed around any of the other subject matter content in the preceding chapters. Parents might negotiate child support to reach an agreement. Couples might negotiate property distribution or alimony to reach a settlement. This chapter frames a negotiation simulation around a shared parenting plan between two parents who have agreed to share custody jointly.

II. OVERVIEW OF THE LAW

Negotiation is an important component of family law practice. Although every legal claim can be settled without contentious litigation, some matters are easier to negotiate than others. Reflect on your studies from the preceding chapters. Some chapters, like child support, had more predictability and consistency in client counseling. Other chapters, like child custody and alimony, had more indeterminacy and subjectivity. Negotiation is particularly effective in helping clients manage uncertainty. Proficient family law lawyers negotiate in the shadows of substantive law and local practice customs, working to bring certainty and resolution to their client's issues. Successful negotiation as a family law attorney requires a strong objective command of the law, effective advocacy skills to assert your client's interests, and a keen ability to anticipate and navigate conflict before it occurs. Negotiation involves a well-developed understanding of power dynamics, leverage, and communication.

Negotiation can occur at the initiation of the parties seeking closure and certainty for themselves. It can also be encouraged and facilitated by the court formally. Negotiation discussions happen outside of the courtroom in a variety of back-and-forth communications between attorneys. This can occur over an extended period of time. Negotiation might alternatively occur in a more structured session, intended to be more expeditious and efficient. The structured meeting is the format that you will use in this simulation exercise.

Negotiation is also a robust component of building your professional identity as a family law lawyer. You will work with family law attorneys in your community on many cases and matters beyond the immediate case at hand. Your ethics, demeanor, professionalism, and judgment are critical components of negotiation. These components of your professional identity are being observed by opposing counsel, opposing clients, your own client, and sometimes the court. Most lawyers are genuinely respectful and professional when appearing in front of a judge because the formalities of the courtroom demand it. Negotiation happens without judicial oversight. Though negotiation happens privately between attorneys, email correspondence and other communications are discoverable. Conflict and discord can occur throughout these interactions. Remember that you are developing and fostering your professional reputation. It is important to remain professional and refrain from negative communication exchanges that do not serve your client's objectives.

This chapter transitions the focus from theoretical family law concepts to the skills and approaches used in family law practice. You will hone and refine negotiation skills every day as you practice family law. If you are considering a career in family law, consider enrolling in a negotiation class to develop this skill further. These courses thoughtfully build out many different aspects of finding middle ground between two parties, including strategies to navigate conflict. They explore psychological and emotional barriers to achieving a settlement. They examine different cooperative and competitive styles to negotiate, as well as analyze the law and ethics of negotiation. They also consider strategies for navigating racial, cultural, and gender differences.

In this simulation, you will negotiate a contract in principle with enough specificity that counsel can draft a comprehensive agreement. In addition to negotiation skills, expert family law lawyers also need strong, sharp drafting skills. It is not enough to just reach an agreement. After the bargaining is complete, the next step is to draft a written agreement reflecting the parties' resolution and secure judicial approval of it.

III. CASE FILE—CODY WILLIAMS V. SARAH WILLIAMS

A. SIMULATION ROADMAP

In this simulation, the class will each represent one parent in a shared custody negotiation. The objective of the assignment is to negotiate on behalf of your client to achieve a shared parenting plan. To assist you in this task, you will review the Ohio statutory law governing shared parenting, practice guidance on custody and visitation negotiation, and some sample models. Both sides will have shared facts from a client intake, and each side will have private facts known just to the lawyer and her client.

We first met Sarah and Cody in Chapter Eight, and we received the following client intake notes from the supervising partner. Sarah and Cody have committed to working together on a shared parenting plan. These are the common facts known to both Sarah and Cody. In Section IV, each client will receive separate negotiation instructions.

B. CLIENT INTAKE MEMO

From the desk of Patricia Partner
CONFIDENTIAL
Attorney Work Product

I met with Cody Williams today. He has hired us to petition for divorce in Ohio from his wife, Sarah Williams. Sarah and Cody Williams were married in Ohio on August YR-10. They met as students at The Ohio State University. They got married immediately after graduation. Sarah came from a very wealthy family, and she held unvested stock options in the family tire business in Ohio, valued at $200,000 in YR-10. Because of this family wealth, her parents pressured her to obtain a prenuptial agreement before marrying. The agreement stated that all of Sarah's stock or proceeds from the stocks in the family tire business would remain her separate property. Cody does not contest or challenge the prenuptial agreement's validity.

When they married, Sarah already owned a condo in the Buckeye Bungalows that her parents bought her as a gift to live in during college (a $120,000 cash purchase). Cody moved in after they married. After graduation, Cody worked as a marketing director for a Columbus medical supply company. He first made $40,000 a year but ultimately progressed to his current salary of $70,000 with $10,000 bonuses annually. Sarah worked as a school guidance counselor making $55,000 a year. Sarah's savings account was $3,500 when they married. She currently has $145,000 in her personal savings account, all of which has come from her parents' annual cash gifts. Cody's savings account had $1,200 in savings when they married. He currently has cash assets of $78,000 spread across his personal checking account, savings account, and investment account. Cody guesses that Sarah's stocks in the family business are presently worth millions, but she says they are "worthless."

In YR-09, Cody's grandpa bequeathed him $30,000. Cody wanted to use that money as a down payment on a larger home for the couple. Due to the poor real estate market, they sold the Buckeye Bungalow condo for $95,000. Sarah and Cody took the $95,000 from the sale and put it in an investment account in their names jointly. Cody manages this account actively. It is presently worth $195,000. Using Cody's $30,000 as the down payment, they jointly bought a four-bedroom home in Cardinal Cul-de-Sac, a trendy up and coming area of Columbus, for $185,000. Today the house is worth $240,000 and they owe $83,250 on their mortgage. Taking advantage of low interest rates, Sarah took out a home equity loan for $50,000 in YR-04 to make some improvements to the property. She used that money to install hard wood floors, redo the kitchen, and convert a half bath into a full. Sarah currently owes $3,900 on the equity line.

Their marriage was happy until YR-05 when their first child, Tate, was born. Sarah nearly died in childbirth after an emergency blood transfusion and a dramatic loss of blood pressure. This scary event, combined with the new joys of parenting, led Sarah to find New Awakenings Church. She became a 'born again' Christian. She ceased all use of alcohol and cigarettes, and she quit her job to focus on 'raising Tate in Christ.'

Although Cody attended church with Sarah, he did not undergo the same transformation she experienced. He continued to smoke cigarettes and drink alcohol regularly. He smoked pot occasionally. This created tension for the couple. Sarah could not see past what she believed to be Cody's 'moral shortcomings.' She worried about the effects of Cody's behavior on Tate and his upbringing. Cody found this frustrating because he used to enjoy game tailgating with Sarah and parties with friends. He felt like she changed the rules in the middle of the marriage, and they no longer had much in common.

In YR-02, Sarah became pregnant with their second child, Ruby Jane. The stress of this pregnancy was too much for them. Cody desperately wanted Sarah to terminate the pregnancy, but Sarah refused and committed to raising the child on her own. She could no longer tolerate living with someone who would even consider ending the pregnancy. Sarah moved out of the marital home on August 1, YR-02. She moved into her grandmother's home in Kentucky, which was vacant after her grandmother relocated to an assisted living facility. Cody and Sarah have lived largely separate lives since. Cody sees the kids every other weekend and they have found a 'new normal' living apart.

In YR-00, however, Cody met his current girlfriend, Isabelle. He now wants to end his marriage so he can remarry someday. Although he and Sarah had lived apart for years, they were never formally separated legally.

Sarah's grandmother's house has four bedrooms. Wanting to serve her community, she connected with the Holy Saints Church in Kentucky. She now uses the fourth bedroom as a refuge for wayward individuals who need a place to stay based on pastoral referrals. During the year she has lived in this house, over 30 different people have stayed in her spare room, including homeless youth, undocumented asylum-seekers, pregnant teens, and mentally ill adults. She charges $15 a night because she wants to teach accountability and responsibility. She donates all the proceeds back to the church though.

Sarah's parents continue to support her with cash gifts of $20,000 annually. This summer, Sarah was diagnosed with Lyme disease. Cody has started to see the kids more because of her fatigue and chronic pain. She mentioned at their last hand-off that her medical bills were piling up.

C. RELEVANT STATUTORY LAW AND PRACTICE GUIDANCE

Your legal research located the following materials to prepare you for this negotiation simulation. You have located a statute governing shared parenting plans, practice guidance offering tips and insights in negotiating shared parenting plans, and model plans located on your state supreme court website. Each of these materials provides insight into the substance and skills you will apply during this negotiation simulation.

1. Ohio Statute

Title 31. Domestic Relations

Chapter 3109: Children

§ 3109.04. Court awarding parental rights and responsibilities; shared parenting; modifications; best interests of child; child's wishes

(A) In any divorce, legal separation, or annulment proceeding and in any proceeding pertaining to the allocation of parental rights and responsibilities for the care of a child, upon hearing the testimony of either or both parents and considering any mediation report filed pursuant to section 3109.052 of the Revised Code and in accordance with sections 3127.01 to 3127.53 of the Revised Code, the court shall allocate the parental rights and responsibilities for the care of the minor children of the marriage. Subject to division (D)(2) of this section, the court may allocate the parental rights and responsibilities for the care of the children in either of the following ways: * * *

(2) If at least one parent files a pleading or motion in accordance with division (G) of this section and a plan for shared parenting pursuant to that division and if a plan for shared parenting is in the best interest of the children and is approved by the court in accordance with division (D)(1) of this section, the court may allocate the parental rights and responsibilities for the care of the children to both parents and issue a shared parenting order requiring the parents to share all or some of the aspects of the physical and legal care of the children in accordance with the approved plan for shared parenting. If the court issues a shared parenting order under this division and it is necessary for the purpose of receiving public assistance, the court shall designate which one of the parents' residences is to serve as the child's home. * * *

(B)(1) When making the allocation of the parental rights and responsibilities for the care of the children under this section in an original proceeding or in any proceeding for modification of a prior order of the court making the allocation, the court shall take into account that which would be in the best interest of the children. In determining the child's best interest for purposes of making its allocation of the parental rights and responsibilities for the care of the child and for purposes of resolving any issues related to the making of that allocation, the court, in its discretion, may and, upon the request of either party, shall interview in chambers any or all of the involved children regarding their wishes and concerns with respect to the allocation.* * *

(D)(1)(a) Upon the filing of a pleading or motion by either parent or both parents, in accordance with division (G) of this section, requesting shared parenting and the filing of a shared parenting plan in accordance with that division, the court shall comply with division (D)(1)(a)(i), (ii), or (iii) of this section, whichever is applicable:

(i) If both parents jointly make the request in their pleadings or jointly file the motion and also jointly file the plan, the court shall review the parents' plan to determine if it is in the best interest of the children. If the court determines that the plan is in the best interest of the children, the court shall approve it. If the court determines that the plan or any part of the plan is not in the best interest of the children, the court shall require the parents to make appropriate changes to the plan to meet the court's objections to it. If changes to the plan are made to meet the court's objections, and if the new plan is in the best interest of the children, the court shall approve the plan. If changes to the plan are not made to meet the court's objections, or if the parents attempt to make changes to the plan to meet the court's objections, but the court determines that the new plan or any part of the new plan still is not in the best interest of the children, the court may reject the portion of the parents' pleadings or deny their motion requesting shared parenting of the children and proceed as if the request in the pleadings or the motion had not been made. The court shall not approve a plan under this division unless it determines that the plan is in the best interest of the children. * * *

(b) The approval of a plan under division (D)(1)(a)(ii) or (iii) of this section is discretionary with the court. The court shall not approve more than one plan under either division and shall not approve a plan under either division unless it determines that the plan is in the best interest of the children. If the court, under either division, does not determine that any filed plan or any filed plan with submitted changes is in the best interest of the children, the court shall not approve any plan.

(c) Whenever possible, the court shall require that a shared parenting plan approved under division (D)(1)(a)(i), (ii), or (iii) of this section ensure the opportunity for both parents to have frequent and continuing contact with the child, unless frequent and continuing contact with any parent would not be in the best interest of the child.

(d) If a court approves a shared parenting plan under division (D)(1)(a)(i), (ii), or (iii) of this section, the approved plan shall be incorporated into a final shared parenting decree granting the parents the shared parenting of the children. Any final shared parenting decree shall be issued at the same time as and shall be appended to the final decree of dissolution, divorce, annulment, or legal separation arising out of the action out of which the question of the allocation of parental rights and responsibilities for the care of the children arose.

No provisional shared parenting decree shall be issued in relation to any shared parenting plan approved under division (D)(1)(a)(i), (ii), or (iii) of this section. A final shared parenting decree issued under this division has immediate effect as a final decree on the date of its issuance, subject to modification or termination as authorized by this section. * * *

(F)(1) In determining the best interest of a child pursuant to this section, whether on an original decree allocating parental rights and responsibilities for the care of children or a modification of a decree allocating those rights and responsibilities, the court shall consider all relevant factors, including, but not limited to:

(a) The wishes of the child's parents regarding the child's care;

(b) If the court has interviewed the child in chambers pursuant to division (B) of this section regarding the child's wishes and concerns as to the allocation of parental rights and responsibilities concerning the child, the wishes and concerns of the child, as expressed to the court;

(c) The child's interaction and interrelationship with the child's parents, siblings, and any other person who may significantly affect the child's best interest;

(d) The child's adjustment to the child's home, school, and community;

(e) The mental and physical health of all persons involved in the situation;

(f) The parent more likely to honor and facilitate court-approved parenting time rights or visitation and companionship rights;

(g) Whether either parent has failed to make all child support payments, including all arrearages, that are required of that parent pursuant to a child support order under which that parent is an obligor;

(h) Whether either parent or any member of the household of either parent previously has been convicted of or pleaded guilty to any criminal offense involving any act that resulted in a child being an abused child or a neglected child; whether either parent, in a case in which a child has been adjudicated an abused child or a neglected child, previously has been determined to be the perpetrator of the abusive or neglectful act that is the basis of an adjudication; whether either parent or any member of the household of either parent previously has been convicted of or pleaded guilty to a violation of section 2919.25 of the Revised Code or a sexually oriented offense involving a victim who at the time of the commission of the offense was a member of the family or household that is the subject of the current proceeding; whether either parent or any member of the household of either parent previously has been convicted of or pleaded guilty to any offense involving a victim who at the time of the commission of the offense was a member of the family or household that is the subject of the current proceeding and caused physical harm to the victim in the commission of the offense; and whether there is reason to believe that either parent has acted in a manner resulting in a child being an abused child or a neglected child;

(i) Whether the residential parent or one of the parents subject to a shared parenting decree has continuously and willfully denied the other parent's right to parenting time in accordance with an order of the court;

(j) Whether either parent has established a residence, or is planning to establish a residence, outside this state.

(2) In determining whether shared parenting is in the best interest of the children, the court shall consider all relevant factors, including, but not limited to, the factors enumerated in division (F)(1) of this section, the factors enumerated in section 3119.23 of the Revised Code, and all of the following factors:

(a) The ability of the parents to cooperate and make decisions jointly, with respect to the children;

(b) The ability of each parent to encourage the sharing of love, affection, and contact between the child and the other parent;

(c) Any history of, or potential for, child abuse, spouse abuse, other domestic violence, or parental kidnapping by either parent;

(d) The geographic proximity of the parents to each other, as the proximity relates to the practical considerations of shared parenting;

(e) The recommendation of the guardian ad litem of the child, if the child has a guardian ad litem.

(3) When allocating parental rights and responsibilities for the care of children, the court shall not give preference to a parent because of that parent's financial status or condition.

(G) * * * A plan for shared parenting shall include provisions covering all factors that are relevant to the care of the children, including, but not limited to, provisions covering factors such as physical living arrangements, child support obligations, provision for the children's medical and dental care, school placement, and the parent with which the children will be physically located during legal holidays, school holidays, and other days of special importance.

2. Practice Guidance—Child Custody Practice and Procedure

Child Custody Practice and Procedure
Linda D. Elrod

(Internal citations omitted)

§ 16:2. Negotiation

* * * Negotiation traditionally has been rooted in the adversarial model which is competitive and has been associated with either hard or soft positional bargaining and "winning" and "losing." Positional (or adversarial) negotiators see negotiations as an exchange of offers and counteroffers for a limited resource, such as number of days of residency with a child. They approach negotiations by viewing that a win for one parent is a loss for the other. The goal is often to "win" as much as possible. The parties seldom speak to each other directly. The lawyer tries to maximize the gain to the client, often capitalizing upon the other party's weaknesses. Any compromises are based on the advice of attorneys based on the perceived chances of winning in a courtroom battle. The lawyers try to reach a settlement without the necessity of a prolonged trial.

Many negotiators are moving toward the problem solving or interest-based approach, where the goal is to separate the parties from the problems and to develop options that will benefit everyone. Recent literature indicates this type of negotiation is more efficient and productive, resulting in less damage to relationships. The problem-based approach requires extensive planning and an understanding of the parties' underlying needs and objectives before solutions can be developed. The four basic principles for problem-solving negotiators are: (1) separate people from the problem; (2) focus on interests, not positions; (3) invent options for mutual gain; and (4) insist on objective criteria to resolve disputes. The keys to successful negotiation are the ability of the lawyer to educate the client and the level of trust and cooperation between the lawyers for the parties.

Any negotiation has four phases:

(1) Planning,

(2) Exchanging information,

(3) Conceding and compromising, and

(4) Reaching an agreement.

The planning stage includes ascertaining the client's goals and objectives as well as considering the means of attaining them. The lawyer needs to learn the facts underlying the dispute and figure out what additional information is needed through formal or informal discovery. Good negotiators are prepared.

After researching or reviewing relevant law, the lawyer can advise the client of the current status and get the client's input on negotiation strategy. The lawyer needs to ascertain the strengths and weaknesses of the client's case before talking with the other lawyer. In exchanging information, the lawyers may talk on the phone, write letters, or meet face to face. The lawyers will discuss their first impressions. The reputation and demeanor of the lawyers may determine the course and tenor of the future negotiations. One of the major considerations will be how the lawyer thinks the judge would decide the case based on the facts.

After exchanging information, the lawyers and the parties explore ways to settle disputed points. Someone has to make the first offer. Although there are strategists who argue that it makes a difference who makes the first offer, in most situations the first offer merely starts the process, and it may not make any difference in the long run, as long as the offer is not so extreme as to alienate and polarize the parties from the outset. In any event, the first offer should set the parameters for negotiation and include room for expansion or reduction.

After the first offer the lawyers and clients can offer counterproposals and the give and take of negotiation gets moving. The lawyer should help the client see the advantages of compromising on some issues to reduce the areas of disagreement. Compromises and concessions are an integral part of the negotiation process. Ethically, the lawyer in the negotiation process must be truthful and not knowingly make a false statement of a material fact or law.

Judges have taken a more active role in recent years in trying to encourage settlement by requiring lawyers and their clients to attend one or more pretrial conferences. The judge, as a neutral party, gives the lawyers and clients a preliminary feel as to how he or she might rule on some issues, such as admission of evidence or importance of an admission of adultery, which may reduce the number of items to be negotiated. * * *

The court has the discretion to accept and incorporate the parties' negotiated agreement. The negotiated agreement of the parties is a contract. In most instances, it will be in writing. Most judges will adopt a settlement agreement of the parties using guidelines that the agreement is "valid, just, and equitable." Because of the *parens patriae* interest in children, the court is not bound by the parties' agreement respecting a child, but must look to see if the agreement is in the child's best interests. If the agreement is unduly burdensome or not in the child's best interests, the court may require the parties to go back to the negotiation table or make a different order in the child's best interest. In most cases, the court will approve the agreement of the parties.

3. Ohio Sample Parenting Plan Schedules

Any time you perform a new family law skill, remember that it is new *to you*, but others have been in your shoes before. Unrepresented clients will also be performing some of these same tasks without having attended law school. There are accordingly many user-friendly guides and materials to help draft parenting plans. The terminology may differ from state to state and over time, but the underlying skills and issues remain the same. Modern terminology is more commonly framed around "parenting time" than "custody or visitation," but follow your local conventions and norms.

The following excerpts are from the Ohio Supreme Court's "Planning for Parenting Time Ohio's Guide for Parents Living Apart." The tool is available online at https://www.supremecourt.ohio.gov/docs/Publications/JCS/parentingGuide.pdf. You may find more useful content by reviewing the full parenting guide document online.

Be prepared in your negotiation simulation to arrive at the simulation exercise knowing which model is preferable for your client.

Parenting Time Schedules

PARENTING TIME SCHEDULES

The following schedules are ***just ideas*** *that may or may not work for your children. Feel free to use one of the numbered schedules or design a schedule that works best for your children, based on work, school, activities and other considerations.*

Use a blank calendar to design the schedule that best meets your needs. See sample of completed schedules on pages 12 and 13. ***For your convenience, a full-sized blank calendar is located on page 80.***

It is recommended that you read the Child Development section that applies to your child before deciding on a parenting time schedule.

Parenting Time Schedule

Sun	Mon	Tue	Wed	Thu	Fri	Sat

Parenting Time Schedules

SUMMARY OF PARENTING TIME SCHEDULES

Schedule Number	Description	PAGE	BIRTH – 2 YEARS	2 – 3 YEARS	3 – 5 YEARS	6 – 9 YEARS	10 – 12 YEARS	TEENAGERS (13 – 18 YEARS)
1	Three periods of 3-5 hours spaced throughout each week	14 25	✓					
2	Two periods of 4-6 hours spaced throughout each week	14 25	✓					
3	Two 3-5 hour periods and one 8-hour period spaced throughout each week	14 26 29	✓	✓	✓			
4	Two periods of 3-6 hours and 1 overnight each week	15 27 29	✓	✓	✓			
5	One period of three to six hours and two non-consecutive overnights each week	15 27 30	✓	✓	✓			
6	An equal parenting time schedule where the child is not away from the other parent for more than two consecutive days ***Caution** – This schedule is designed <u>**only**</u> for those parents who can agree on this schedule.	16 27	✓*	✓*	✓*			
7	One period of 3-6 hours and two consecutive overnights each week	17 31		✓	✓			

Parenting Time Schedules

Schedule Number	Description	PAGE	BIRTH – 2 YEARS	2 – 3 YEARS	3 – 5 YEARS	6 – 9 YEARS	10 – 12 YEARS	TEENAGERS (13 – 18 YEARS)
8	Two days with one parent (including overnights) followed by 3 days with the other parent (including overnights) with this schedule continuing over time	17 31		✓	✓			
9	Two consecutive overnights every other week. An additional three- to six-hour period or overnight may be added each week.	18 33 38 43 51			✓	✓	✓	✓
10	Three consecutive overnights every other week and an additional 4-6-hour period each week	18 33 38 43 51			✓	✓	✓	✓
11	Four consecutive overnights during Week 1 and one overnight during Week 2	19 34 39 44 51			✓	✓	✓	✓
12	Split each week and weekend	20 35 40 45 51			✓	✓	✓	✓
13	Each parent has the same 2 consecutive weekday overnights each week and alternates the weekends	21 35 36 40 45 51			✓	✓	✓	✓
14	The parents share time with the child during alternating 7-day periods. A midweek overnight period is optional with the parent who does not have parenting time that week.	22 40 41 45 46 52				✓	✓	✓

Parenting Time Schedules

SAMPLE A: COMPLETED SCHEDULE FOR CHILDREN AGES 8-10

Parenting Time Schedule

Sun	Mon	Tue	Wed	Thu	Fri	Sat
	Mom	Mom Dad 4:30-7:30 p.m.	Mom	Mom Dad 4:30 p.m. Overnight	Dad	Dad
Dad Mom 6 p.m.	Mom	Mom Dad 4:30-7:30 p.m.	Mom	Mom Dad 4:30-7:30 p.m.	Mom	Mom
Mom	Mom	Mom Dad 4:30-7:30 p.m.	Mom	Mom Dad 4:30 p.m. Overnight	Dad	Dad
Dad Mom 6 p.m.	Mom	Mom Dad 4:30-7:30 p.m.	Mom	Mom Dad 4:30-7:30 p.m.	Mom	Mom
Mom	Mom	Mom Dad 4:30-7:30 p.m.	Mom	Mom Dad 4:30 p.m. Overnight	Dad	Dad

Parenting Time Schedules

SAMPLE B: COMPLETED SCHEDULE FOR CHILDREN AGES 8-10

<table>
<tr><th colspan="7">Parenting Time Schedule</th></tr>
<tr><th>Sun</th><th>Mon</th><th>Tue</th><th>Wed</th><th>Thu</th><th>Fri</th><th>Sat</th></tr>
<tr><td rowspan="2"></td><td rowspan="2">Mom</td><td rowspan="2">Mom</td><td>Mom</td><td rowspan="2">Dad</td><td rowspan="2">Dad</td><td rowspan="2">Dad</td></tr>
<tr><td>Dad
6 p.m.</td></tr>
<tr><td>Dad</td><td rowspan="2">Mom</td><td rowspan="2">Mom</td><td>Mom</td><td rowspan="2">Dad</td><td>Dad</td><td rowspan="2">Mom</td></tr>
<tr><td>Mom
6 p.m.</td><td>Dad
6 p.m.</td><td>Mom
6 p.m.</td></tr>
<tr><td rowspan="2">Mom</td><td rowspan="2">Mom</td><td rowspan="2">Mom</td><td>Mom</td><td rowspan="2">Dad</td><td rowspan="2">Dad</td><td rowspan="2">Dad</td></tr>
<tr><td>Dad
6 p.m.</td></tr>
<tr><td>Dad</td><td rowspan="2">Mom</td><td rowspan="2">Mom</td><td>Mom</td><td rowspan="2">Dad</td><td>Dad</td><td rowspan="2">Mom</td></tr>
<tr><td>Mom
6 p.m.</td><td>Dad
6 p.m.</td><td>Mom
6 p.m.</td></tr>
<tr><td rowspan="2">Mom</td><td rowspan="2">Mom</td><td rowspan="2">Mom</td><td>Mom</td><td rowspan="2">Dad</td><td rowspan="2">Dad</td><td rowspan="2">Dad</td></tr>
<tr><td>Dad
6 p.m.</td></tr>
</table>

Child Development and Suggested Parenting Schedules

3 TO 5 YEARS

Three- to five-year-olds are attached to their regular caregivers, and separation may make them uncomfortable and anxious. They also may be fearful about unfamiliar activities and objects and may experience night fears like "monsters" under the bed.

Three- to five-year-olds may show increased emotional discomfort when moving between parents' homes. Some of these children may become very upset at these times. This behavior does not necessarily mean that the other parent is not a good parent or that the child does not want to be with the other parent. Parents can make exchanges easier for children by following predictable schedules and making sure the child is not exposed to conflict between the parents.

Children are more likely to resist going to the other parent if the parents are tense, hostile or argue with each other at the exchange. If tension is present, the child might become difficult to manage or might act out negative feelings. If parents cannot be nice to each other, or at least civil, they should avoid talking to each other at these exchanges. Parents must not use the child as a messenger to communicate with the other parent. Children also may feel more secure if they can take favorite stuffed toys, family photos or other objects that will remind them of the other parent.

After age three, children become more aware of holiday celebrations. Parents should schedule holidays, which may be religious, cultural, or national, that are meaningful to the child and the family. Parents should also include birthdays, Mother's Day and Father's Day in the parenting schedule.

Three- to five-year-olds may benefit from structured time with children their own age, away from parents. This time helps them develop social skills and learn that they can be safe and happy away from both parents.

Research the Law: You are preparing for a negotiation with your opposing counsel of a shared custody arrangement applying Ohio law. Many states have drafting tools, software, and templates available for practitioner and public use. These tools can provide a useful starting point in your drafting and ensure that your settlement results are robust and comprehensive. These tools also remind us that the typical online legal research tools that you study and work with in introductory legal research and writing courses play a critical role in locating statutes, cases, and some secondary sources. There are other practice-specific tools too. As you develop expertise in a particular field you will also become familiar with publicly available tools and resources through your state courts.

Research whether Ohio has a reputable, publicly available tool for drafting shared parenting plans. You will not use this tool in this negotiation exercise, but you may find it helpful to prepare for a thorough and comprehensive negotiation. If you anticipate practicing in another jurisdiction after law school, you are welcome to research your home state instead of Ohio to locate a parenting plan or shared custody drafting tool or template.

IV. THE SIMULATION

A. NEGOTIATING A PARENTING PLAN

In this simulation, you will represent either Sarah or Cody in a negotiation of a shared parenting agreement. You should only read the following instructions designated for ***your client***. This document describes your client's objectives and desired outcomes in the visitation exercise. Your professor may conduct this negotiation exercise during class time or outside of class time. Either way, from the moment the exercise begins, you are role-playing as a practicing family law lawyer representing your client. Bring a strong sense of professional commitment to sound ethics, judgment, and sensitive communication while negotiating in a zealous client-centered approach.

Your goal is to agree to as many terms as is feasible within the time frame that you have. Isolate any narrow issues that remain for resolution. You need not draft the agreement in its entirety, but you should discuss the agreement with enough precision and specificity to make the drafting process self-executing after your negotiation is complete. For example, saying that Dad gets "weekends" is far too general and imprecise. Instead, clarify what time and day marks the beginning of the weekend and the end of the weekend, consider how you will handle "holiday" weekends, and consider where the exchange will occur. Negotiate preventatively too. How will deviations in the schedule work? How will conflicts be resolved? What if one parent is going out of town and leaving the kids with a sitter during their parenting time? Should the other parent have a right to acquire that additional parenting time? Use clear-cut language that offers the flexibility necessary for your client to deal with normal parenting issues that may arise among parents raising children in separate homes.

The models provided in Section IV.C. provide a very useful starting point for your negotiations. Avoid starting with a narrow focus. Consider agreeing upon a general scheduling framework first. The full online parenting guide (citation provided in IV.C.) can also be a useful tool to work through specific issues.

You should work creatively and collaboratively with your opponent to reach an agreement. If you cannot agree on particular terms, just note those at the end of your agreed order notes.

Do not read the instructions for your opponent or discuss the content in advance of the simulation. You must follow the objectives and directives of your client. You may (and must) make reasonable concessions, so long as these concessions do not conflict with your client's stated objectives. Be resourceful. Maintain a client-centered focus.

CONFIDENTIAL Negotiation Instructions FOR SARAH

Sarah would like Cody's weekends to be shorter with the kids. She is worried about the geographic hardships. Just last week, Tate started a basketball league at their church on Sunday afternoons at 2:00 p.m. She would ideally like the kids to return in time to attend church and other activities in Kentucky on Sundays. Sarah believes Cody should bear the responsibility of transporting the children back and forth since he is the one who initiated the divorce. She would like Cody to drive and drop the kids off at her church by 9:45 a.m. on Sunday. She is willing to allow this for two to three weekends of the month in these shorter segments (Friday night to Sunday morning). This will allow Tate and Ruby Jane to still see friends and attend outings on Sundays. She does not want the kids' friendships and extra-curricular activities to be compromised by the distance. She is also open to Cody coming down to Kentucky once a week to meet the kids for dinner. She was just in a car accident this summer and has suffered some minor back injuries. Sitting in the car for long periods of time is very hard for her currently. Her recovery time is likely another two to three months.

The most important issue to Sarah is the kids' religious upbringing. She has been taking the kids to the New Awakenings Church in Kentucky. She'd like the children to return to her on Sunday in time for her to take them to 10:00 morning services in Kentucky. There are also three branches of this same church in Columbus. She herself attends the one near their marital home occasionally when she is in Ohio. Were the kids ever in Columbus on a Sunday morning, she would like a provision requiring that Cody take the children to New Awakenings Church every Sunday morning for ***both*** Sunday school (10:00) and church services (11:00), with no exceptions for any reason whatsoever other than illness, which she wants disclosed to her. She does not believe that any other church will be acceptable other than New Awakenings. She wants this provision enforced even on vacation, while traveling, etc. She will happily help Cody find a suitable nearby church to attend if he is traveling.

She would also like Cody to read the Bible to the kids every night at bedtime and help them with their prayers daily. She wants him to pre-approve with her any movies or shows that he allows the kids to watch to ensure that they are appropriate to foster the children's moral upbringing. She is very worried about Cody's swearing and overall lack of religious grounding. She wants Cody to be with the kids at church for supervision, but she wants him to divert any questions about the church and its teachings to her for discussion.

She wants Cody to have no alcohol or signs of alcohol in the house while the kids are there. Strongly opposed to sex outside of marriage, Sarah wants Cody to refrain from any overnight dates while the kids are at the house. She wants to meet any of Cody's girlfriends before the children do.

Sarah is worried about the time the kids spend with Cody's parents. Cody's mother has been diagnosed with bipolar disorder and can be quite unstable at times. In a prior encounter when Cody's mom was in a manic state, Cody's mother threw Tate in the pool thinking she was being playful, but she forgot that he could not swim and did not have on a life jacket. Sarah had to jump in to help Tate. Sarah believes that Cody's father is an alcoholic and that he binge drinks regularly. She wants to limit the unsupervised time Tate and Ruby Jane spend with Cody's parents.

Sarah has begun to date someone named Jonathan. He was one of the guests who visited her house this past spring. He was working as a missionary in Honduras. He spends lots of time with Tate and Ruby Jane, but Sarah has not yet told Cody about this. Sarah thinks he is a great influence on her kids. She anticipates that Jonathan will likely propose to her within the year. He has stayed over in the house before as a boarder. He has never stayed with Sarah overnight in her area of the house; their faith does not condone cohabitation or premarital sex among unmarried couples. Sarah knows that Cody will want restrictions on the boarders. Because Sarah anticipates that Jonathan will occasionally stay there as a boarder, she is very uncomfortable with restrictions that would negatively impact Jonathan's relationship with the kids. She is fine with other reasonable restrictions about the boarders. She would prefer not to reveal her relationship with Jonathan to Cody yet.

CONFIDENTIAL Negotiation Instructions FOR CODY

Cody lives three hours away from Sarah in Columbus, Ohio. He is very worried about the burdens of driving given his professional obligations. He wants to have longer and more sustained visits with the kids because he recognizes how hard it will be to drive six hours (round trip) for just a dinner or just a few hours with the kids. He would like visitation from Friday after Tate gets out of school until Sunday night. He would like to see them at least every other weekend. He would also like to be able to take the kids with him on his four weeks of vacation, including one around Christmas, one in the Spring, and two weeks in the summer. His family has an annual family reunion over the Fourth of July every year in Pennsylvania.

Cody knows that church attendance will be a sticking point for Sarah. He is not a strong believer himself, but he is willing to take the kids to a church in Ohio if that is a sticking point for her. He will not, however, take the kids to the New Awakenings Church in Columbus. His reasoning for this is because Sarah attends that church occasionally when she is back in town, and he believes that Sarah has defamed him throughout the congregation.

He is worried about the kids' safety at Sarah's house. He wants to be sure adequate protections are taken with all the guests who stay in Sarah's house. He would like better locks and separators put in place to ensure that the renters are separated from the spaces where his children will be. He also does not want—under any circumstances—to have the kids left alone with any of these houseguests for any reason at any time.

He is very frustrated and concerned with the ways Sarah has badmouthed him to the kids for his lack of religious faith. He wants to be sure that this behavior stops.

Because Sarah has more free time and is the one who elected to leave Columbus, he would like Sarah to drive to Columbus for all childcare exchanges. He is very bitter about the amount of money he is paying in child support and thinks that she is doing very little to ease the transition of their divorce. His vacation time and hours are managed very strictly at his company. If he needed to travel to Kentucky, he would have to take a half-day vacation every Friday. He usually gets off from work at 6:00 p.m., so if he had to then drive to Kentucky and back, he would not meaningfully see the kids on Friday. Tate's school day ends at 2:45 p.m. He believes that Sarah could easily drive to Columbus and have the kids there when his workday ends.

Cody has been actively dating. He strongly believes that this is his life to live. Sarah cannot control his actions anymore. He knows that Sarah is "poisoning" the kids' minds with negative comments about Cody and his lifestyle. He will not agree to any restriction about his life that is not equally imposed on Sarah. He does not want to be regulated by "Sarah's self-righteousness," he says. If Sarah has any intentions to regulate his conduct and behavior, he wants the exact same regulations applied to her.

CHAPTER TEN

MEDIATION

I. INTRODUCTION

Civil and family courts regularly use mediation to resolve legal claims. While there are various alternative dispute resolution (ADR) options for family law matters, such as arbitration and collaborative law, mediation is the most common form of ADR. Mediation can be informal or formal. It typically lasts either a half or whole day. Most civil and family courts mandate mediation prior to a final trial to control the court docket. Mediators are either appointed by the court or jointly chosen by the parties. All parties must come together in good faith to make mediation successful and to bring the litigation to an end. This chapter will present the rules of mediation and engage you in how to strategically prepare for a mediation in a family law case involving a divorcing couple struggling with their parenting plan and the distribution of their family home.

Learning Outcomes:

(1) Use the common rules of mediation and apply effective mediation skills.

(2) Draft a Mediation Plan Memorandum to prepare for mediation.

(3) Mediate to reach a final settlement agreement for resolvable issues and retain any remaining issues for judicial resolution.

II. OVERVIEW OF THE LAW

Mediation can be used to resolve all of the disputes within the marital dissolution process. Even if there are some issues that are not settled, it can help to resolve some of them so that the final trial is shorter and narrowly limited to particular legal issues. Mediation is usually more successful for clients if you introduce the concept and the purpose of it early during your representation. Lawyers play a critical role in explaining, framing, and visualizing the experience and the possible outcome for the client. Likewise, lawyers can begin mentally preparing for mediation and strategizing approaches as they work through the case.

Mediation is a process, rather than an event. It requires trust-building between the parties, their attorneys, and the mediator. Parties prepare for mediation in various ways depending on the attorney's experience level. Most new attorneys create a mediation plan or notebook that includes relevant laws, cases, documents, and notes from client meetings. Senior attorneys may only prepare a short memorandum due to their experience and knowledge of the law. For mediation to be a productive process, your client should already have been introduced to the concept at the outset of the case so that the idea of prioritizing objectives and potentially compromising on the final outcome of the legal issues is familiar.

Most mediators send a mediation packet to the lawyers prior to the mediation date. This packet will include the mediator's rules and information about attendance, time, cost, and location. Mediators typically request electronic copies of the live pleadings, inventories, calculations, important discovery documents, and any prior written agreements. At the beginning of mediation, parties are allowed to make opening statements, although some mediators begin with separate caucuses or meetings with the parties to save time. Mediators work to identify the issues in the dispute and the motivations of the parties. They help each side assess risk, suggesting creative and collaborative solutions that preserve the values and objectives of each side.

Mediators are neutral, independent third parties who assist adversarial parties in moving toward agreement by facilitating dialogue and compromise. Unlike Chapter Nine negotiations, where attorneys negotiate directly on behalf of their clients, Chapter Ten introduces a trained mediator to help settle disputes. Mediators vary in their experience and familiarity with family law; some are former judges or retired attorneys, while others are practicing family lawyers trained in mediation at various stages of their careers. Most states require family law mediators to complete a state-authorized certification process. Effective mediators possess deep knowledge of family law and strong interpersonal skills that enable them to help parties navigate emotionally charged issues. Drawing on the "shadow of the law" concept from Chapter Three, skilled mediators help parties understand the risks of judicial outcomes and the advantages of settlement. Ethical mediators do not impose decisions but use active listening, empathy, and strategic communication to identify each party's values and motivations, find common ground, and guide the parties toward a mutually acceptable resolution.

III. CASE FILE—PAULA JONES V. KELVIN JONES

A. SIMULATION ROADMAP

In this chapter, you will meet new clients, Kelvin and Paula Jones who live in Boston, Massachusetts. This state initiated the Pathways Case Management System, a case management process in all divisions of their family and probate courts that uses a problem-solving approach to assist with resolving cases earlier.[1] There are three pathways for each case: (1) case management conference, (2) guided resolution, and/or (3) judicial intervention. Pathway 1 involves a Case Management Conference conducted virtually on Zoom by a judicial designee. If an agreement is not reached, the matter could be referred to Pathway 2, which is a guided resolution with court personnel, including a referral to mediation, conciliation, or another form of alternative dispute resolution program. The court has referred the case to mediation. You will work to mediate two intertwined issues—the parenting time schedule and the valuation and disposition of the family home. Both are 'big ticket' items that carry a lot of emotional attachment and are hard for couples to resolve.

To understand the process of family law mediation, you will review a standard set of guidelines for family and divorce mediation. You will also review a mediator skills checklist so that you will be

[1] Probate and Family Court of Commonwealth of Massachusetts, *Pathways Case Management Initiative in the Probate and Family Court* (April 25, 2023), https://www.mass.gov/info-details/pathways-case-management-initiative-in-the-probate-and-family-court#initiation-of-action.

clear on the role of the mediator. Finally, you will review instructions and a checklist for preparing a Mediation Plan Memorandum, which will help you critically analyze the best possible outcomes for your client and help guide your client through the mediation process.

You will represent either Kelvin or Paula in a class simulation of a mediation. There will be a set of facts to which you agree and others which you contest. The agreed set of facts is set forth in the Mediator Memorandum. You will also have a set of values driving your priorities and your client's subjective understanding of what a "successful" mediation means. The mediation client objectives for each client will be provided to you by your professor in a mediation packet. In addition to these objectives, the relevant Massachusetts Family Code sections for parenting time and disposition of real property will be provided in the mediation packet, along with a child custody assessment completed by a court-appointed child custody evaluator.

You will participate in a simulated mediation session with your classmates. In preparation for the mediation simulation, you will prepare a Mediation Plan Memorandum to guide you and your client. The Mediation Documents in Section IV.C. provide the ground rules for the mediation process and assist in memorializing a settlement.

B. MEDIATOR MEMORANDUM

MEMORANDUM

To: Mediator Assigned to Jones Case

From: Modern Mediations, LLC

As we discussed, next week you will be mediating a case for Paula and Kelvin Jones. Paula and Kelvin have been married for five years and have three children, April (7), Damien (4), and Patricia (1). Kelvin is African-American and Paula is a Jamaican-born immigrant. Paula is an anesthesiologist with a premiere hospital in Boston, Massachusetts. When they met, Paula lived in Beacon Hill, an affluent enclave for young medical professionals. She owned a townhome valued at $240,000 at that time. Kelvin worked part time as a free-lance writer for magazines and blogs. Before they married, Kelvin lived in a one-bedroom condominium in Dorchester, a more affordable neighborhood in Boston boasting one of the most diverse zip codes in the region. Kelvin was born and raised in this area. His parents and siblings still live within blocks of this property.

Shortly after they first started dating, the couple conceived their first daughter, April. Uncertain about whether to marry or not, Kelvin rented his condo for a year to local college students and moved in with Paula. One reason straining their decision to marry was Kelvin's mom, Barbara, who was angry and resentful toward Paula for the pregnancy. Barbara, a deeply spiritual woman, believed that Paula was 'hoodwinking' Kelvin to get him to marry her. Barbara resented Paula's immigrant roots and believed that she was not the right woman for Kelvin.

Paula and Kelvin nonetheless married when April was two years old. Kelvin continued to lease his condominium because he was bringing in $3,000 a month in rent, and he was only paying $1,200 monthly on his mortgage. Kelvin continued to work from home as a writer, but he dreamed of starting his own business as a men's clothing designer. He generated his business plan and also acted as the primary caretaker of the couple's three children.

The couple believes deeply in teaching the children about their combined cultural heritage. Paula has traveled home to Jamaica every summer for three weeks to give her children time with their cousins and extended family. She has spent time cultivating a love of Jamaican food, culture, and heritage with their children. Kelvin has worked hard to foster a diverse network of friends and playmates for their children. He regularly returns to his Dorchester neighborhood to take the kids to parks and kid-friendly programs.

Kelvin's mother regularly watches the kids at her home in Dorchester. She watches the children three to four times a week while Kelvin works at a local coffee shop on his writing pursuits and business plan. Her caregiving is vital to Kelvin's ongoing career pursuits. The kids are deeply attached to Barbara. Barbara has also worked to raise the children spiritually as well. She regularly takes the children to her local church. The church, a revered predominantly Black church in the neighborhood, offers the children a critical sense of community and spiritual growth.

Paula is often at work for long shifts spanning into the nights and weekends. Kelvin is tired of effectively functioning as a single parent. He left Paula seven months ago and moved back in with his mother until the lease on his condo expires next month. He filed for divorce, hoping that perhaps it would jolt Paula into focusing less on her career and more on raising her children and saving their marriage. It did not.

Paula instead began a large-scale renovation of the townhome. This renovation was based entirely on plans and designs that Kelvin had developed while their marriage was strong. Paula took Kelvin's designs, hired a contractor, and renovated the kitchen from its 1930s original design into a chic, modern design. She also began the renovation on the townhome's two bathrooms and refinished the hardwood floors. Kelvin's cousin, Jimmy, runs AAAA Contracting in the Boston area. Jimmy did the work for Paula at a substantially discounted rate based on his family relationship with Kelvin.

Kelvin and Paula reconciled with brief periods of intimate relations and cohabitation approximately four to five times during the months of the renovation. Due to Paula's demanding work schedule, Kelvin met the contractors to let them into the unit at least a dozen times. After a dispute between Paula and the contractor, the contractor walked off the job. Kelvin worked carefully and tirelessly to resolve the dispute with Jimmy to get the contractors back out to the townhome to finish the job on time.

Disputed Issues:

1. Shared Parenting Time

Paula is seeking joint physical custody with Kelvin. She does not want Barbara to have unrestrained time with the children. She worries that Barbara is indoctrinating the children through religion and poisoning the children against Paula.

Kelvin wants sole physical custody of the children and the right of first refusal for situations when Paula would merely outsource the kids' care to nannies or babysitters. Kelvin knows that the kids are very attached to their grandmother. His mother is in the early stage of Parkinson's Disease, so he knows that their time with Barbara as a caregiver may be somewhat limited by changes in her mobility.

2. Classification and Value of Family Home

Paula hired a valuation expert to appraise the townhome. Paula's expert concluded that the townhome was worth $670,000 as a combination of both Paula's improvements and passive appreciation. This expert concludes that Kelvin's contributions were merely passive and do not change the separate property classification of the townhome.

Kelvin has hired a valuation expert who agrees that the townhome is worth something in the range of $670,000, but attributes the significant increase in property value to the improvements that the expert says were made on the home using marital income, Kelvin's renovation designs, and a discounted cost for renovations due to Kelvin's family connection to the contractor. Kelvin wants his fair share of the increase in value to the townhome, which the valuation expert estimates is a minimum of $250,000.

Party Agreements:

The couple have already agreed to the following points:

– No alimony will be awarded.

- The couple will have joint *legal* custody of the children.
- Each party will keep their respective separate property.
- The marital property will be divided 50–50.
- Kelvin will buy Paula out of her share of the Boston Red Sox season tickets and the related rights.
- Paula will retain all her personal possessions.
- Kelvin will retain all his personal possessions.

C. GOVERNING SOURCES

State statutes governing the use of ADR and mediation in family law are usually part of both the rules of civil procedure and the family code. Typically, a mediated settlement agreement is binding on the parties. If children are involved, the best interests of the child standard is the overarching consideration for the court.

1. Guidelines for Mediation

In addition to being familiar with the state and local rules for ADR, family law lawyers should also consult the mediation guidelines issued by the Association of Family and Conciliation Courts (AFCC). These guidelines can be found at this link: https://www.afccnet.org/Portals/0/PDF/ModelStandardsOfPracticeForFamilyAndDivorceMediation.pdf?ver=v77klmUz90N86n5wjQye7g%3d%3d. Read this document to understand how family mediations should be conducted, what participants should expect from mediation, and how the mediation process can be used to resolve family disputes.

Rules for mediation are commonplace for lawyers, but most laypersons are not aware of these rules. The mediation rules to be used for this simulation, as well as the Mediation Confidentiality, Waiver, and Consent Agreement, are located in Section IV.C. Family law lawyers should explain the mediation process to clients as well as the ethical boundaries concerning what is communicated between the parties during mediation. A vital part of mediation is good faith. Each party should come to mediation with the intent to make every effort to settle the case.

One of the most frequent complaints about attorneys is their failure to communicate with clients. It is incumbent upon you as the attorney to keep your client apprised of the documents that you are generating and receiving regarding their case. Ongoing communication is vital so that your client does not encounter any surprises that will inhibit their good faith efforts during mediation.

2. Mediator Skills Checklist

The Massachusetts Uniform Rules on Dispute Resolution adopt the following rules governing mediation values and skills.[2] This excerpt from the Mediator Skills Checklist explains what roles mediators play and how they interact with parties in a mediation.

Philosophy: Mediators have an obligation to the public and the profession to conduct their practice in a competent and ethical manner. Central to the code of behavior required of mediators is a commitment to and respect for the parties and the mediation process. Central also is the personal integrity with which each mediator enhances the quality of the process.

The following list of observable behaviors is not intended as an exhaustive list, but as a reflection of the minimum requirements for basic mediator competency. The skills evaluation checklist should be used to evaluate mediators during training, mentoring, and evaluation:

---

[2] Commonwealth of Massachusetts Trial Court Standing Committee on Dispute Resolution, *Supreme Judicial Court Rule 1.18*, Uniform Rules on Dispute Resolution 75–76 (Jan. 2020).

A. Managing the Process

The mediator:

1. Is able to explain the mediation process and role of mediator
2. Sets a tone that helps to put people at ease
3. Guides transitions between stages
4. Has a good sense of timing
5. Is flexible in tailoring the process to the needs of the parties
6. Respects the parties' rights to make their own decisions
7. Upholds the parameters of confidentiality

B. Managing Interactions

The mediator:

1. Maintains an open, honest and supportive atmosphere
2. Treats parties with respect and affirmation
3. Maintains neutrality
4. Demonstrates effective active listening skills
5. Uses clear language
6. Maintains composure when challenged
7. Avoids appearance of bias or favoritism
8. Handles conflict and strong emotions effectively
9. Helps parties to see things positively
10. Helps parties to see problems from the others' point of view
11. Is able to ask tough questions in a non-threatening manner
12. Avoids giving opinions or making judgments
13. Works cooperatively with co-mediator
14. Keeps discussions focused on issues relevant to the negotiations
15. Demonstrates patience and persistence

C. Managing Information

The mediator:

1. Asks relevant and open-ended questions
2. Presents and re-frames information clearly
3. Seeks understanding of underlying needs
4. Determines areas of flexibility
5. Keeps track of new information and changing perspectives
6. Develops strategic direction

7. Introduces brainstorming or role reversal to encourage re-evaluation of positions and development of options and development of options
8. Encourages parties to develop new solutions
9. Identifies common interests
10. Encourages collaborative efforts between parties
11. Recognizes potential areas of agreement
12. Summarizes at appropriate times
13. Supports parties' control of the outcome
14. Helps to frame a clear, balanced, specific and future-oriented agreement

IV. THE SIMULATION

A. MEDIATION ROLE-PLAY

Your professor will divide you into different groups. One group of students will role-play as Kelvin and his attorneys in the mediation pursuing his goals and objectives. Another group of students will role-play as Paula and her attorneys in the mediation pursuing her goals and objectives.

You should read the Rules for Mediation and review them with your client prior to mediation. A Mediation Confidentiality, Waiver and Consent Agreement will be signed by all parties before mediation begins. You should also read this document and review it with your client before you arrive to the mediation. There are copies of these documents included in Section C.

Each party will have three minutes to make an Opening Statement. Be concise and to the point regarding the client's mediation goals. Either the attorney or the client can make the Opening Statement. This is an opportunity to generally state your client's overall objectives for mediating the case and what your client hopes to achieve with settlement of the disputes at hand.

The Mediator will caucus with each spouse and their attorneys after the opening statements to reach a resolution. Students should stay focused on helping their client ensure a successful mediation outcome, whatever that might mean for your client. Be creative and client-centered. Any issues that can be negotiated will be memorialized in a binding settlement agreement. A sample binding settlement agreement is in Section C.

B. DRAFTING A MEDIATION PLAN MEMORANDUM

Preparing for mediation requires strategically considering how the case will proceed with the facts and evidence at trial. The best way to develop a plan for a successful mediation is to draft a mediation plan memorandum for your case. Each client-attorney group is responsible for writing a Mediation Plan Memorandum. The memorandum should be a short guide for you and your client as you go through the mediation process.

A mediation plan memorandum consists of an outline of client goals and strategies to achieve those goals during mediation. Alongside each client goal, it is helpful to note 1) any specific statutory provision that might impact the goal, 2) any factual or legal support or impediment that will impact the client's objectives, including any case precedent and/or public policy that may affect the outcome of the case. Your strategy should include a plan for addressing any negative facts or legal impediments during mediation. A checklist for preparing your mediation plan memorandum is as follows:

Mediation Plan Preparation Checklist:

- Read Rules of Mediation.
- Read Mediation Confidentiality, Waiver, and Consent Agreement.
- Read mediation packet for your assigned role (provided by your professor), containing client's facts and objectives, a child custody assessment, and relevant provisions of Massachusetts law.
- Determine mediation goals and strategy.
- Identify any impediments to client goals and develop a plan for overcoming these obstacles.

C. MEDIATION DOCUMENTS

RULES FOR MEDIATION

1. **Definition of Mediation**: Mediation is a process during which an impartial, neutral person, the mediator, facilitates communication between the parties in a dispute to assist reconciliation, settlement, or understanding among them. The mediator may suggest ways of resolving the dispute but may not impose his or her own judgment on the issues or on either of the parties.

2. **Agreement of Parties**: The parties involved in the mediation of the dispute agree to these Rules by their signatures on the Mediation Confidentiality, Waiver and Consent Agreement.

3. **Consent to Mediator**: The parties consent to the appointment of the individual named as mediator in their case. The Mediator may not act as an advocate for any party to the mediation.

4. **Conditions Precedent to Serving as Mediator**: The mediator shall not serve as mediator in any dispute in which he/she/they has or have any financial or personal interest in the result of the mediation. Prior to accepting an appointment, the Mediator shall disclose any circumstances likely to create a presumption of bias or prevent a prompt meeting with the parties. If the parties disagree as to whether the Mediator shall serve, the Mediator shall not serve.

5. **Authority of Mediator**: The Mediator does not have the authority to decide any issue for the parties but will attempt to facilitate the voluntary resolution of the dispute by the parties. The Mediator is authorized to conduct joint and separate meetings with the parties and to offer suggestions to assist the parties to achieve settlement. If necessary, the Mediator may also obtain expert advice concerning technical aspects of the dispute, provided that the parties agree. Arrangements for obtaining such advice shall be made by the Mediator or the parties, as the Mediator shall determine.

6. **Commitment to Participate in Good Faith**: While no one is asked to commit to settle his/her/their case in advance of mediation, all parties commit to participate in the proceedings in good faith with the intention to settle, if at all possible.

7. **Parties Responsible for Negotiating Their Own Settlement**: The parties understand that the Mediator will not and cannot impose a settlement in their case and agree that they are responsible for negotiating a settlement.

8. **Authority of Representation**: Each party representative agrees that he or she has authority to settle the dispute involved in the mediation and that all persons necessary to the decision to settle shall be present at the mediation.

9. **Time and Place of Mediation**: A mediation coordinator shall coordinate the time of each mediation session. The mediation shall be held at the offices of the mediator, or any other convenient location agreeable to the Mediator and the parties, as the Mediator shall determine.

10. **Identification of Matters in Dispute**: If requested, prior to the first scheduled mediation session, each party shall use his or her best efforts to provide the Mediator and all attorneys of record with an Information Sheet on the form provided by the Mediator, setting forth its position regarding the issues that need to be resolved.

11. **Privacy**: Mediation sessions are private. The parties and their representatives may attend mediation sessions. Other persons that attend such as family members, school personnel, and others will be required to sign a confidentiality agreement.

12. **Confidentiality**: The Mediator shall not divulge confidential information disclosed to the Mediator by the parties or by witnesses during the mediation. All records, reports or other documents received by the Mediator while serving in that capacity shall be confidential. The Mediator or his/her/they employees, agents shall not be requested or compelled to produce or divulge such records or to testify about the mediation in any adversary proceeding or judicial forum. Any party that violates this agreement shall pay all fees and expenses of the Mediator, his/her/they employees, agents, and other parties, including reasonable attorneys' fees, incurred in opposing the efforts to request or compel testimony or records from the Mediator, his/her/they employees, agents. The parties shall maintain the confidentiality of the mediation and shall not rely on, or introduce as evidence in any trial, judicial or other proceeding: a) views expressed or suggestions made by another party with respect to a possible settlement of the dispute; b) admissions made by another party in the course of the mediation proceedings; c) proposals made or views expressed by the Mediator; or d) the fact that another party had or had not indicated willingness to accept a proposal for settlement made by the Mediator.

CONFIDENTIALITY EXCEPTIONS: any allegations of abuse or neglect and any statements of threatened harm to any individual are exceptions to the confidentiality agreement and will be reported by the mediator to the appropriate authorities.

13. **No Stenographic, Audio, Videotape, or AI Record**: There shall be no stenographic record, tape-recording, videotaping, or artificial intelligence (AI) recording of the mediation process.

14. **No Service of Process at or Near the Site of the Mediation Session**: No subpoena, summons, complaints, citations, writs, or other process may be served upon any person at or near the site of any mediation session or upon any person entering, attending, or leaving the session.

15. **Termination of Mediation**: The mediation shall be concluded: a) by the execution of a settlement agreement by the parties; b) by declaration of the Mediator to the effect that further efforts at mediation are no longer worthwhile; or c) by a written or verbal declaration of a party or parties to the effect that the mediation proceedings are terminated.

16. **Exclusion of Mediator**: The Mediator is not a necessary or proper party in judicial proceedings relating to the mediation.

17. **Interpretation and Application of Rules**: The Mediator shall interpret and apply these rules.

18. **Parties to Rely on Own Counsel**: If the mediation is concluded by a settlement agreement, the parties are advised and agree to have the agreement independently reviewed by their own attorneys and counsel before executing the agreement in final form. The parties understand and agree that the Mediator is not acting as an advocate for any party and each party holds that they have not relied upon legal advice or counsel from the Mediator in entering into the settlement agreement.

19. **Weapons and Firearms Ban**: The possession of weapons and firearms is prohibited on the premises of the offices of the Mediator and in all other locations where the mediation may take place.

MEDIATION CONFIDENTIALITY, WAIVER AND CONSENT AGREEMENT

CAUSE NO. ______________________ MEDIATOR: ______________________________

STYLE OF CASE: ____

This Confidentiality, Waiver and Consent Agreement is executed in exchange for participation by the mediator(s) in the mediation pertaining to the above referenced Cause. This agreement pertains only to the matters arising as a result of the mediation of the above referenced Cause.

1. I understand that the mediator is not a legal advisor and is not to provide legal advice to any party involved in mediation. I agree to hold the said mediator harmless for any observations, suggestions or implications that he/she/they may make in the course of mediation. I specifically agree to obtain legal advice on any issue of interest to me from my own attorney and not to rely upon the mediator for such advice.

2. I waive any right of action that I may have against the mediator for any allegation of wrongful conduct on his/her/their part or on the part of his/her/their employees, while acting during the mediation.

3. I agree to the necessity that mediation be confidential and, therefore, agree that I will keep all information disclosed in this mediation confidential within the limits of the law and as provided in this agreement. I will not divulge to persons not present in this mediation what was said or presented at mediation unless permitted by law or this agreement. I will not call the mediators, or their agents or employees who serve on my case to act as witnesses in any court of competent jurisdiction to testify to facts concerning or relating to the subject matter here being mediated, and neither will I subpoena documents or information about my case which may have been retained. **I understand and agree, however, that any allegations of child abuse or neglect and any statements of threatened harm to any individual are exceptions to this confidentiality agreement and will be reported to appropriate authorities.**

4. I agree to treat as confidential anything said by any party as part of an offer to compromise and settle the dispute being mediated. I further agree that statements made during mediation shall be treated as offers to settle and shall not be admissible should this matter result in litigation.

5. I specifically agree, however, that a fully executed settlement agreement can be admitted to any court proceeding without my objection as evidence of such settlement and that any such agreement is enforceable in the same manner as any other written contract.

6. I acknowledge receipt of the Rules for Mediation and agree to abide by them. I consent and agree to these terms of this agreement and waive the rights herein specified, and I acknowledge that I have the right to consult legal counsel before executing this document.

____

Petitioner

____

Petitioner's Attorney

____

Respondent

____

Respondent's Attorney

CAUSE NUMBER

______________________________	§	**IN THE DISTRICT COURT OF**
V.	§	____________________ **COUNTY**
______________________________	§	

BINDING MEDIATED SETTLEMENT AGREEMENT

This settlement agreement resolves the legal issues of Paula Jones and Kelvin Jones, and is in the best interests of their children, April Jones, Damien Jones, and Patricia Jones, Cause No. _______________. **THIS SETTLEMENT AGREEMENT IS NOT SUBJECT TO REVOCATION.** IT IS A BINDING, MEDIATED SETTLEMENT AGREEMENT AMONGST THE SIGNED PARTIES BELOW.

The parties agree to the following terms regarding the physical custody of the children April Jones, Damien Jones, and Patricia Jones:

____
____
____
____
____
____
____
____

The parties agree to the following terms regarding the shared parenting of the children April Jones, Damien Jones, and Patricia Jones:

____
____
____
____
____
____
____
____
____
____
____
____
____
____

The parties agree that it is in the best interests of the children for the following persons to have access to the children April Jones, Damien Jones, and Patricia Jones. The terms of this access are as follows:

____
____
____
____
____
____
____

The parties agree to resolve the property dispute regarding the townhome appreciation as follows:

____

Petitioner

____

Petitioner's Attorney

____

Respondent

____

Respondent's Attorney

CHAPTER ELEVEN

FINAL ORDERS

I. INTRODUCTION

This chapter moves us toward closure in family law matters. Matters may reach closure because the parties reached a private agreement resolving all issues or because a court brought remaining disputes to resolution through a bench or jury trial. Case closure may also come from a combination of the two. The parties might negotiate or mediate most components of the case and need the judge or factfinder to resolve the final outstanding items. The final order in a family law case is the capstone document of the litigation process. It is important for you to effectively and clearly state the final resolution of the case so that the parties have accurate documentation for the future. The final order is like the roadmap for a divorced couple regarding child custody and support, division of property, and any other matters before the court.

Learning Outcomes:

(1) Prepare a final order addressing the resolution of a dissolution of marriage.

(2) Draft an Income Withholding Order for Child Support.

II. OVERVIEW OF THE LAW

Family law matters may come to closure through private agreement or judicial resolution. Regardless of how a case ends, a final order must be executed by the presiding judge. As mentioned in Chapters Nine and Ten, informal negotiations, mediation, arbitration, or a collaborative law process can bring parties together to resolve all issues before the court. If the parties agree to binding mediation or arbitration, the court must execute an order reflecting the mediated settlement agreement or the arbitrator's award. If there is a bench or jury trial on all matters before the court, the final decree of divorce should reflect the findings of fact and conclusions of law, as well as the judge's final orders on all claims.

Whether a private agreement or a judicial resolution, all issues in the case need to be resolved in the final court order. Final orders often incorporate private agreements and/or judicial findings, and they are subject to contempt and enforcement proceedings. The final order is the starting point for any lawyer seeking to modify or enforce the decision of the court. State statutes governing final orders and enforcement of orders are usually part of the rules of civil procedure and the family code. There will also be relevant state law that governs how orders can be enforced if there is a breakdown in the agreement or a violation of the final order.

Preparing the final orders in a divorce, child custody or child support matter is of utmost importance. This final document memorializes the judgment of the court and/or the agreement of the parties, and both parties will refer to it for guidance regarding how to conduct themselves going forward. Final orders are the culmination of many months or years of litigation. It is vital to pay attention to detail and write clearly to meet your client's objectives and resolve the case. If you are tasked with preparing these orders, it is important that you take accurate notes of the judge's ruling, check your notes with the docket sheet where the judge records his or her ruling, and forward a draft of the document to opposing counsel to make sure that there is a mutual understanding of what the judge ruled.

When your final order is complete, you will need to submit the original document to the judge for review and signature, as well as make a certain number of copies. Generally, each party and attorney should receive a copy of the final order, with the original order remaining in the court file. There are different local rules and practices regarding when a judge signs the final order and how the clerk of the court executes copies of the order with the judge's signature stamp. You will need to confirm what the practice is in your jurisdiction.

Once you obtain copies of the final order, you will need to have a few of these copies certified by the court clerk. A certified court order has a raised or stamped seal on each page, verifying that the document is an official, accurate copy of the final order signed by the judge.[1] As noted in Chapter Four, if there is a protective order included in the final order, a certified copy must be delivered to other persons or entities besides the respondent, such as appropriate members of law enforcement, schools, and childcare exchange facilities. Attorneys should also retain a certified copy because it is often a necessary exhibit on a motion to enforce or a motion for contempt. Certified copies require a specific fee, and typically the client bears the cost of this expense.

After a final order has been submitted to the court for signature, there may be other documents that need to be drafted or filled out to effectuate the order. For example, if there has been a change of name after the divorce, the order alone will not change a party's name. A form usually must be filled out and sent, along with the court order, to the state Bureau of Vital Statistics so that the legal name change can take effect for all other government-issued identification. Family law lawyers must also ensure that the appropriate orders or forms are submitted to the appropriate government and private entities (typically the obligor's place of employment) for child support to begin.

Final orders are final judgments ripe for appeal, if appropriate. Family law matters are rarely appealed because the governing standards of review are quite difficult. Appeals involving factual findings, such as a court's conclusion that a mother has bipolar disorder or that the house is worth $98,000, are reviewed under the clearly erroneous standard. The appellate court will only overturn these findings if there is a clear and unmistakable mistake. Only significant factual errors can be challenged on appeal. Appeals based on errors of law such as a court's failure to apply the presumption of shared custody are reviewed using a *de novo* standard. In this instance, the appellate court provides an independent evaluation of the legal issue without deferring to the trial court's decision. However, errors regarding factual findings and errors of law are quite rare.

Finally, appeals of discretionary decisions, such as determining that joint custody of the children is in their best interests, are subject to an abuse of discretion standard. This is the most highly deferential standard for trial court judges. It governs many aspects of family law, such as *how much* alimony is awarded or what a *reasonable* visitation plan looks like. These issues are very difficult to win on appeal. Judges are allowed a wide latitude of discretion regarding family law matters, and appellate courts are reluctant to step into the role of fact finder and change the outcome of a case unless there is an egregious decision that clearly departs from case precedent or public

1 Certified copies typically require a fee. Clients often need these official copies to provide to various entities such as banks, schools, or government agencies to verify account changes, child custody arrangements, or other legal matters.

policy. It should be reiterated that the final order should reflect the accurate judgment of the court and/or agreement of the parties because any appeal will be based on what is set forth in this document.

III. CASE FILE—KATRINA FLETCHER V. MICHELLE SANTOS

A. SIMULATION ROADMAP

After a contested hearing in the Katrina Fletcher v. Michelle Santos case from Chapter Six, the judge issued a final order granting a divorce with final resolution on property distribution, child custody and access, and child support. The judge asked the parties to draft a final order accurately documenting these rulings. Read the following trial notes you documented. You may also need to refer to the client intake in Chapter Six for additional information.

B. TRIAL NOTES

Date: November 15, YR-00
Cause No.: YR-00-3270
Dade County, FL
Circuit Judge Renee Jackson

Final Court Hearing: *In re: The Marriage of Katrina Fletcher vs. Michelle Santos*:

- No-fault divorce granted.
- Value of Michelle's separate property as of the hearing last month calculated at $75,000, including her Toyota Prius ($7,500), her personal savings ($25,000), her retirement account ($45,000), and her grandmother's antique bedroom furniture ($2,500).
- Value of Katrina's separate property as of the hearing last month calculated at $480,000, including her Range Rover ($20,000), her pre-marital N.Y.C. co-op apartment used as a rental property ($600,000), her personal savings ($100,000), and her student loan debt (-$240,000).
- Marital property divided in 55–45 split between Michelle and Katrina, respectively. No award of alimony. The parties agreed to a disproportionate split in the marital assets in lieu of alimony. The judge was concerned that Michelle had contributed greatly to childcare and was presently without a job or permanent housing.
- Marital assets include:
    - $6,700 cash
    - $45,000 E-Trade investment account
    - $50,000 furniture
    - $150,000 life insurance policies
    - $5,000 modern art collection
    - $900,000 N.Y.C. townhome
- Marital debts include:
    - Visa credit card -$14,500
    - Mastercard credit card -$3,580
    - Macy's department store card -$960

- Mortgage on N.Y.C. townhome -$670,000

– The couple agreed that Michelle would retain possession of the home at 92nd & Amsterdam Ave. in N.Y.C. and refinance the mortgage in her name solely. Michelle has until the end of the calendar year to pick up her possessions from the N.Y.C. residence. She must provide Katrina with one week's notice before retrieval.

– The parties will split the costs of hiring an accountant to manage their tax liabilities for the previous and current year.

– Katrina and Michelle are granted joint legal custody of the four children, twins Kaitlyn and Kassidy (DOB 4/17/YR-02), and twins Mason and Monte (DOB 04/30/YR-00). Michelle is granted sole physical custody of all four children and can determine the primary residence of the children. Katrina is granted visitation rights.

– Katrina will travel at her own expense to Florida to visit the children every weekend from 5:00 p.m. Friday until 8:00 p.m. Sunday. Once Michelle secures an apartment, Michelle will vacate the apartment on the weekends, residing instead with her parents, to preserve continuity for the children and to allow Katrina to visit with the children at the apartment. Katrina will have custody of the children for two weeks during each summer, on alternating holiday weekends, and on alternating school holidays with a duration of one week or longer.

– Michelle will have parenting time with the children from 8:00 p.m. Sunday night through 5:00 p.m. Friday. Michelle agrees to FaceTime one weeknight a week with Katrina and the children. The court will incorporate the detailed parenting plan that the parties negotiated.

– Katrina agreed to pay $3,550 monthly in child support. An order of wage withholding will be entered to administer payment. Child support will commence on January 1, YR+01.

– Katrina's employer is Pope, Simpson and Wheeler, LLC. The employer's address is 51 West 52nd Street, Manhattan, New York 10019. Katrina agrees to supply any additional employer information necessary to complete the Income Withholding Order for Child Support.

– Katrina agrees to cover the children on her employer's health and dental insurance policy.

– Both parties agreed to pay their own attorney's fees and costs.

IV. THE SIMULATION

A. PREPARING A FINAL ORDER

The state court website offers the following form for use in family law matters. Less complex forms are available for simpler cases. Use this form to prepare a draft order finalizing the judge's decisions in the case. When drafting the final order, pay attention to what content should be reflected in the document. The client file may be missing some dates or other specific information. Students should use the information provided and add placeholders for any missing information. All substantive content should be incorporated thoroughly and accurately.

IN THE CIRCUIT COURT OF THE ______________________ JUDICIAL CIRCUIT
IN AND FOR ______________________ COUNTY, FLORIDA

Case No.: ______________________
Division: ______________________

In Re: The Marriage of:

______________________,
Petitioner,

and

______________________,
Respondent.

FINAL JUDGMENT OF DISSOLUTION OF MARRIAGE WITH DEPENDENT OR MINOR CHILD(REN)

This cause came before this Court for a trial on a Petition for Dissolution of Marriage. The Court, having reviewed the file and heard the testimony, makes these findings of fact and reaches these conclusions of law:

FINDINGS:

1. The Court has jurisdiction over the subject matter and the parties.
2. At least one party has been a resident of the State of Florida for more than 6 months immediately before filing the Petition for Dissolution of Marriage.
3. The marriage between the parties is irretrievably broken.

ORDERED AND ADJUDGED:

SECTION I: DISSOLUTION AND RESTORATION

A. The marriage between the parties is dissolved and the parties are restored to the status of being single.

Florida Supreme Court Approved Family Law Form 12.990(c)(1), Final Judgment of Dissolution of Marriage with Dependent or Minor Child(ren) (02/18)

B. Former Name. *{If applicable}* ☐ Petitioner's ☐ Respondent's former name of *{full legal name}* ______________________________ is restored.

SECTION II. MARITAL ASSETS AND LIABILITIES

A. **Date of Valuation of Property.** The assets and liabilities listed below are divided as indicated. The date of valuation of these assets and liabilities is, unless otherwise indicated:

1. ☐ date of filing petition for dissolution of marriage.
2. ☐ date of separation.
3. ☐ date of final hearing .
4. ☐ other: *{specify date}*______________________________

B. **Division of Assets.**

1. **The assets listed below are non-marital assets.** Each party shall keep, as his or her own, the assets found to be non-marital, and the other party shall have no further rights or responsibilities regarding these assets.

ASSETS: DESCRIPTION OF ITEM(S) **Please describe each item as clearly as possible.** **You do not need to list account numbers.**	**Current Fair Market Value**	**Petitioner's Non-marital Property**	**Respondent's Non-marital Property**
	$	$	$
Total Non-marital Assets	$	$	$

2. **The assets listed below are marital assets.** Each party shall keep, as his or her own, the assets awarded in this section, and the other party shall have no further rights or responsibilities regarding these assets. **Any personal item(s) not listed below are awarded to the party currently in possession or control of the item(s).**

ASSETS: DESCRIPTION OF ITEM(S) **Please describe each item as clearly as possible.** **You do not need to list account numbers.**	**Current Fair Market Value**	**Petitioner Shall Receive**	**Respondent Shall Receive**
Cash (on hand or in banks/credit unions)	$	$	$

Florida Supreme Court Approved Family Law Form 12.990(c)(1), Final Judgment of Dissolution of Marriage with Dependent or Minor Child(ren) (02/18)

ASSETS: DESCRIPTION OF ITEM(S) **Please describe each item as clearly as possible. You do not need to list account numbers.**	**Current Fair Market Value**	**Petitioner Shall Receive**	**Respondent Shall Receive**
Stocks/bonds			
Notes			
Business interests			
Real estate: (Home)			
Automobiles			
Boats			
Furniture & furnishings			
Jewelry			
Life Insurance (cash surrender value)			
Retirement Plans (Profit sharing, Pension, IRA, 401(k)(s), etc)			
Other assets			

Florida Supreme Court Approved Family Law Form 12.990(c)(1), Final Judgment of Dissolution of Marriage with Dependent or Minor Child(ren) (02/18)

ASSETS: DESCRIPTION OF ITEM(S) Please describe each item as clearly as possible. You do not need to list account numbers.	Current Fair Market Value	Petitioner Shall Receive	Respondent Shall Receive
Total Marital Assets	$	$	$

C. **Division of Liabilities/Debts.**

1. **The liabilities listed below are nonmarital liabilities** and, therefore, are owed as indicated. Each party shall owe, as his or her own, the liabilities found to be nonmarital, and the other party shall have no responsibilities regarding these debts.

LIABILITIES: DESCRIPTION OF DEBT(S) Please describe each item as clearly as possible. You do not need to list account numbers)	Current Amount Owed	Petitioner's Non-marital Liability	Respondent's Non-marital Liability
	$	$	$
Total Non-marital Liabilities	$	$	$

2. **The liabilities listed below are marital liabilities** and are divided as indicated. Each party shall hold the other party harmless and pay, as his or her own, the marital liabilities awarded below.

LIABILITIES: DESCRIPTION OF DEBTS Please describe each item as clearly as possible. You do not need to list account numbers.	Current Amount Owed	Petitioner Shall Pay	Respondent Shall Pay
Mortgages on real estate: (Home)	$	$	$
(Other)			
Charge/Credit card accounts			

Florida Supreme Court Approved Family Law Form 12.990(c)(1), Final Judgment of Dissolution of Marriage with Dependent or Minor Child(ren) (02/18)

LIABILITIES: DESCRIPTION OF DEBTS **Please describe each item as clearly as possible. You do not need to list account numbers.**	**Current Amount Owed**	**Petitioner Shall Pay**	**Respondent Shall Pay**
Auto loan			
Auto loan			
Bank, Credit Union loans			
Other			
Total Marital Liabilities			
	$	$	$

D. Contingent assets and liabilities will be divided as follows: ______________________________

____

____.

E. The distribution of assets and liabilities in this final judgment is equitable; if each party does not receive approximately one-half, the distribution is based on the following facts and reasoning:

____

____

____

____

F. Beneficiary Designation (By completing this section, the beneficiary designations continue after Entry of Final Judgment of Dissolution of Marriage.)

The designation providing for the payment or transfer at death of an interest in the assets described below to or for the benefit of the deceased party's former spouse is **NOT VOID** as of the date of entry of the Final Judgment of Dissolution of Marriage.

The Final Judgment of Dissolution of Marriage shall provide that the designations set forth below remain in full force and effect.

☐ 1. The ☐ Petitioner ☐ Respondent shall acquire or maintain the following assets for the benefit of the other spouse or child(ren), to be paid upon his/her death outright or in trust. This provision only applies if other assets fulfilling such requirement for the benefit of the other spouse or child(ren) do not exist upon his/her death and unless precluded by statute. *{Describe the assets with specificity}*:____

____

____

____.

☐ 2. The ☐ Petitioner ☐ Respondent shall not unilaterally terminate or modify the ownership of the following assets, or their disposition upon his/her death. *{Describe the assets with specificity}*: ____

____

____

____.

SECTION III. EXCLUSIVE USE AND POSSESSION OF HOME

*{Indicate **all** that apply}*

A. The ☐ Petitioner ☐ Respondent , as a condition of support, shall have exclusive use and possession of the dwelling located at the following address:______________________________

____

until: *{date or event}* ____

____

____

____.

B. The ☐ Petitioner ☐ Respondent may make visits to the premises described in the paragraph above for the purpose of obtaining any items awarded in this Final Judgment. These visits shall occur after notice to the person granted exclusive use and possession of the dwelling and at the earliest convenience of both parties or as ordered in paragraph 4 below.

C. ☐ Upon the termination of the right of exclusive use and possession, the dwelling shall be sold and the net proceeds divided _____% to Petitioner and _____% to Respondent, with the following credits and/or setoffs being allowed:

____

____

____

____.

D. ☐ Other: ____

____

____.

Florida Supreme Court Approved Family Law Form 12.990(c)(1), Final Judgment of Dissolution of Marriage with Dependent or Minor Child(ren) (02/18)

SECTION IV. PARENTING PLAN ESTABLISHING PARENTAL RESPONSIBILITY AND TIME-SHARING WITH DEPENDENT OR MINOR CHILD(REN)

A. **Jurisdiction.** The Court has jurisdiction to determine parental responsibility, to establish or adopt a Parenting Plan, and a time-sharing schedule with regard to the minor child(ren) listed in paragraph 2 below.

B. **The parties' dependent or minor child(ren) is (are):**

Name	**Birth date**

C. **Parenting Plan.** The parties shall comply with the Parenting Plan which is attached and incorporated herein as Exhibit _______.

SECTION V. ALIMONY

A. ☐ The Court denies the request(s) for alimony;

OR

B. ☐ The Court finds that ☐ Petitioner ☐ Respondent, (hereinafter Obligee), has an actual need for, and that ☐ Petitioner ☐ Respondent, (hereinafter Obligor,) has the present ability to pay, alimony as follows: *{Indicate **all** that apply}*

1. ☐ **Permanent Periodic.**

a. The Court finds that no other form of alimony is fair and reasonable under the circumstances of the parties.

b. As a marriage of: *{Choose only **one**}*

☐ **Long Duration** (17 years or greater) alimony is appropriate upon consideration of all relevant factors;

☐ **Moderate Duration** (greater than 7 years but less than 17) alimony is appropriate based upon clear and convincing evidence after consideration of all relevant factors; or

☐ **Short Duration** (less than 7 years) alimony is appropriate based upon the following exceptional

Florida Supreme Court Approved Family Law Form 12.990(c)(1), Final Judgment of Dissolution of Marriage with Dependent or Minor Child(ren) (02/18)

circumstances:____.

c. Obligor shall pay permanent periodic alimony to Obligee in the amount of $__________ per month, payable ☐ in accordance with Obligor's employer's payroll cycle, and in any event, at least once a month, or ☐ other *{explain}* ____
beginning *{date}* ____________________. This alimony shall continue until modified by court order, death of either party, or remarriage of Obligee, whichever occurs first. The alimony may be modified or terminated based upon either a substantial change in circumstances, or the existence of a supportive relationship in accordance with section 61.14, Florida Statutes.

2. ☐ **Bridge-the-Gap.** Obligor shall pay bridge-the-gap alimony to Obligee in the amount of $______________per month, payable ☐ in accordance with Obligor's employer's payroll cycle, and in any event, at least once a month, or ☐ other *{explain}*__________________ beginning *{date}*______________________and continuing until: *{date}*____________________ *{a period not to exceed two (2) years}*; death of either party; or remarriage of the Obligee, whichever occurs first.

3. ☐ **Rehabilitative.** Obligor shall pay rehabilitative alimony to Obligee in the amount of $______________ per month, payable ☐ in accordance with Obligor's employer's payroll cycle, and in any event, at least once a month, or ☐ other *{explain}*_______________ beginning *{date}*____________________. This rehabilitative alimony shall continue until: modified by court order; the death of either party; or until *{date/event}* ____,
whichever occurs first. The rehabilitative plan presented demonstrated the following: ____.

4. ☐ **Durational.** Obligor shall pay durational alimony to Obligee in the amount of $_____________ per month payable ☐ in accordance with Obligor's employer's payroll cycle, and in any event, at least once a month, or ☐ other *{explain}*___________________________ beginning *{date}*______________________and terminating on *{date}*_______________________, the death of either party, remarriage of the Obligee, or until modified by court order in accordance with section 61.08(7), Florida Statutes, whichever occurs first.

5. ☐ **Lump Sum.** Obligor shall pay lump sum alimony to Obligee in the amount of $______________, which shall be paid as follows:____.
beginning *{date}*_____________________and terminating on *{date}*___________________, the

death of either party, remarriage of the Obligee, or until modified by court order, whichever occurs first.

6. ___ **Retroactive.** Obligor shall pay retroactive alimony in the amount of $___________ for the period of *{date}*_____________, through *{date}* ________________, which shall be paid pursuant to paragraph D. below.

C. **Reasons for ___ Awarding ___ Denying Alimony.** The Court has considered all of the following in awarding/denying alimony:

1. The standard of living established during the marriage;
2. The duration of the marriage;
3. .The age and the physical and emotional condition of each party;
4. .The financial resources of each party, including the nonmarital and marital assets and liabilities distributed to each;
5. The earning capacities, educational levels, vocational skills, and employability of the parties and, when applicable, the time necessary for either party to acquire sufficient education or training to enable such party to find appropriate employment;
6. The contribution of each party to the marriage, including, but not limited to, services rendered in homemaking, child care, education, and career building of the other party;
7. The responsibilities each party will have with regard to any minor or dependent children they have in common;
8. The tax treatment and consequences to both parties of any alimony award, including the designation of all or a portion of the payment as a nontaxable, nondeductible payment;
9. All sources of income available to either party, including income available to either party through investments of any asset held by that party and
10. Any other factor necessary to do equity and justice between the parties: *{explain}*

____

____

____

____.

___ Please indicate here if additional pages are attached.

D. **Retroactive Alimony and/or Arrearages.**

1. ___ There is no alimony arrearage at the time of this Final Judgment.

OR

2. ___ The ___ Petitioner ___ Respondent shall pay to the other spouse the sum of:

$___________ for retroactive alimony, as of *{date}*____________________;

$___________ for previously ordered unpaid alimony, as of *{date}* _______________.

The total of $ ________ shall be paid in the amount of $_________ per month, payable ___ in accordance with Obligor's employer's payroll cycle, and in any event at least once a month, or ___ other *{explain}* ____

____

Florida Supreme Court Approved Family Law Form 12.990(c)(1), Final Judgment of Dissolution of Marriage with Dependent or Minor Child(ren) (02/18)

beginning *{date}*__________________________, until paid in full including statutory interest.

E. ☐ **Life Insurance (to secure payment of support).** To secure the alimony obligations set forth in this judgment, Obligor shall maintain life insurance on his/her life naming Obligee as the sole irrevocable beneficiary, so long as reasonably available. This insurance shall be in the amount of at least $__________ and shall remain in effect until the obligation for alimony terminates.

F. ☐ **Other provisions relating to alimony, including any tax treatment and consequences:**
1. The award of alimony ☐ does not ☐ does leave the Obligor with significantly less net income than the net income of the recipient/Obligee. If the award **does** leave the Obligor with significantly less net income than that of the Obligee, the Court finds the following exceptional circumstances: ____________________________
____
____
____.

2. Other____
____
____.

SECTION VI. CHILD SUPPORT

A. ☐ The Court finds that there is a need for child support and that the ☐ Petitioner ☐ Respondent (hereinafter Obligor) has the present ability to pay child support. The amounts in the Child Support Guidelines Worksheet, Florida Family Law Rules of Procedure Form 12.902(e), filed by the ☐ Petitioner ☐ Respondent are correct;

OR

☐ The Court makes the following findings:
Petitioner's net monthly income is $__________, (Child Support Guidelines ____%).
Respondent's net monthly income is $__________, (Child Support Guidelines ____%).
Monthly child care costs are $____________.
Monthly health/dental insurance costs are $___________.

B. Amount.
Child support established at the rate of $_________per month for the _______children *{total number of parties' minor or dependent children}* shall be paid commencing ____________________ *{month, day, year}* and terminating __________________________________ *{month, day, year}*. Child support shall be paid in the amount of $________ per _______________ *{week, month, other}* consistent with the Obligor's current payroll cycle.

Upon the termination of the obligation of child support for one of the parties' children, child support in the amount of $__________for the remaining __________children *{total number of remaining children}* shall be paid commencing __________________________________ *{month, day, year}* and terminating_______________________________ *{month, day, year}*. This child support shall be paid in the amount of $________per __________ *{week, month, other}* consistent with the Obligor's current payroll cycle.

{Insert schedule for the child support obligation, including the amount, and commencement and termination dates, for the remaining minor or dependent children, which shall be payable as the obligation for each child ceases. Please indicate whether the schedule ☐ appears below or ☐ is attached as part of this form.}

____
____
____
____
____
____.

The Obligor shall pay child support until all of the minor or dependent children: reach the age of 18; become emancipated, marry, join the armed services, die, or become self-supporting; or until further order of the court or agreement of the parties. The child support obligation shall continue beyond the age of 18 and until high school graduation for any child who is dependent in fact, between the ages of 18 and 19, and is still in high school, performing in good faith with a reasonable expectation of graduation before the age of 19.

If the child support ordered deviates from the guidelines by more than 5%, the factual findings which support that deviation are: ____
____
____
____.

C. Retroactive Child Support and/or Arrearages.

1. ☐ There is no retroactive child support or child support arrearage at the time of this Final Judgment.

OR

2. ☐ There is either retroactive child support or child support arrearage.

☐ Petitioner ☐ Respondent shall pay to the other spouse child support in the amount of:
$_________ for retroactive child support, as of *{date}* ______________;
$_________ for previously ordered unpaid child support, as of *{date}* ________________.

The total of $____________ in child support shall be paid in the amount of $__________ per month, payable ☐ in accordance with Obligor's employer's payroll cycle, and in any event at least a month, or ☐ other *{explain}* ______________________________________ beginning *{date}*________________________, until paid in full including statutory interest.

D. Insurance.

1. ____ **Health/Dental Insurance.** ____ Petitioner ____ Respondent shall be required to maintain ____ health and/or ____ dental insurance for the parties' minor child(ren), so long as reasonable in cost and accessible to the child(ren). The party providing insurance shall be required to convey insurance cards demonstrating said coverage to the other party;
   OR

   ____ health and/or ____ dental insurance is not reasonable in cost or accessible to the child(ren) at this time.

2. ____ Reasonable and necessary **uninsured medical/dental/prescription drug costs** for the minor child(ren) shall be assessed as follows:
   ____ Shared equally by both spouses.
   ____ Prorated according to the child support guideline percentages.
   ____ Other *{explain}*: ____
   ____

   As to these uninsured medical/dental/prescription drug expenses, the party who incurs the expense shall submit request for reimbursement to the other party within 30 days, and the other party, within 30 days of receipt, shall submit the applicable reimbursement for that expense, according to the schedule of reimbursement set out in this paragraph.

E. ____ **Life Insurance (to secure payment of support).** To secure the child support obligations in this judgment, ____ Petitioner ____ Respondent ____ Each party shall maintain life insurance, in an amount of at least $____________, on his/her life her life naming minor child(ren) as the beneficiary(ies) **OR** naming ____ Petitioner ____ Respondent, or ____ other *{name}* ______________________________ as Trustee for the minor child(ren), so long as reasonably available. The obligation to maintain the life insurance shall continue until the youngest child turns 18, becomes emancipated, marries, joins the armed services, dies, or becomes self-supporting.

F. **IRS Income Tax Exemption(s).** The assignment of any tax exemption(s) for the child(ren) shall be as follows: ____
____
____.

Each party shall execute any and all IRS forms necessary to effectuate the provisions of this paragraph.

G. **Other provisions relating to child support:** ____________________________________
____
____.

SECTION VII. METHOD OF PAYMENT

Obligor shall pay court-ordered alimony and child support, including any retroactive support or arrearages as follows:

A. **Place of Payment.**

1. ☐ Obligor shall pay court-ordered support directly to either the State Disbursement Unit or the central depository, as required by statute, along with any fee required by statute.

2. ☐ Both parties have requested and the court finds that it is in the best interests of the child(ren) that support payments need not be directed through either the State Disbursement Unit or the central depository at this time; however, either party may subsequently apply, pursuant to section 61.13(1)(d)3, Florida Statutes, to require payment through either the State Disbursement Unit or the central depository.

B. **Income Deduction.**

1. ☐ **Immediate.** Obligor shall pay through income deduction, pursuant to a separate Income Deduction Order which shall be effective immediately. Obligor is individually responsible for paying this support obligation until all of said support is deducted from Obligor's income. Until support payments are deducted from Obligor's paycheck, Obligor is responsible for making timely payments directly to the State Disbursement Unit or the Obligee, as previously set forth in this order.

2. ☐ **Deferred.** Income deduction is ordered this day, but it shall not be effective until a delinquency of $____________, or, if not specified, an amount equal to one month's obligation occurs. Income deduction is not being implemented immediately based on the following findings: Income deduction is **not** in the best interests of the child(ren) because: *{explain}*

____

____

____,

AND

There is proof of timely payment of a previously ordered obligation without an Income Deduction Order in cases of modification,

AND

☐ There is an agreement by the Obligor to advise the Title IV-D agency, the clerk of court, and the Obligee of any change in Payor and/or health insurance

OR

☐ there is a signed written agreement providing an alternative arrangement between the Obligor and the Obligee and, at the option of the IV-D agency, by the IV-D agency in IV-D cases in which there is an assignment of support rights to the state, reviewed and entered in the record by the court.

C. **Bonus/one-time payments.** ☐ All _______% ☐ No income paid in the form of a bonus or other similar one-time payment, up to the amount of any arrearage or the remaining balance thereof owed pursuant to this order, shall be forwarded to Obligee pursuant to the payment method prescribed above.

D. **Other provisions relating to method of payment.**
____
____
____.

SECTION VIII. ATTORNEY'S FEES, COSTS, AND SUIT MONEY

A. ☐ Petitioner's ☐ Respondent's request(s) for attorney's fees, costs, and suit money is (are) denied because: ____
____.

OR

B. ☐ The Court finds there is a need for and an ability to pay attorney's fees, costs, and suit money. ☐ Petitioner ☐ Respondent is hereby ordered to pay to the other spouse $____________ in attorney's fees, and $ __________ in costs. The Court further finds that the attorney's fees awarded are based on the reasonable rate of $ _________ per hour and _________ reasonable hours. Other provisions relating to attorney's fees, costs, and suit money are as follows:
____
____.

SECTION IX. OTHER PROVISIONS

Other Provisions.
____
____
____.

The Court reserves jurisdiction to modify and enforce this Final Judgment.

DONE AND ORDERED in ________________________, Florida, on ________________________.

____
CIRCUIT JUDGE

Florida Supreme Court Approved Family Law Form 12.990(c)(1), Final Judgment of Dissolution of Marriage with Dependent or Minor Child(ren) (02/18)

I certify that a copy of this **Final Judgment of Dissolution** was ___ mailed ___ faxed and mailed ___ e-mailed ___ hand delivered to the parties listed below on *{date}*____________________.

by___________________________________
{Clerk of court or designee}

___ Petitioner (or his/her attorney)
___ Respondent (or his/her attorney)
___ Central Depository
___ State Disbursement Unit
___ Other ________________________________

Florida Supreme Court Approved Family Law Form 12.990(c)(1), Final Judgment of Dissolution of Marriage with Dependent or Minor Child(ren) (02/18)

B. DRAFTING AN INCOME WITHHOLDING ORDER FOR CHILD SUPPORT

To set up child support payments, the court needs to issue an order directing Katrina's employer to withhold payments from her salary. Draft an Income Withholding Order for Child Support for the court to sign and enter. You should search the state family law code for the appropriate statutory requirements and language. You may also search the internet for a sample form or order. You may not have all the specific information needed for every part of the Income Withholding Order for Child Support. You should accurately and thoroughly prepare the substance of the order and insert placeholders for any missing information.

It should be noted that in addition to the Income Withholding Order for Child Support, there is an Income Withholding Support Form (IWO) issued by the federal Office of Management and Budget (OMB) that must be completed by the attorney representing the party receiving child support and signed by the presiding judge. This form is the standard format prescribed in accordance with 42 U.S.C. § 666(b)(6)(A)(ii). The IWO can be found on the Office of Child Support Services website, which is a sub-section of the U.S. Department of Health and Human Services, Administration for Children and Families webpages. This form is used for income withholding in tribal, intrastate, and interstate cases as well as all child support orders that were initially issued in the state on or after January 1, 1994. The OMB-approved IWO must be issued to employers or other income payers to collect child support.